RFK JR.

ALSO BY ISABEL VINCENT

*Gold Bar Bob: The Downfall of the Most Corrupt
US Senator* (with Thomas Jason Anderson)

*Overture of Hope: Two Sisters' Daring Plan That Saved
Opera's Jewish Stars from the Third Reich*

Dinner with Edward: A Story of an Unexpected Friendship

*Gilded Lily: Lily Safra: The Making of One
of the World's Wealthiest Widows*

*Bodies and Souls: The Tragic Plight of Three Jewish
Women Forced into Prostitution in the New World*

Hitler's Silent Partners: Swiss Banks, Nazi Gold, and the Pursuit of Justice

See No Evil: The Strange Case of Christine Lamont and David Spencer

RFK JR.

THE FALL AND RISE

ISABEL VINCENT

WILLIAM MORROW
An Imprint of HarperCollinsPublishers

Without limiting the exclusive rights of any author, contributor or the publisher of this publication, any unauthorized use of this publication to train generative artificial intelligence (AI) technologies is expressly prohibited. HarperCollins also exercise their rights under Article 4(3) of the Digital Single Market Directive 2019/790 and expressly reserve this publication from the text and data mining exception.

Insert photographs: pages 1 and 2 (*top*): John F. Kennedy Presidential Library and Museum; page 2 (*bottom*): The Archives of Falconry, Boise, Idaho; page 3 (*top*): Getty Images; page 3 (*bottom*): Liz Hafalia, San Francisco Chronicle/Hearst Newspapers, Getty Images; page 4: Jose Jimenez/Primera Hora, Getty Images News; page 5: courtesy of the author; page 6 (*top*): Paul Hawthorne, WireImage, Getty Images; page 6 (*bottom*): Jim Spellman, Getty Images; page 7 (*top*): Michael M. Santiago, Getty Images; page 7 (*bottom*): J.C. Rice; page 8: Win McNamee, Getty Images News

RFK JR. Copyright © 2026 by Isabel Vincent. All rights reserved. Printed in the United States of America. No part of this book may be used or reproduced in any manner whatsoever without written permission except in the case of brief quotations embodied in critical articles and reviews. For information, address HarperCollins Publishers, 195 Broadway, New York, NY 10007. In Europe, HarperCollins Publishers, Macken House, 39/40 Mayor Street Upper, Dublin 1, D01 C9W8, Ireland.

HarperCollins books may be purchased for educational, business, or sales promotional use. For information, please email the Special Markets Department at SPsales@harpercollins.com.

hc.com

FIRST EDITION

Library of Congress Cataloging-in-Publication Data has been applied for.

ISBN 978-0-06-347228-0

26 27 28 29 30 LBC 5 4 3 2 1

No sympathy for the devil; keep that in mind. Buy the ticket, take the ride.
> —Hunter S. Thompson, *Fear and Loathing in Las Vegas: A Savage Journey to the Heart of the American Dream*

Whether you call someone a hero or a monster is all relative to where the focus of your consciousness may be.
> —Joseph Campbell, *The Power of Myth*

CONTENTS

PREFACE: "Just like the President"	xi
CHAPTER 1: **Prison Diary**	1
CHAPTER 2: "History Was Happening All Around Us"	19
CHAPTER 3: "Everybody Takes Their Licks"	43
CHAPTER 4: "I Bought the Ticket; I Took the Ride"	70
CHAPTER 5: **The Riverkeeper**	93
CHAPTER 6: "The Sirens Were on Every Rock"	117
CHAPTER 7: "Things Fall Apart"	142
CHAPTER 8: "My Voice Is Gone"	165
CHAPTER 9: **Vaccine Warrior**	191
CHAPTER 10: "They Had No Clue What They Were Doing"	217
EPILOGUE: **A Work in Progress**	237
ACKNOWLEDGMENTS	245
BIBLIOGRAPHY	247
NOTES	248
INDEX	264

PREFACE

"Just like the President"

On the eve of Robert F. Kennedy Jr.'s Senate confirmation hearings over his appointment as secretary of health and human services, his cousin Caroline Kennedy released an extraordinary letter. "He lacks any relevant government, financial, management, or medical experience," wrote the daughter of John F. Kennedy in her scathing January 28, 2025, missive to the senators investigating Kennedy. "His views on vaccines are dangerous and willfully misinformed. These facts alone should be disqualifying. But he has personal qualities related to this position which, for me, pose even greater concern." A video of the poised and bespectacled former ambassador to Australia and Japan reading the letter posted to her son, Jack Schlossberg's, Instagram and X accounts quickly went viral.

In addition to calling Kennedy "a predator" and likening him to the birds of prey he has long kept as pets, she dug deep, going back to her cousin's childhood and adolescence. She described how he would show off to his cousins by placing baby chicks and mice in a blender to feed his hawks. She blamed him for encouraging them "down the path of substance abuse," leading them to addiction, illness, and, in the case of Kennedy's younger brother David, death. And she accused him of expropriating the assassinations of both their fathers. "Bobby continues to grandstand off my father's assassination, and that of his own father," she wrote. "It is incomprehensible that someone who is willing to exploit their own painful family tragedies for publicity would be in charge of American life-and-death situations."

For his part, Schlossberg accused his cousin of "trading in on Camelot, celebrity, conspiracy theories and conflict for personal gain and fame."

The letter and Schlossberg's incessant and seemingly unhinged social media attacks against his cousin in the run-up to his own campaign for Congress in New York City were evidence of a long-rumored split within the storied Kennedy dynasty, which is itself a kind of American aristocracy. The boisterous and scrappy Hyannis Port heirs of Robert F. Kennedy and the much more aloof and intellectual Martha's Vineyard descendants of John F. Kennedy were clearly deeply divided. Upon reading Caroline's letter and her son's social media attacks, one might be hard pressed to believe that they had ever once been the "close family" that she took pains to describe.

But the shrill, emotionally charged letter was significant for another reason: It echoed the desperation of Democrats and even some Republicans eager to block at any cost Kennedy's appointment as the country's powerful health czar, overseeing an annual budget of nearly $94 billion and more than eighty-three thousand employees in his bid to Make America Healthy Again—part of the rallying cry of Donald Trump's historic presidency.

Kennedy is dangerous, and his unwillingness to back vaccinations that he felt were harmful could lead to national health emergencies, such as the resurgence of a measles epidemic, argued the experts. "With global measles cases surging more than 20% in a year, the specter of an anti-vaccine leader like Robert F. Kennedy Jr. at the helm of US health policy has alarmed public health experts," said an article in the renowned medical journal *The Lancet* that appeared the same month as Caroline's letter. "Kennedy, a well-known vaccine skeptic, has long promoted dangerous misconceptions about vaccines, and his influence could worsen an already dire situation."

Earlier, some of Kennedy's siblings had raised the alarm about Bobby Jr. They felt his controversial views on vaccine-related autism were so dangerous that they broke the family's long-held code of silence and began to speak up against him. The opposition had begun on a hysterical note when Kennedy had decided to cut his ties to the family's sacred Democratic Party—as important to them as their Catholic faith—and run as an independent candidate for president. And then, in an unforgivable betrayal that had further strained his family relationships and lost him lifelong friends, he had boldly endorsed Trump in the 2024 race. "We want an America filled with hope and bound together by a shared vision of a brighter future, a future defined by individual freedom, economic promise and national pride," said a post on X signed by five of Kennedy's siblings—Kathleen Kennedy Townsend, Courtney Kennedy, Kerry Kennedy, Chris Kennedy, and Rory Kennedy—months before the 2024 election. "We believe in Harris and Walz," the statement continued, referring to Democratic presidential candidate Kamala Harris and her vice presidential running mate, Tim Walz. "Our brother Bobby's decision to endorse Trump today is a betrayal of the values that our father and our family hold most dear. It is a sad ending to a sad story."

But for Kennedy, now in his seventies, who was coming into his own as a controversial national power broker, it was actually a new beginning—an appointment with destiny and one that he had been mulling over since the death of his father nearly sixty years ago.

"Bobby always aroused very strong emotions," said a good friend. "And in many ways, he's a pretty determined guy."

Kennedy's break with his family's deeply held political views was a long time coming and chronicled in a collection of three diaries that were entrusted to me in 2013, a year after I had begun covering the death of Mary Richardson, Kennedy's second wife, for the *New York Post*.

In the spring of that year, I found the diaries in a plastic shopping bag hanging from my chair at an Upper East Side restaurant in New York City, where I had met a trusted source who knew the Kennedy family well. The journals, from 1999, 2000, and 2001, are red-bound volumes festooned with stickers from exotic destinations: the Maui Dive Shop in Hawaii; Ushuaia, Argentina; San Ignacio Lagoon, Baja, California; Antártida. One book features a red, white, and blue "Gore 2000" campaign sticker. There is also a Continental Airlines baggage tag stuck to the cover of one, on which Richardson had scribbled her name and included two phone numbers with the Westchester County 914 area code, the word "REWARD" written in capital letters.

Before she was found hanging in a barn on the couple's Westchester estate on May 16, 2012, Richardson had been involved in a bitter divorce from Kennedy. At some point, he had barred her from seeing their four children over her bouts of drinking and abusing prescription drugs, although she was reportedly sober and studiously frequenting Alcoholics Anonymous meetings. On the eve of her death, she had been looking forward to putting the divorce behind her and moving on to see her children on a regular basis, sources had told me. But when Kennedy had refused to disclose his assets, many of them tied up in a secret family trust started by patriarch Joseph P. Kennedy in the mid-1940s, Richardson had seized the diaries "for insurance," according to my source. She had threatened to expose her cheating husband to the world if he did not cooperate in the divorce negotiations.

Initially, the *Post* was interested mainly in Kennedy's philandering, grappling with what he called his "lust demons," and perhaps for the first time the diaries offered proof that he was fulfilling a long-held tradition of womanizing, tacitly and even openly encouraged by generations of Kennedy men. At the back of the diaries, he kept ledgers of his romantic conquests, assigning numbers from 1 to 10 to rate their performance. Sometimes there were as many as three trysts in a single day. Richardson had told my source that the numbers corresponded to sex acts, with 10 denoting intercourse. In some cases, he scrawled the word "victory" followed by exclamation points in columns without a woman's name—a sign that he had successfully resisted being "mugged" by a woman, which was his term for seduction. In September 2013, when the *Post* published its first story on the diaries, Kennedy went from denying that he had a diary—in this case from 2001—to later admitting that it was indeed his. "The diary served as a tool for self-examination and for dealing with my spiritual struggles at the time," he said regarding the 2001 journal. "It also contains unedited, unfiltered stream-of-consciousness musings about current events and people."

For Richardson, the contents of the diaries were truly valuable because they documented years of her husband's infidelities with multiple women—which drew national scrutiny a dozen years after her death, when Kennedy announced his plans to run for president. In the weeks after he ended his campaign and endorsed Trump in August 2024, there was a renewed focus on his personal life. In September, *New York* magazine reporter Olivia Nuzzi revealed to her editors that she had been involved in a "personal relationship" with Kennedy, whom she had profiled a year earlier for the magazine. The sexting scandal in which Kennedy had allegedly told her that he wanted to "possess" and "impregnate" her led to her ouster at *New York* and resulted in the breakup of her engagement to another journalist. Kennedy, who is married to his third wife, the actress Cheryl Hines, denied the tryst.

Around the same time, Kennedy offered a rare apology to a former family babysitter who had accused him of groping her on several occasions when she went to work for him in 1998, while he was married to Mary Richardson. He claimed to have no memory of the incidents, which were eerily reminiscent of his grandfather

Joe Kennedy's treatment of many of his sons' girlfriends, "even coming into their bedrooms at night and kissing them full on the lips." Jack Kennedy and his siblings often warned friends that their father "prowls at night."

Despite their devotion to the Roman Catholic Church and its edicts against adultery, the womanizing seems to have been encouraged among Kennedy men. In the late 1920s, Joe Kennedy had a well-documented affair with the Hollywood actress and reigning sex goddess Gloria Swanson. In letters to his father, John Kennedy would often boast about his own romantic conquests, noting in one instance on a visit to Palm Beach that there had been "three girls to every man so I did better than usual." As for Kennedy's own father, Bobby Sr., rumors have swirled for decades of his liaisons with the glamorous women in his orbit, including Marilyn Monroe and his sister-in-law Jackie Kennedy.

Robert F. Kennedy Jr. was tormented by his womanizing and agonized in his diaries over how to become a better person. In a particularly perceptive entry on July 25, 2001, he noted, "I bought the ticket, as Hunter [S. Thompson] says, and I took the ride. The seeds of it were easy. The restlessness, the shattered dreams, the empty hole that had to get filled with women." Through it all, he knew that he was failing the one person he had always wanted to impress. "I knew daddy was watching me and that he loved me," he wrote the same day. "But I also felt I was disappointing him—when I told a lie, had a sexual thought, got a bad grade."

In fact, Kennedy's diary entries are evidence of a lifetime spent grappling with the weight of his family's legacy and his quest to carve out a distinct identity as an environmental crusader, public health critic, and political maverick. "Still trying to be a political and moral force," he wrote in his diary on October 14, 2000, during a hectic ten-day cross-country lecture tour, describing his conquests as an environmental lawyer suing corporations and others for polluting forests and waterways. "I am letting slip the opportunity for real power, and fear that I will become a kind of gentleman environmentalist without any real import or prestigious office."

He enumerated a series of "random encounters" he'd had on a speaking tour that had taken him from California to Puerto Rico and Canada in which people who had heard him speak in the past told him he had changed their lives. One woman told him she had changed careers and become an environmental lawyer. Another lawyer had decided to take on a pro bono case against a real estate developer after attending one of Kennedy's speeches. "This happened a half dozen times and in the past five days," he wrote.

A year earlier, on May 21, 1999, he had confessed his deep-seated fear that his life would have no meaning unless he took the leap to enter politics. "The thing that scares me most in life is that I might squander the great life I've been given—the extraordinary access to any CEO or head of state on Earth, the enormous reserve of public good towards my father's children, the powerful political power and the wealth, etc.," he wrote. "Will I use these things to the maximum effect possible to improve people's lives and bring benefits to others? Will I leave my children anywhere near the wealth and power I was given? I worry that the answer to both of these is 'no.' That is the fear that makes me want to run for political office."

Besides that, he needed the cash. When his father was killed in 1968, the family was left with little. "My father, when he died, had spent virtually all of his money on the 1968 election," he said in a deposition during negotiations over his second divorce. "My family did not have money. It was the only Kennedy family that didn't have money."

He claimed under oath in the same 2012 deposition that the family had been so cash strapped that his mother, Ethel Kennedy, was also broke and could not afford the upkeep on her home at the family's summer compound in Hyannis Port. "Those of us who stay at her house pay her, and she doesn't know she's being paid," he said. "It would be a great embarrassment if she were to know." Ethel Kennedy died in October 2024.

Since childhood, he had been told that he was the Kennedy most likely to follow in his tragic uncle's footsteps, the most likely to become president of the United States. As Caroline Kennedy conceded in her blistering letter to the Senate, Kennedy is "charismatic—able to attract others through the strength of his personality, willingness to take risks and break the rules."

His father would have agreed and might have admired his son's risk taking and probing of accepted wisdom. He certainly encouraged all of his rarefied interests, buying him a red-tailed hawk when he expressed a fascination with falconry and arranging an after-school job at Washington, DC's, National Zoo as well as lessons with a local falconer. As a child, Kennedy identified with Saint Francis of Assisi, a lover of animals and birds who had been awakened every morning by the shrill cries of a peregrine falcon on Mount Alverna. Kennedy, who grew up hearing the stories of Saint Francis from his parents, recalled his childhood experiences fondly, describing in his diary on July 25, 2001, exploring the woods near the family's Virginia estate "with my knife and cowboy boots, turning over every rock."

Marveling at his son's curiosity and fascination with animals and the natural world, Bobby Sr. had once said of his third child, "He's just like the president," referring to his older brother Jack Kennedy. It was an opinion shared by Kirk LeMoyne "Lem" Billings, Jack Kennedy's best friend and a Kennedy family devotee who became a surrogate father to Kennedy after Bobby Sr.'s assassination when Kennedy was fourteen years old. It was Lem who accompanied his charge on an African safari and river trip to the Peruvian Amazon when he was a teenager, encouraging him to keep a journal and write articles about their adventures. And it was Lem who told him that he could have a greater impact on the world than his father.

Still, Robert Francis Kennedy was a hard man to emulate.

The former attorney general in his brother's administration

and junior senator from New York became a martyr, shot dead in his prime, on the cusp of greatness shortly after his victory in the Democratic presidential primary in California in June 1968. Bobby Sr. was beloved by the poor, by African Americans fighting for civil rights, union leaders and anti–Vietnam War activists. He quoted the Greek tragedian Aeschylus in a speech announcing the death of Martin Luther King Jr. at a rally in Indianapolis in April 1968, even though as attorney general he had authorized the CIA to wiretap the civil rights leader's phones.

Bobby Sr. had also grown up in the shadow of the Kennedy legacy. He was the trusted confidant of his older brother, running his political campaigns from behind the scenes and guiding him through the various crises of his short-lived administration. He was a complicated, conflicted man whose world fell apart after his brother's assassination. Five years after his brother's death, he would follow in his footsteps and run for the presidency. He received numerous death threats but was determined to continue with the race, campaigning largely from an open convertible, reminiscent of the one in which his brother had been shot dead in Dallas in 1963. "At stake is not simply the leadership of our party and even our country," he told a cheering crowd in the Senate when he announced his run in the Democratic primary. "It is our right to moral leadership of this planet."

Despite his lofty goals, Bobby Sr. was no doctrinaire liberal. He began his career going after Communists in the United States when he worked for family friend Senator Joseph McCarthy, promoted hard-line positions against Cuban leader Fidel Castro during the Cuban Missile Crisis, even as his greatest legacy was the promotion of equality for Black Americans. "I never vote for the party," he once said. "I always vote for the man." As a result, he included many trusted Republicans among his advisers, including John Doar, deputy assistant attorney general for civil rights in the Kennedy and Lyndon Johnson administrations, and former Secretary of Defense Robert S.

McNamara, who had started off as a Republican when he worked in the Kennedy administration but later became a Democrat.

Years later, in 2007, Kennedy would give a similar answer to a reporter who asked if he would consider following in his father's footsteps. "I wouldn't be a reliably liberal senator," he said. "My father was never a liberal. He was a devout Catholic with an open mind."

In an interview with Fox News executive and family friend Roger Ailes in 1995, Kennedy refused to commit to a timeline to go into politics or even identify himself as either Republican or Democrat. "I live my life one day at a time," he said. "I love what I'm doing and keep doing that until the signs are right. I wouldn't characterize myself with either of those labels. I believe in free market economics where we liberate people."

In fact, his diary entries show how he gradually became disillusioned with the Democratic demigods and civil rights heroes that he and his family had once embraced. Nearly a quarter century before running for political office, he became deeply critical of everyone from Bill and Hillary Clinton to Jesse Jackson and even his former brother-in-law Andrew Cuomo, a former governor of New York.

In 2021, Kennedy launched his biggest attack against Democrats and the Joe Biden administration, targeting Anthony Fauci, the longtime director of the National Institute of Allergy and Infectious Disease. He accused him of "the catastrophic mismanagement" of the HIV epidemic and the COVID-19 pandemic in his book *The Real Anthony Fauci: Bill Gates, Big Pharma, and the Global War on Democracy and Public Health*. While it was derided by most critics and experts, the book touched a chord with many Americans who weren't entirely convinced that the social distancing and masking protocols mandated by Fauci and his cronies would do anything to keep them healthy. *The Real Anthony Fauci* argued that Fauci had pushed COVID-19 vaccines that had not been properly tested and compared the strict vaccine mandates in the United States to living under the rule of the Nazi Party in Germany. The book also blamed billionaire Bill Gates for the "forced" vaccinations of millions of African children. *The Real Anthony Fauci* went on to sell more than 1.1 million copies. More than anything, it jump-started his run for the presidency.

Fauci replied to the charges against him in the book by dismissing Kennedy completely and contrasting him to his martyred and heroic father. "I don't think he is inherently malicious," he said about Kennedy following the book's publication. "I just think he's a very disturbed individual. . . . And it's a shame because he comes from such an extraordinarily distinguished family, many members of whom I know personally, and I was very close to Senator Ted Kennedy, who was such an extraordinary person and a real warrior for public health. And to have RFK Jr. just spouting things that make absolutely no sense."

In that same year, Kennedy wrote a letter to President Biden noting that the latter had promised to give Americans a COVID vaccine program that was "rooted in honesty, transparency and rigorous science"—principles that Biden had abandoned in the first few months of his presidency. "The sad reality is vaccines cause injuries and death," he wrote.

Kennedy's obsession with vaccines began gradually in 2003 when a woman showed up at his summer home in Hyannis Port with a Bankers Box of studies on mercury and vaccines. Sarah Bridges told Kennedy that her son had experienced brain damage after being vaccinated. Although Kennedy at first claimed that he needed convincing, in 2015 he had joined the World Mercury Project, a nonprofit that eventually became Children's Health Defense, a controversial anti-vaccine advocacy group that with Kennedy's help had launched dozens of lawsuits across the country challenging pharmaceutical companies that made vaccines, raking in millions of dollars in damages and making Kennedy a millionaire several times over. "It took me a long time," he told the broadcaster Megyn Kelly following Trump's victory in 2024.

Still, during his Senate hearings he hesitated when asked whether he would vaccinate his children today with the MMR (measles, mumps, and rubella) vaccine, eventually saying that he probably would. "I am not going to just tell people everything is safe and effective if I know there are issues," he said, promising to work with Vermont's independent senator, Bernie Sanders, to make sure that the United States pays similar prices for drugs as do other countries, which often pay lower prices because their single-payer health care systems negotiate the deals.

It may have been a rare form of compromise on his part. Among the traits he inherited from his father are a reputation for hardheaded stubbornness and determination as well as a willingness to challenge accepted wisdom. He has repeatedly questioned the assassination of his father, suggesting that his assassin, Sirhan Sirhan, couldn't have fired the bullet that ultimately killed him. His diaries show that throughout his career as an environmental lawyer, he has been known for his obdurate views, often ignoring scientific evidence that could disprove them. His diary entries relate combative meetings with members of Riverkeeper, the environmental nonprofit he joined in the mid-1980s as part of his required community service following a drug bust and conviction.

He has also inherited the Kennedy family's sense of entitlement. One source recalled a meeting in his Manhattan office over lunch. Kennedy had sat and eaten his lunch and then left all the wrappers from his burger and fries on a conference table. "He had wrappers all over his side of the table and he just left them there, and then he just walked out," said the source. "I cleaned up after him. Everything else about Bobby is consistent with that."

In his diary, Kennedy related the story of his mother, whom he referred to by her initials, ESK—Ethel Skakel Kennedy—who had been caught for speeding by a trooper near the family home in Maryland. She had told the trooper to send the bill "to the New York office." When the confused trooper had asked what that was, she had simply said, "That's where they pay all the bills." And then she had left.

Despite his feeling of entitlement, Kennedy has a deep love for his country and a keen sense of patriotism that was forged largely while he was a college student in Alabama. Many of his diary entries are more aligned with the ideas of Bible Belt Republicans than with the progressive principles embraced by most of his family. He spent more than a year in Montgomery and Hayneville, Alabama, to work on his senior thesis for Harvard University beginning in 1975 and returned to help organize his uncle Teddy's presidential campaign five years later. "I felt close to these people because of their sentimentality, their strong bond with the land, the attachment to . . . values and love of country and pride in our traditions—patriotism and humility and love of God," he wrote on July 25, 2001. Everyone drove American cars, he continued. "No BMWs like in Cambridge." Instead, people were "rooted in the conviction that this country was great and were suspicious of Europeans."

For Kennedy, who was suspended from just about every boarding school he attended after his father's death, the teacher he credits with having the most influence on his life was no liberal. His biology teacher Skip Lazell was a right-wing scientist who was an expert on amphibians, a supporter of the Vietnam War, and a member of the John Birch Society, a secretive group that believed the fluoridation of drinking water was a Communist plot. Kennedy has long argued that fluoride is responsible for a host of health problems, including neurodevelopmental disorders, thyroid disease, and cancer.

With these kinds of sentiments, it may not have been a huge leap for Kennedy to embrace the Trump credo to "Make America Great Again" when he saw an opportunity to profit from Trump's campaign, ending his own attempt at the presidency in exchange for wielding his authority over the country's health ministry. "For 20 years, I've gotten up every morning on my knees and prayed that God would put me in a position where I can end the childhood chronic disease epidemic in this country," he said on February 13, 2025, when he was sworn in as secretary of health and human services.

Kennedy may have prayed for divine inspiration, but he also dug deep into his soul—a process that began in earnest when he found himself in prison for a daring act of disobedience on the island of Vieques in 2001. Alone in his cell in Puerto Rico, the forty-seven-year-old began a process of intense soul-searching. In his prison diary—musings scrawled on a collection of yellow legal pads—he questioned his legacy and the nature of heroism and justice, invoking everyone from his father to the Buddha and the Trappist monk Thomas Merton. "The true disciples are often found on the front lines fighting for justice," he wrote on July 8, days after he was sentenced.

Four days later, on July 12, he questioned what it really meant to be a hero, citing his uncle Jack's Pulitzer Prize–winning book *Profiles in Courage*: "I've been thinking about heroics lately, how the subject has fascinated us," he wrote. "*Profiles in Courage* and my father surrounding himself with war and sports heroes. How our spiritual longing is really a search for heroes. . . . My father found it in the endurance and perseverance of the poor in Appalachia and the ghetto who faced and overcame challenges that he knew he would never know. He urged us to be heroes and put us constantly in strenuous situations to nurture those qualities."

His constant questioning about his responsibility in the world was something that was well known to his closest friends. "There's a deeper aspect to him than people give him credit for," said a friend, who was close to him for nearly twenty years. "I believe that he believes he's doing right for the world."

In his quest to radically reform the US health care system, Kennedy is clearly taking inspiration from his father, so much so that he has started dressing like the former senator and presidential candidate, donning trim suits and skinny retro ties. "When people look at his position, the subtlety they are missing is that he is now a member of the president's cabinet," said the former close friend. "In his deep consciousness, this is more important for him. Bobby reveres the presidency. He has had a lifelong passion to collect items that are signed by all the presidents, and he believes that one of the highest callings he can have is national service. It's his family-driven mission."

Like Fauci, critics who have denounced Kennedy have done so largely by comparing him to his crusading uncles and father—the failed heir who could never live up to their heroic legacy. But like most heroes, the Kennedys were no saints. They were entitled and wealthy, with a family who could buy their way into Ivy League universities, pull strings with the military, and even buy their books in bulk to ensure that they made it onto the bestseller lists. Massachusetts Senator Ted Kennedy may have been a big proponent of health care, but he left a young woman to drown at Chappaquiddick in 1969. Jack and Bobby Sr. escalated the United States' involvement in the conflict in Vietnam, presided over the disastrous Bay of Pigs invasion of Cuba, which ultimately led to the missile crisis that took the country and the world to the brink of nuclear conflagration. They wiretapped civil rights leader Martin Luther King Jr.'s phone and hotel rooms, eager to prove that he was a Communist and hoping to discredit him by exposing his various romantic trysts. Jack, Bobby Sr., and Ted took their inspiration from their father and engaged in their own marital infidelities.

In their explosive statement on their brother, Kennedy's siblings noted that "Bobby might share the same name as our father, but he does not share the same vision, values or judgment." Or maybe he shares all of them. And perhaps that's what's really making his family and his other critics so apoplectic. For in many ways, Kennedy may be exactly like his father. "Other people's opinions of me are not my business," he told a reporter in the days before his Senate hearings. "I know what I have to do."

CHAPTER 1

Prison Diary

In his prison mug shot, Robert Kennedy Jr. wore an easy smile. The square jaw and the rugged good looks that mark him as a scion of America's most storied family were on display in the black-and-white photo that federal prison administrators affixed to a name tag that also included information about his height (six feet, one inch), his weight (180 pounds), and the colors of his eyes (blue) and hair (brown). But there was something beyond the Kennedy mystique in that very comfortable smile, the way he fixed the camera with a steady gaze. Was it pride? A sense of accomplishment? No doubt it was both—the very things that had eluded him for most of his very privileged life, the things that his family's wealth and connections couldn't buy. Now, in the summer of 2001, the forty-seven-year-old former heroin addict who had carved out a career as an environmental crusader was about to spend a month in federal prison at Puerto Rico's Metropolitan Detention Center in Guaynabo, on the outskirts of San Juan. He was political prisoner 21553-069. And he couldn't have been happier.

"I was exultant," he wrote on July 6, 2001, in his diary, after US District Court Judge Hector Manuel Laffitte sentenced him to thirty days in prison on trespassing charges and ordered federal marshals to take him into custody. Not only was he thrilled about doing time for a cause he believed in, but the sentence would be completed by early August, allowing him to enjoy the last month of summer with his family at the Kennedy compound in Hyannis Port.

Judge Laffitte had been harsh with some of the other Vieques protesters who had been sentenced before him, and Kennedy had feared the worst during his court appearance in San Juan. A day before the sentencing, he had participated in a betting pool with the other protesters convicted of trespassing on Vieques. They had all met for dinner, and Kennedy bet five dollars that he would get at least thirty days from Laffitte, who was known for being tough. He feared that he would be singled out for harsher punishment because of his last name. Whatever happened, he was prepared to take a stand. On the morning of July 5, he had told his lawyers that he didn't want them to challenge the evidence "particularly vigorously," which the other protesters had been doing. Following the meeting with his legal team, he seemed largely unperturbed. He wrote in his diary that he had gone for a swim in the ocean with a fellow protester.

The next day, he boarded a bus with the other convicted trespassers, clutching a sheet of paper with the scribbled notes of the comments he wanted to make in court in a hearing that would last some seven hours. "I was dead sure that when he entered the courtroom, we were going to do 40—maybe 45—maybe even 60 days," he wrote in his diary on July 6, 2001, referring to Judge Laffitte. "But there were to be several before us." When it finally came to Kennedy and his co-conspirator Dennis Rivera, the powerful Puerto Rico–born president of New York's Service Employees Union Local 1199, who was among the leaders of the protesters, "all he [Laffitte] said was 30 days."

Puerto Rican state senator Norma Burgos, whose hearing came right before theirs, received a sixty-day sentence after an outburst in which she began to criticize the proceedings and told Judge Laffitte that he should have put the navy on trial instead of the protesters. Burgos, who was a member of the pro-state party in Puerto Rico, had originally been sentenced to forty days in prison. "You're being defiant," Judge Laffitte said. "It does not behoove you to defy the court." He added twenty days to her sentence, which she later successfully appealed.

As he was driven off to prison with the other protestors, Kennedy was pleased with himself. During his first few days in the lockup, his wife, Mary, who was days away from delivering their fourth child, had managed to get through to him on the phone. She told him that she had received many calls from friends expressing their outrage at his sentence. Everyone except Kennedy's own family condemned his treatment, she said. "Well, it's Bobby's own choice to be there," his younger sister Kerry had told Mary following news of his sentence.

Mary told her husband that his mother, Ethel Kennedy, was "very proud of me"—likely for the first time in his life. His mother was planning to visit him at Guaynabo, Mary said. So was Hillary Clinton, who was six months into her first term as the junior senator from New York. His uncle Ted Kennedy, the senator from Massachusetts, was also planning a visit, as was Mark Green, New York City's public advocate and a fellow environmentalist who was running in the Democratic primary for mayor of New York City.

And there were other things to look forward to. Days later, on July 12, Kennedy noted on the yellow legal pad that now served as his makeshift prison diary, "My life is so fast paced. I really needed a break and this place is perfect."

He spent most days alone in his cell, working on an article about his part in the protest on Vieques, an island nature preserve off the coast of Puerto Rico that had been used as a weapons training ground for the US Navy since 1941, when it had taken over 26,000 acres of the island's eastern and western shores, forcing local residents to move to the center of the territory. For years, the bombing had been playing havoc with the island's biodiversity, and Kennedy, along with Rivera, Burgos, the Hollywood actor Edward James Olmos, and others, including the civil rights activists Jesse Jackson and Al Sharpton, had been part of the protests, which had taken place at the end of April and beginning of May. Sharpton, who had previously been arrested for civil disobedience, was originally sentenced to ninety days. His attorney, Johnnie Cochran, who had successfully defended the football star O. J. Simpson in his murder trial six years earlier, appealed the sentence. He was unsuccessful, although Sharpton was allowed to serve most of his prison time at a facility in Brooklyn.

Jacqueline Jackson, the wife of the Baptist minister and failed presidential candidate, had also been sentenced for trespassing. Jackson, the firebrand reverend, dominated the Vieques protests, insisting upon headlining press conferences even though he had not risked arrest on the island. Kennedy, who despised Jackson, spent much of his time avoiding him, he wrote.

Jackson was using Vieques for his own purposes. Months earlier, he had admitted to having an affair with a campaign worker at his Rainbow/PUSH Coalition offices in Washington. The affair with Karin Stanford, a professor of political science, had produced a daughter. Pontificating about Vieques at every press conference he could find proved to be a convenient distraction from the scandal after Sharpton, once a fawning protégé, broke with his mentor over the affair. As Kennedy noted, the scandal had weakened Jackson in the Black community and paved the way for Sharpton to emerge as Black Americans' leader. "Jesse is trying to rehabilitate himself from the disclosure that he has an out-of-wedlock child," he wrote on July 5, a day before his trial and incarceration. "I don't really want to be the instrument of his rehabilitation."

Or caught in between the epic battle of the reverends for dominance within the Black community. Although Sharpton was in prison, he raged against his former mentor through one of his supporters. "While arch-rival Sharpton languishes in a federal lockdown in Brooklyn for protesting the U.S. Navy's bombing of Vieques, Jackson has been quietly buttressing an alliance with Dennis Rivera, leader of the powerful Local 1199 health care workers union, who is the cochairman of Jackson's Rainbow/PUSH Coalition," wrote columnist Peter Noel in *The Village Voice*, an article that helped inflame the conflict between the two men even more. "Rivera is Jackson's point man in the city. And privately, several of Jackson's critics have asked Black activists to avoid Rivera at all cost." In addition, he dubbed Jackson "the pimp of Vieques" and quoted a former campaign worker who had accused him of using his wife in a political stunt by "forcing" her to protest at Vieques. "Anyone who believes that this situation was not staged to take the spotlight off Sharpton must be crazy," Noel wrote. Jacqueline Jackson received a ten-day sentence.

In Harlem, where Jackson's affair was sharply criticized, Sharpton seized the spotlight. Like his former mentor, he was using Vieques for his own purposes. A day before he was arrested for trespassing there, he had announced that he was contemplating a run for president in 2004. "The condemnation of the Harlem ministers emboldened Sharpton to attack his teacher," wrote Kennedy in his diary on July 5. "Sharpton presented himself as the new heir to Martin Luther King and came to Vieques."

According to Kennedy, both Sharpton and Jackson had little interest in the issues behind the protests at Vieques and had embraced the cause in order to increase their exposure on national media. "I may be cynical about his motives," he wrote of Sharpton, "but I believe he came to Vieques because he saw cameras here and determined to be in front of them."

In a long passage in his diary, Kennedy explained that Jackson's rise to power had been directly related to his own family and had taken place as early as 1979, when his uncle Ted Kennedy had challenged Jimmy Carter in the Democratic presidential primary. Carter's people had seen Jesse on TV and hired him to travel across the country and "counterbalance Teddy's popularity among Black voters," he wrote, adding that in the long run it hadn't worked for Carter, who had won the Democratic primary but lost the election to Ronald Reagan. But it had given Jackson national exposure as a self-styled civil rights leader and jump-started his own presidential campaign in 1984, which had ultimately failed.

Sharpton, who had begun preaching at age four and worked as a youth director for Jackson's Operation Breadbasket in the late 1960s, had taken his lessons on developing a national base from Jackson. "When he came to New York, Al Sharpton would meet him at the airport and study him," wrote Kennedy on July 5 in his diary. In 1996, when Jackson had introduced his Wall Street Project "to end the multi-billion dollar trade deficit with minority vendors and consumers," Sharpton had begun a similar campaign among New York City advertising firms known as the Madison Avenue Initiative. "Both these guys give me the creeps," wrote Kennedy, adding that Jackson had a "desperate and destructive addiction to publicity."

Kennedy had soured on Jackson in 1993, when he had been a pallbearer at Cesar Chavez's funeral. Kennedy's family had had a special relationship with the California labor organizer since 1966 when his father, Robert Kennedy, then a senator with a seat on the Subcommittee on Migratory Labor, had reluctantly visited Chavez in California.

"By the end of the day, Kennedy had embraced Chavez and La Causa," wrote historian and RFK biographer Arthur M. Schlesinger Jr. Kennedy *père* had famously broken bread with the labor leader in 1968 following Chavez's twenty-five-day hunger strike to raise awareness of the slavelike conditions that farm workers were forced to endure. Later, when Robert Kennedy ran for president, Chavez and his United Farm Workers were crucial in organizing votes for him.

At Chavez's funeral in 1993, which drew more than thirty-five thousand mourners, Jackson "pushed Cesar's friends and family out of the way to make himself lead pallbearer," wrote Kennedy on July 5 in his diary. He had attended the funeral with his mother and older brother, Joseph Kennedy II, then a congressman.

Kennedy's disenchantment with the civil rights leader continued after Jackson opposed an initiative to clean up the Everglades three years later, in 1996. Kennedy had backed the Save Our Everglades campaign, which had proposed a penny-a-pound tax on sugar to finance the cleanup of the Florida wetlands. Jackson campaigned against the tax measure on the ballot—Florida Amendment 4—arguing that it would hurt minorities.

Kennedy wasn't the only one who had issues with the reverends. Both Rivera and Hillary Clinton were fierce critics of the civil rights leaders, according to his prison diary entries, although they dared not go against them in public. In their private conversations with Kennedy, Rivera described Sharpton as "psychotic" and Clinton said that "she was tired of all the politicians running to him [Jackson] and wanting to see what he will do." According to Kennedy, she was one of those politicians.

"Al Sharpton has done more damage to the Black cause than George Wallace," wrote Kennedy on July 5, referring to the pro-segregation former governor of Alabama, whom he had met while he was a student at Harvard working on his senior thesis about Judge Frank M. Johnson Jr., who had ruled in landmark civil rights cases.

The day before Kennedy was sentenced, he wrote in his journal that he had lost respect for Sharpton after the Tawana Brawley scandal. In 1987, Brawley, a Black teenager in upstate New York, had falsely accused four white men of kidnapping and raping her. Sharpton had helped bring the case to national prominence, but a grand jury had concluded a year later that no rape had taken place. "Even the most deserving causes he has championed since then becomes suspect by his association with the Tawana Brawley stench," he wrote on July 5.

Despite the media circus surrounding the two civil rights leaders in Puerto Rico, there was true solidarity among the other protestors. In Guaynabo, the Vieques prisoners were known as *los disobedientes* (the disobedient ones) and were beloved for their stand at Vieques. "We were greeted by about 60 cellmates—mostly disobedientes—who cheered us as we entered the cell block and played the drums and gave us abrazos [hugs]," he wrote on July 6, the day he reported to jail, where he was issued a set of prison clothing, sheets, pillowcases, a blanket, and "a ragged mattress."

Despite the bare-bones living conditions, there was singing every night by his fellow prisoners and general excitement when one of their comrades was released after serving their time. Three days after he arrived at the prison, a fellow protestor completed his sentence and was on his way out when the other prisoners—there were forty Vieques protestors among the fifty-six prisoners in his cell block—shouted *"Afuera Tito!"* ("Out Tito!") His fellow cellmates threw him a bon voyage party, and by the time he left, Tito was sobbing, according to Kennedy.

Among his fellow prisoners were the activists Rubén Berríos, the president of the Puerto Rico Independence Party, and another Tito—Tito Kayak—who was serving a year in prison for a daring act of civil disobedience in which he had climbed to the top of the Statue of Liberty in New York City with a group of Vieques protestors to hang a Puerto Rican flag on the statue's top deck in November 2000. Kayak, whose real name was Alberto de Jesús Mercado, had long been associated with the Vieques cause.

A sense of warmth and camaraderie existed among the Vieques prisoners and the prison workers. When Kennedy went for a routine checkup with the prison medic, his caseworker allowed him to use the phone in his office to call Mary. "I said 'thank you,'" he wrote on July 11 in his diary. "He said, 'no, thank you for what you did.' This is pretty typical of everyone who works in this joint." At night, troops gathered outside the prison to wave to the Vieques prisoners through the fence and picket their incarceration, he wrote. When protestors were released from the prison, they were sent off with singing and hugs, with those remaining in the cell block shouting the rallying cry of the movement, *"Vieques o muerte!"* ("Vieques or death!")

To them, Bobby Kennedy was a hero who had risked his life for their cause. Months earlier, he had participated in his own daring invasion of Vieques. On April 28, he had boarded a thirteen-foot fiberglass panga fishing boat at Esperanza on the southern coast of Vieques and sped to the bombing range where the US Navy was exploding five-hundred-pound bombs. Olmos, Rivera, and the Puerto Rican pop star Robi Draco Rosa had accompanied him on the risky mission, trailed by a boat "packed with journalists and photographers."

For Kennedy, who by then had worked for eighteen years as a lawyer and environmental activist, his trespassing on Vieques—the first act of civil disobedience in his life—came after he and others had "exhausted every legal and political avenue" to end the navy bombings, which had resulted in thousands of pounds of exploded bombs each year, eventually dwarfing the explosive power of the atomic bomb dropped on Hiroshima, he wrote in an article about the adventure for *Outside* magazine. The bombs had destroyed the island's rainforests and poisoned fish and wildlife, interfering with the local fishing industry, he said.

The battle to remove the navy from Vieques had been going on since the bombings had begun in 1941 and was tied to the movement for Puerto Rican independence. It gained momentum in the early 1970s when the lawyer and human rights activist Berríos staged a protest on Culebra, an island east of the Puerto Rican mainland, which was also used for navy target practice. In 1971, Berríos and twelve other protestors entered a major navy bombing target area on Flamenco Beach and set up an encampment, where they remained for several weeks. The protestors had also convinced a white-shoe Washington law firm, Covington & Burling, to represent them for free in federal court. By December 1975, the protest and the legal challenge had worked, and the navy ceased all military operations on Culebra.

On Vieques, protests continued, led by a grassroots group of local fishermen who regularly risked arrest by launching flotillas in restricted waters around the island in order to interfere with the bombings following the death of the Puerto Rican independence leader

Angel Rodriguez Cristobal in a Florida prison in 1979. The thirty-three-year-old member of Puerto Rico's Socialist League was found dead in his Tallahassee cell while serving a six-month sentence for trespassing on navy land in Vieques while military maneuvers were taking place. The official cause of death was suicide, but in a "fiery" graveside speech, the Puerto Rican Nationalist Party's secretary general, Juan Antonio Corretjer, said that he had been murdered and the movement would avenge his death by driving the navy from Vieques. "The sounds and odors of gunpowder will prevail until the Navy has been driven from Vieques and the U.S. from Puerto Rico," he declared at Rodriguez Cristobal's funeral.

Two months later, in January 1980, a bomb exploded at the Puerto Rico Bar Association, destroying its glass doors. Alex Joseph de la Zerda, a navy lieutenant serving as a liaison between the military and the residents of Vieques, was arrested for the crime. He was also charged, along with two anti-Castro Cubans, with attempting to bomb a commuter plane that ferried passengers between San Juan and Vieques. Both the commuter plane company and the bar association were considered sympathetic to the movement to remove the navy from Vieques.

Protests continued and reached a fever pitch on April 19, 1999, when navy planes accidentally dropped bombs during a nighttime training mission. The blasts killed David Sanes Rodríguez, a Puerto Rican security guard who worked as a civilian employee for the navy. According to a congressional report, a Marine Corps F-18 on a training mission dropped two five-hundred-pound bombs that struck the security post, killing Sanes and injuring four others. By December, President Bill Clinton had ordered a temporary stop to the explosions on the island, and the navy ceased their bombing exercises. Two months later, in February 2000, more than 150,000 people took to the streets of Puerto Rico to protest any further military exercises on Vieques. The protests drew everyone from lawmakers to the singer Ricky Martin, the boxer Félix "Tito" Trinidad, and the daring activist and environmentalist Tito Kayak, who had been fighting for the removal of the US military from Vieques for years.

Kennedy became involved in April 2000, traveling to the island to meet with fishermen, scientists, and local leaders who represented the 9,300 residents. He was accompanied by Rivera, who had made Vieques an urgent issue among his union members in New York. On that first trip, Kennedy donned scuba gear and dived to examine the effects of the bombings on the ocean floor. He found what "looked like an army-navy store, the reef bristling with dud bombs," he wrote in his story for *Outside* magazine, adding that he had immediately agreed to represent local leaders in the battle against the navy. "The bombardment of Vieques is bad military policy and disastrous for public health and the environment. But the most toxic residue of the Navy's history on Vieques is its impact on our democracy. The people I met there are United States citizens, but the Navy's abusive exercise of power on the island has left them demoralized, alienated, and feeling that they are neither part of a democracy nor the beneficiaries of the American system of justice."

In addition, the Vieques bombings were causing other long-term problems. The 1999 Special Commission on Vieques report for the Puerto Rican governor's office found that Vieques had the highest infant mortality rate in the commonwealth. The report also cited a Puerto Rico Department of Health study that had found that between 1980 and 1989, the risk of developing cancer was higher on Vieques than in any other part of Puerto Rico.

During his civil disobedience on Vieques in April 2001, Kennedy hid from navy police under a demolished truck. But he worried that if bombing resumed, he might take a direct hit. When he fled from his hiding place, he heard a soldier call his name. He was arrested and joined Rivera, who was already in handcuffs. Later, the navy police officers who had arrested him and Rivera asked to have their pictures taken with Kennedy and even asked for his autograph, Kennedy said.

But the authorities soon dispensed with the celebrity treatment.

"Our captors drove us all to the naval compound at Camp Garcia, where they turned us over to a less refined crowd," he wrote in his article. "Our new guards made us kneel upright on sharp gravel, searched us, and took our shoes, socks, and belts. Then they marched us toward a chain-link enclosure containing 24 other male protesters." Hours later, they were transported by boat and bus to Guaynabo, where they were strip-searched and "marched to our cell block." Two days later, on April 30, they were released on $3,000 bail each.

Neither Kennedy nor Rivera had thought to resist arrest. For his part, Kennedy was determined to go to prison, even as friends and supporters arranged for Mario Cuomo, New York's governor from 1983 to 1994, to handle his and Rivera's defense at trial. Cuomo, a skilled attorney and the father-in-law of Kennedy's younger sister Kerry, who was married to Cuomo's son Andrew at the time, had brokered a deal whereby Kennedy would plead guilty to trespassing charges and waive all defenses and appeals. The judge would then likely sentence him to a short time in prison after Mary had her baby. She was due in mid-July. "I rejected the deal—much to Mario's chagrin," wrote Kennedy on July 5, the day before his court appearance in San Juan. "I need to go to jail. Now! If I don't it will look like I made some backroom deal. I need to go to jail. If I won my case on some other technicality, it would look like I was being treated differently from the others [and] that would discredit the movement."

He was already prepared to serve his time behind bars. Before flying to San Juan, he had gone shopping at Barnes & Noble with Bobby, his eldest son from his marriage to his first wife, Emily Black. He had bought Spanish grammar and yoga books and packed the ointment that he needed for a skin condition that caused pustules and sores on his face. Bobby jokingly warned his father not to do any yoga poses where anyone could see him and asked him to continue the skin care regimen "to make my face look scary" and to tell his roommate that he was suffering from

AIDS, syphilis, and dysfunctional bowel syndrome. "He's getting a perverse enjoyment about my predicament," wrote Kennedy on July 1. "He keeps talking about my girlfriend Tito."

Three days later, he spent the July Fourth holiday with his children and Peter Kaplan, his former roommate at Harvard and the editor of the *New York Observer*, at Van Cortlandt Manor, a museum in Westchester County. "We watched revolutionary war reenactments and Conor and Finn drilled with a minuteman squadron and we watched an artillery team shoot a cannon across the Croton River," he wrote on July 4.

Despite his skin problems, which made him look like a "*monstro*" to his fellow inmates, his early days behind bars were serene and peaceful, removed from distractions and a problem that had dogged him for years: his serial womanizing. "I'm so content here," he wrote in his diary on July 6. "I have to say it. There's no women. I'm happy! Everybody here seems happy. It's not—misogyny. It's the opposite! I love them too much."

He took yoga classes and attended daily Mass in the prison chapel. After he was released, he told a reporter that compared to the other prisoners, who had lost much-needed jobs and couldn't provide for their families while they were in jail, he and his celebrity activists had had it pretty easy. "Really, I escaped my cell phone," he told CNN. "I got a lot of time to do some reading."

He was immersed in Alan Schom's biography of Napoleon Bonaparte, which he found beautifully written but rather pessimistic. "His is not an inspiring life," he wrote on July 12 of the Corsican general. According to Schom, Napoleon was worse than Adolf Hitler, who "at least had a purpose outside himself." Napoleon had been so obsessed with his own life that he had failed to see the suffering and death that he was leaving around him, Kennedy noted. He found Karen Armstrong's *Buddha*, which he also read in prison, much more inspiring. He also dipped into the works of Thomas Merton, an American Trappist monk whose 1948 autobiography and most important work, *The Seven Storey Mountain*, relates his spiritual journey and conversion to Catholicism.

Merton had an interesting bond with Kennedy's maternal grandmother, Ann Skakel, and his mother, Ethel, who had befriended the monk's mentor, philosophy professor Daniel Walsh, who had been one of Ethel's professors at Manhattanville College. At one point Ethel had wanted to become a nun and she was a member of the Legion of Mary, a global lay Catholic organization. Her parents, Ann and George Skakel, had befriended Merton and had been major donors to the Abbey of Gethsemani, a Trappist monastery in Kentucky. Ann, a fervent Catholic who had attended secretarial school as a young woman, volunteered to type the monk's manuscripts. Often described as an "honorary beatnik," Merton had embraced many of the beliefs of the beat poets, including Eastern mysticism, a rejection of materialism and questioning of authority. He had corresponded with Jack Kerouac and Lawrence Ferlinghetti, who had been deeply influenced by his autobiography. Both Ethel and her mother had remained close to both Walsh and Merton, who had corresponded with them throughout John F. Kennedy's presidency with insights about the Cold War and the dangers of the nuclear arms race. Merton died on a spiritual pilgrimage in Asia in December 1968, six months after Robert Kennedy was assassinated. In a letter to Ethel, he called the presidential candidate's death "Bobby's tragic immolation."

Kennedy copied many of Merton's dictums to his diary as part of his attempt to use his jail time to become a better person. "Never despise anyone, never condemn anybody. Never speak evil of anyone and the Lord will give you peace," he wrote on July 21, quoting the monk. "I like this because it's a defect (gossip, criticism) that I need to begin addressing."

On most days, Kennedy would head to the prison yard, where a "sinewy Dominican" prisoner often played guitar, sitting cross-legged against a backdrop of stucco walls and a canopy of concertina wire.

"He played beautifully" while other prisoners stood around him in the courtyard, he wrote on July 25.

Kennedy's only complaint about his time in prison was the food, which was mostly starch, which led to a general sense of lethargy among the inmates. "It's like the land of the Lotus Eaters," he wrote on July 9.

Throughout his detention, Kennedy was in regular communication with his family. Mary had told him that back at their home in Westchester, his children held a nightly vigil led by Conor, his eldest son with Mary. According to his diary, Conor sat in his father's chair and assembled his younger siblings, Kyra and Finn, leading them in prayers for their father. "I am so lucky," wrote Kennedy on July 9, underlining the sentence three times in his diary.

In addition to his mother, Mary was firmly behind him, and regaled him with messages from his supporters in New York, including Mario Cuomo, who complained to Mary about his wayward client, describing Kennedy as "troublesome and hard-headed," he noted in a July entry in his diary. Cuomo was upset that he had lost his case in Puerto Rico and blamed Kennedy for the defeat, Mary said. After all, Cuomo had "mesmerized the courtroom audience with his characteristic eloquence," noted a reporter for the *New York Times* during the presentencing trial. He spoke about Independence Day and praised the history of civil disobedience in the United States in order to cast Rivera and Kennedy in a noble light. "We ask the court to recall that our nation was conceived in the civil disobedience that preceded the Revolutionary War," Cuomo said. "And that the acts of civil disobedience involved in the Fugitive Slave Act of 1793, the famous sit-down strikes of 1936 and 1937, the valiant struggle for civil rights in the 1960s and the movement against the Vietnam War were always treated by the courts—not like crimes committed for personal gain or out of pure malice—but as technical violations designed to achieve a good purpose."

Judge Laffitte was unmoved, although Cuomo still gave himself credit for getting Kennedy a relatively short sentence. Kennedy had confided in Mary that it was really due to Norma Burgos's outburst in court right before his own sentencing, which had distracted the judge and resulted in his monthlong sentence. Burgos continued her defiance in prison and ended up in "the hole," or solitary confinement, for three days—which both Kennedy and Rivera were quick to protest to the prison spokesman. They threatened that their entire unit would volunteer to go to "the hole" if they didn't let Burgos out immediately.

Mario Cuomo had told Mary, "'I'm so happy to be rid of those guys (me and Dennis). It was like a bad love affair. Have you ever had that experience—where you know that the relationship is not good for you, but can't extract yourself?'" Kennedy noted in his diary on July 9.

In addition to Cuomo's conversations with Mary, Kerry sent Kennedy inspiring quotes by Evelyn Waugh and Henry David Thoreau, which he committed to his journal. "Under a government which imprisons any unjustly, the true place for a just man is also in prison," he wrote on July 18, quoting Thoreau in his diary.

On July 13, Mary had their fourth child. "He came around 6pm," wrote the ecstatic Kennedy in his diary on the same day. "I was calling all day with special permission from the warden (We are only allowed 10 minutes a day)." In fact, he was able to spend between two and three hours on the phone with his wife while she was in labor. "I felt at least in some sense, like I was there with her when she was having the baby," he told a reporter following his release, referring to Mary as the real hero, who had "shouldered the burden of my imprisonment," taking care of their children on her own while he was away.

Kerry and Mary's sister Nan Richardson were both in the delivery room during the birth of Aidan Caomhán Kennedy, who weighed seven pounds, ten ounces and was named for two Irish saints. "I am so proud of my Mary," he wrote on July 13. "She has become the woman I fell in love with through hard work. She has overcome her fear, enshrined her faith, abandoned self pity and blame and immersed herself in gratitude and God gave her a baby commensurate with her victory and her struggles—a beautiful, serene and happy soul. I am so happy. I couldn't be happier or more grateful for the life and the wife God has given me."

The couple had married in 1994, shortly after Kennedy had divorced his first wife and while Mary was pregnant with their son Conor. By 1999, the marriage was in trouble, with Kennedy frequently complaining in his diary entries about Mary's mood swings and her stints at rehab facilities to treat her addiction to alcohol.

Two days after the happy news, Kennedy and Rivera welcomed a steady stream of visitors that included Hillary Clinton as well as the archbishop of Puerto Rico, who spoke to all the Vieques inmates. Benicio del Toro, the Puerto Rican actor, also visited with his father, a prominent criminal lawyer. Clinton met with both Kennedy and Rivera for more than an hour, and they were allowed to use the warden's office for their conversation, he said.

Ethel Kennedy visited a few days later, on July 19. "Mommy came at noon," he wrote. "She was kind of stressed by my face but said that I should tell future visitors that the guards here were fierce and had roughed me up." After he sneaked a look at himself in a mirror just before his mother's visit, he admitted to looking like "Robert the Bruce's leprosy-ridden father in Braveheart."

During her visit, one of the guards apologized for her son's imprisonment. "He came to help us and our children and our children's children," said the guard. Kennedy told a reporter that the guard had tears in his eyes when he spoke to his mother.

At the end of her visit, Ethel gave an interview to Puerto Rican reporters. Kennedy watched on a prison TV as his mother, clearly proud of her son's civil disobedience and incarceration, said she hoped that Kennedy would name his new son "Vieques Libre Kennedy." Kennedy and his wife would end up taking Ethel's advice, giving Aidan "Vieques" as one of his middle names, although they left out "libre" on the birth certificate. "It would give him a context of his birth, and that he would know that his father was in jail doing a term for a choice of conscience," Kennedy told an interviewer after his release. "And it would give him something good to think about."

While he waited for Mary to arrive with their newborn—she was due in with his other children, his friend Peter Kaplan, and his sister Kerry—Kennedy admitted that he wasn't achieving the serenity that he had hoped for. "I'm not getting the kind of spiritual respite and growth that I had hoped for," he wrote on July 17. "I need to come out strong and resolved and I don't feel that anymore."

In a poignant admission toward the end of his incarceration, he confessed that he had failed to live up to the Kennedy family legacy, crippled by his addictions to sex and drugs. "After daddy died I struggled to be a grown-up," he wrote on July 25. "I felt he was watching me from heaven. Every time I was afflicted with sexual thoughts, I felt a failure. I hated myself. I began to lie—to make up a character who was the hero and leader that I wished I was."

The longer he remained in detention, the more frequently he returned to the distant past and the defining moments of his life. In his diary, he recalled the "smell of mint growing near a creek" during the time he had spent in Alabama with Kaplan working on the Harvard senior thesis that would turn into his first book. He recalled his restlessness and emptiness then and worried that he was disappointing his father with his lack of discipline and restraint.

With his face "as grey as a hornet's nest," he vowed to execute a "three-point plan" for "fixing his lust demons" and becoming a better father and husband. But he never wrote down the plan, and he left the subsequent days of his diary—the remainder of his time in prison—blank.

CHAPTER 2

"History Was Happening All Around Us"

As a child, growing up with a swarm of siblings and a menagerie of unusual pets, Robert F. Kennedy Jr. dreamed of becoming a veterinarian. It wasn't until his father was assassinated that he began to change his mind. He began thinking about a career in public service and following in his vaunted footsteps, he told TV executive and longtime friend Roger Ailes decades later.

Bobby, the third child and second son of RFK and Ethel Skakel, was born at Georgetown University Hospital on January 17, 1954. As the namesake of his crusading father, he was expected to rise to greatness.

At the time of his birth, his twenty-nine-year-old father was poised to become chief counsel for the Democratic minority on the Senate committee investigating the conduct of Wisconsin's Republican Senator Joseph McCarthy, a family friend who, like the Kennedys, was a fervent Irish Catholic—a rarity among US lawmakers at the time and often seen as a liability in political circles dominated by moneyed Protestants.

McCarthy had given Robert Kennedy, or Bob, as he was known to his friends, a job in December 1952 on his Permanent Subcommittee on Investigations at the behest of his father, Joseph Kennedy, a businessman and former ambassador to the United Kingdom during the early years of the Second World War. After managing the successful Senate campaign of his older brother John earlier in the year, Bob was casting about for a government position when he became one of fifteen staffers on the subcommittee that aggressively investigated Communist infiltration in the US at the height of the Cold War. According to some accounts, he couldn't stomach much of the Cold War hysteria and brutal investigation tactics that characterized the committee's work.

Or at least that was the myth that he and his family later spun to suit his crusading image. The reality was that Robert Kennedy was at times more doctrinaire and reckless than McCarthy himself. RFK spent less than seven months working for McCarthy and resigned largely over friction with McCarthy's chief counsel, Roy Cohn. The ruthless former prosecutor was on the legal team that prosecuted Ethel and Julius Rosenberg in Manhattan federal court. In 1952, the electrical engineer and his secretary wife were convicted of spying for the Soviet Union and executed a year later. The tough Bronx-born attorney, who would go on to be a mentor to the young Donald Trump, had little time for the imperious and entitled Harvard grad. "He walked in, sat down, and he looked me over very carefully as though, you know, sizing up a piece of merchandise," said Cohn, describing his first meeting with Bobby Kennedy in an interview for the John F. Kennedy Library in 1971.

When Bobby returned to McCarthy's committee as counsel for the Democratic minority in February 1954, he was determined to go after Cohn in front of millions of Americans who were watching the thirty-six-day Army-McCarthy hearings on television. Before the beginning of the hearings, RFK told McCarthy's secretary, Mary Driscoll, to assure the senator that he would do everything to protect him. "I'm really going to get that son-of-a-bitch Cohn," he said, according to an interview with Cohn years later. At one point, things got so out of hand that Cohn threw a punch at RFK in the hearing room lobby during a break in the hearings.

In Cohn's recollection of events, RFK was more militant than his boss and known to hold a grudge. After conducting an investigation for the committee on the transshipment of goods by Greek ship owners to Communist countries, RFK insisted that the Dwight D. Eisenhower administration crack down with an iron fist on the Greek ship owners, which would have resulted in the United States' breaking diplomatic ties with Greece. Even McCarthy refused to back the plan. "In later years when he had become a 'liberal,' he tried to indicate that he had resigned . . . from the committee because he disapproved of McCarthy's methods," said Cohn. "Well, this is total nonsense. The exchange of letters between him and Senator McCarthy at the time of his resignation make it crystal clear they were on the most cordial friendly terms."

Still, Cohn's reckless pursuit of Communists in the US Army was heavily criticized and ultimately led to his resignation and McCarthy's censure in the Senate in December 1954.

But for Kennedy, there was little room for nuance in his early memories of his father. RFK was the valiant hero lawyer. Although he had never practiced law, Robert Kennedy had fearlessly taken on Cohn, McCarthy, and a string of mobsters and corrupt union leaders, including Jimmy Hoffa, when he had later headed up investigations on the labor racketeering committee led by Democratic Senator John McClellan of Arkansas, beginning in 1956.

"My dad believed the 'enemy within'—a dark force infiltrating American politics and business, unseen by the public and out of reach of democracy and the justice system—posed a greater threat to our country than any foreign enemy," wrote Kennedy, describing how his mother would take him—a toddler at the time—and his older siblings, Kathleen and Joe, to the Senate hearings to support her husband. Kennedy's younger brother David was born a year before the hearings began. During the nearly three years of the Mob and labor union investigations and hearings, Ethel would give birth to three more children: Courtney in 1956, Michael in 1958, and Kerry in 1959. "Pointing at Teamster bosses Jimmy Hoffa and Dave Beck, and their shady mob associates, my mother declared, 'Those are the bad guys,'" wrote Kennedy. "She didn't need to tell us that my father, Uncle Jack, and dour old Senator John McClellan were the good guys." Later in his diary, in a section he called "memories from childhood," he remembered "Teamsters backfiring in front of our house" as a warning to his father that they would come after him and his family unless he backed down.

From the time they could read and write, the Kennedy children were expected to be immersed in current affairs. According to Kennedy, they had to read for an hour each day, record three current events from the newspapers in their daybooks, and be prepared to speak about them at the dinner table. On Sundays, they read poetry, he said. If Bobby caught any of his children reading a comic book, he was quick to admonish them and tell them to do something useful instead. "America has been very good to the Kennedys," he was fond of saying. "We all owe the country a debt of gratitude and public service."

In his family memoir, *American Values: Lessons I Learned from My Family*, Kennedy described an idyllic childhood at Hickory Hill, the family's thirteen-bedroom estate on twelve acres in McLean, Virginia. The sprawling mansion where his family moved when he was three years old had been owned by Robert E. Lee's father, Henry, a former governor of Virginia. His parents had purchased the five-story home in 1956 from his uncle Jack and his wife, Jackie, who had moved to a smaller residence in Georgetown.

The home was decorated with shrines to Saint Francis, for whom Kennedy and his father were named. "Franciscan iconography decorated our home, and the garden bristled with shrines and statuary celebrating Francis and his friars," wrote Kennedy.

The home boasted a stable, two swimming pools, a tennis court, and an obstacle course and zip line built by the Green Berets at his father's request to be used during charity events at the property, although on occasion Major Francis Ruddy Jr., the head of the Army Special Forces, who was close to the Kennedy family, would bring in soldiers wearing camouflage and black greasepaint for demonstrations that delighted the Kennedy children. Later, after Jack was assassinated in 1963, Ruddy famously took off his beret and left it on his coffin at Arlington National Cemetery.

Kennedy described horseback riding with both his parents before breakfast in the fields near Hickory Hill. He rode a horse named Geronimo, while his father rode alongside on Attorney General, he wrote. On other mornings, the Kennedy children pretended to shave with their busy father while he got ready to go to work. Kennedy recalled in his diary on July 25, 2001, "the dogs and kids piled into my father's black convertible" and rather cruelly "egging" his dog Otis to run next to their car. There were also games of Botticelli at the dining room table among the brood of ten children. His youngest sister, Rory, was born in 1968, after their father's death.

When he was attorney general, Robert Kennedy drove himself to work every day in the family convertible, often taking one of his children and their dog and speeding down the George Washington Parkway. He drove so fast that his aides were worried that he might be arrested. In order to prevent an embarrassing situation involving the attorney general breaking the law, his aides Nicholas Katzenbach and Burke Marshall came up with a solution. "Nick said that when my dad was AG he drove to work by himself (especially on Saturdays) in his convertible—with the big dog in the front seat with him—very fast," wrote Kennedy in his diary years later. "His aides were worried he'd be arrested and mentioned the problem to Stu [sic] Udall, secretary of the interior, who raised the speed limits on the parkway to avoid the issue."

In the summer, the clan decamped to Cape Cod, to the family

compound at Hyannis Port, where the Kennedy patriarch, Joe Sr., had bought a small white cottage on Marchant Street in 1928 and immediately proceeded to double its size. Other members of the family had began scooping up nearby homes, soon forming a sizable beach compound where the Kennedy children were "subjected to a daily regimen of athletic training supervised by a rotund former Olympic diver, Sandy Euler," wrote Kennedy in one of his memoirs. "Three times a week we would have riding lessons at my grandfather's farm in Osterville, or go on long rides through the scrub pine forest and sandy marshlands with him and his horse." Every day, his parents would take the children sailing on their twenty-six-foot wooden boat for a picnic on a nearby island. When his uncle was president, his Marine One helicopter carrying him, his brother Bobby, and their aides would land at the compound to spend the weekends.

Kennedy also wrote about the entire clan getting behind his uncle's 1960 campaign for president, helping him shore up votes in their home state of Virginia and elsewhere. Jack Kennedy ran with Lyndon B. Johnson as his vice presidential running mate, a senator and skilled politician from Texas who the campaign was counting on to bring in votes from key states in the South. Kennedy was in second grade at Our Lady of Victory School in Washington, DC, where the campaign for the first Catholic president in the country's history was akin to a religious crusade among the priests and nuns, he said. Across the country, Jack and his wife, Jackie, symbolized glamor and hope, encapsulating the campaign's "A time for greatness" slogan and set to the soundtrack of Frank Sinatra's Oscar-winning song "High Hopes." Sinatra turned the song about an ambitious ant into a rallying cry for JFK. "Everyone is voting for Jack/He's what all the rest lack" were the opening lyrics of the tune blasted at every campaign rally. Kennedy wore a red, white, and blue "Kennedy for President" button on the lapel of his school blazer, and he and his siblings stuck stickers of Kennedy's opponent, Richard Nixon, onto neighborhood stop signs during the campaign.

During the spring of 1960, Kennedy's parents "disappeared" for six weeks to campaign for his uncle in West Virginia, which had the smallest Catholic population in the country. JFK ended up winning the state with 65 percent of the vote and the rest of the country by a slim margin in one of the tightest races in US history.

Amid widespread cries of nepotism, Jack appointed Bobby as his attorney general. He was already his older brother's most important confidant, a skillful tactician who had managed his political campaigns. "Call Bobby, get together with him and come back with an idea on this" was the familiar command that Jack would give to his advisers. Now, at just thirty-five, Bobby Kennedy, an intense strategist who fixed "the steely blues" on anyone he needed to convince to his way of thinking, became "assistant president," said George Stevens Jr., a Hollywood filmmaker who later worked on propaganda films for Bobby's campaign for New York senator, which tried to soften his "ruthless" demeanor and dispel his opponents' charges that he was a carpetbagger candidate who had never really lived in the state.

Walter Lippmann, an influential newspaperman, had his doubts. "Bobby is a very attractive human being, but his greatest weakness, the thing I worried about before he was appointed is that when he's bent on what he thinks is the right course, he's rather ruthless in action," he said.

One of those ruthless acts involved allowing the FBI to wiretap the phone of civil rights leader Martin Luther King Jr. Authorities also bugged his hotel rooms when he was on the road leading marches. The agency was collecting information about his numerous extramarital affairs and his connections to the Communist Party in order to discredit his entire movement. The surveillance began soon after King's March on Washington in August 1963. More than half a million people descended on the National Mall for King's "I Have a Dream" speech. "The whirlwinds of revolt will continue to shake the foundations of our nation until the bright day of justice emerges," said King, sending shock waves to authorities, who convinced themselves that the Baptist leader was promising some kind of Communist revolution.

From the beginning of the Kennedy administration, Hickory Hill doubled as an extension of the White House.

During the University of Mississippi crisis, when the first African American student registered for university at Ole Miss, many of the planning meetings to prepare for the riots that were expected to take place at the school took place at Hickory Hill, with legal advisers who included Deputy Attorney General Katzenbach and Associate Justice of the Supreme Court Byron White, among others. Kennedy, who was eight years old at the time, eavesdropped on the meetings from behind a sofa. "History was happening all around us," he wrote in his memoir *American Values*. "During the years that Uncle Jack was president, our home at Hickory Hill was a satellite White House. Many of the most momentous governmental decisions were made there by men in swimming trunks on the pool-house patio."

James Meredith, a twenty-nine-year-old civil rights activist and air force veteran, decided he wanted to test the federal government's commitment to desegregate schools after the landmark 1954 Supreme Court ruling *Brown v. Board of Education*, which had declared that segregation was illegal, by registering at the University of Mississippi in Oxford. He was twice denied admission to the public university in 1961. That year, he wrote an extraordinary letter to the Department of Justice, outlining his segregated education in Attala County, where he had grown up, and the nine years he had spent in the air force serving his country. He was seeking federal intervention to allow him and other African Americans to enroll at the school. "I have no great desire to protect my hyde [*sic*], but I do hope to see the day when the million Negroes who live in the state of Mississippi will have cause not to fear as they fear today," he wrote on February 7, 1961.

With the help of Medgar Evers, an army veteran and civil rights activist who was the head of the Mississippi chapter of the National Association for the Advancement of Colored People (NAACP), Meredith sued the school in Mississippi federal court. The case went all the way to the Supreme Court, which ruled in Meredith's favor. On September 13, 1962, Meredith tried to enroll in classes, much to the anger of Mississippi's Democratic governor, Ross Barnett, who tried all manner of ways to prevent him from attending the university, including charging him on a trumped-up voter fraud violation. On September 25, Meredith attempted to register again but was blocked from entering the university's admissions office. Three days later, the Court of Appeals found Barnett in civil contempt and ordered his arrest and a fine of $10,000 per day if he continued to refuse to admit Meredith to the school. Following a flurry of phone calls among Barnett, Bobby Kennedy, and the president, Barnett finally relented, although he made a fiery speech at a football game in which he encouraged people to continue to block Meredith's entry. On September 30, riots broke out when three thousand white protestors, including members of the Ku Klux Klan, clashed with federal marshals at the school. A phalanx of five hundred federal marshals escorted Meredith to his dorm room. Two people died in the violent melee. The next day, President Kennedy dispatched more than thirty thousand federal troops to quell the riot and protect Meredith, who graduated a year later.

Days after the Mississippi crisis, on October 16, 1962, the Kennedy brothers confronted arguably the most consequential moment of Jack's presidency and the most dangerous episode of the Cold War when intelligence operatives discovered the presence of Soviet missile bases in Cuba. The nuclear missiles there were capable of traveling more than three thousand miles and were aimed directly at the United States.

More than a year before the Cuban Missile Crisis, Jack had already relied on his brother for foreign policy advice when he had consulted Bobby on the failed Bay of Pigs operation in April 1961—an incident that ultimately led to the missile crisis. Beginning in the Eisenhower administration, the CIA had trained a group of Cuban exiles in Guatemala to invade the island and topple Communist leader Fidel Castro, who had come to power in 1959 and begun expropriations of everything from major industries to the homes of ordinary Cubans the following year. Brigade 2506 was made up of 1,334 exiles, and they counted on US airpower to take over the island in a daring invasion. The mission was a disaster, largely because the Kennedy administration failed to provide air cover, resulting in 114 exiles being killed and more than 1,100 captured by Castro's forces.

Following the debacle, Robert Kennedy defended the actions of the exiles in legalistic terms, citing the United States' neutrality laws in a press release, even though he was fully aware that the exiles had been trained and funded by the US government—a violation of those very laws. "There is nothing in the neutrality laws which prevents refugees from Cuba from returning to that country to engage in the fight for freedom," he said. "Nor is an individual prohibited from the United States, with others of like belief, to join still others in a second country for an expedition against a third country." Later, Jack put his brother in charge of Operation Mongoose, a series of undercover operations to undermine Castro's government through support for exile groups, sabotage, and assassination.

After the Bay of Pigs invasion, Castro had reached a secret deal with Soviet leader Nikita Khrushchev to place Soviet nuclear missiles in Cuba to prevent another US incursion onto the island. But they were not defensive missiles; they were squarely aimed at the United States. At first, Bobby was determined to bomb Cuba, but after much consideration he helped his brother achieve a last-ditch diplomatic solution that saw the Kennedy administration order a naval "quarantine" of the island and demand that Khrushchev remove the missiles. In the tense days when the world found itself on the brink of nuclear war, it was Bobby who met secretly with the Soviet ambassador to the United States, Anatoly Dobrynin, to defuse the crisis. He told Dobrynin that the United States was planning to remove its intermediate-range ballistic Jupiter missiles from Turkey—one of Khrushchev's key demands—but it could not be made public and seen to be part of the deal to avert the nuclear showdown. The Soviets backed down and agreed to remove their IL-28 bombers from Cuba on November 20. Five months later, in April 1963, the United States removed its Jupiter missiles from Turkey.

"We didn't see my dad during most of the Cuban Missile Crisis," wrote Kennedy in his family memoir. "For thirteen days and twelve nights he stayed at the White House. At the height of the crisis, the government made plans to evacuate public officials and their families. We all knew that the capital would be vaporized in the first minutes of a nuclear exchange." When US marshals arrived at Hickory Hill to transport the family to a bombproof bunker, Bobby refused to allow them to leave, even though Kennedy and his older brother, Joe, were eager to visit the underground caverns. "My dad told us we needed to be 'brave soldiers' and show up at Our Lady of Victory School, that our absence would be noticed and might cause panic in the capital."

Just as the Cuban Missile Crisis was being defused, another segregation drama was unfolding at the University of Alabama, where the state's governor, George Wallace, seemed to aim his fiery inaugural speech at the Kennedy brothers when he promised "segregation now, segregation tomorrow, segregation forever" in January 1963. Months later, when three Black students applied to the University of Alabama at Tuscaloosa, Bobby Kennedy called the governor in an effort to avoid an armed confrontation like the one at Ole Miss a year earlier. After numerous phone calls from the president, which Wallace refused to answer, Bobby traveled to the state capital in Montgomery for a face-to-face meeting. The Confederate flag was flying at the state capitol on April 25 when Bobby arrived for his meeting with Wallace, making his way past a menacing phalanx of state troopers in steel helmets emblazoned with the Confederate flag.

"If this country means anything, if our society's going to hang together at all, it's going to hang together because of the law, and observance of the law," said Bobby. "And that's what we are interested in. This transcends the question of segregation or integration or desegregation. This is a question of law and order in the United States."

A few minutes before Bobby's arrival, police arrested eighteen white demonstrators in front of the capitol building carrying signs saying "Mississippi Murderer" and "No Kennedy Congo Here." "Inside the executive office, Wallace placed a tape recorder on the table between them and endeavored to goad my dad into threatening to send troops into the state, a provocation Wallace could use to political advantage," Kennedy wrote in his family memoir.

Wallace remained firm that he would not allow the federal government to interfere with Alabama, and Bobby returned to Washington.

The confrontation at the university ended nearly two months later, when Katzenbach, accompanied by two federal marshals and a contingent of National Guard, confronted Wallace on the steps of the school in front of the national press. Katzenbach presented Wallace, who was standing at a lectern with a microphone, backed by state troopers, with a proclamation from the US president threatening to charge him with obstruction of justice if he did not allow African American students Vivian Malone and James Hood to enter Foster Auditorium to register for their classes. Wallace gave a prepared speech, refusing to step aside. "Governor, I'm not interested in a show," said Katzenbach. Wallace eventually backed down, declaring "I can't fight bayonets with my bare hands," and allowed Malone and Hood to pass.

The Kennedy family's proximity to power informed Kennedy's childhood. For one thing, the Kennedy children kept largely to themselves. "When I was growing up, my brothers and sisters were my friends," he told an interviewer in 2007. And they made friends with some powerful adults. William O. Douglas, an associate justice of the Supreme Court, taught Kennedy how to fly fish. "In 1962, Justice Douglas took us kids, many of my cousins, aunts and uncles and my father on a ten-day pack trip to Whiskey Bend in the San Juan range on Washington's Olympic peninsula," he wrote. "We lived on trout that we caught with salmon eggs and drank from the streams. Afterward, we fished for salmon in Puget Sound and caught more fish than I'd ever seen."

In addition, everyone from the actor and activist Harry Belafonte to Lauren Bacall and the football player Roosevelt Grier were guests at soirées at Hickory Hill. "One winter a contingent of Alaskan Inuit arrived for lunch during an unusual Washington snowstorm and spent the afternoon with my father in the backyard building a great igloo," wrote Kennedy in his memoir.

His powerful family nurtured his fascination with animals and nature, with his uncle inviting him to the Oval Office for a private meeting about the environment. A black-and-white photo in the archives of the John F. Kennedy Library & Museum shows the nine-year-old Kennedy in a blazer, matching shorts, and a tie presenting a salamander to his uncle. Other pictures show the lifeless amphibian floating in a vase as Kennedy and his uncle examine it closely. After that meeting in March 1961, Jack Kennedy arranged for his nephew to meet with Secretary of the Interior Stewart Udall to present his concerns about extinction. The encounter of the young Kennedy scion and the country's leading environmentalist resulted in news stories in both *Time* magazine and *The Saturday Evening Post*.

By the time he was eleven and immersed in T. H. White's *The Once and Future King*, Kennedy became obsessed with falconry, hunting wild game with a trained bird of prey, such as a hawk or a falcon. He eventually trained with a local falconer and acquired his own hawk. The hawk, named Morgan after King Arthur's half sister, joined a menagerie of animals at Hickory Hill that at one point included a sea lion named Sandy, who lived in one of the pools and was fed a diet of fresh mackerel. Although she devoured the fish, she had issues with their eyeballs, which were "scattered like marbles across the pool, patio and lawn." Eventually, things got so out of hand with Sandy prowling through the neighborhood with a pack of dogs and, at one point, causing a traffic jam that the family donated her to the Washington National Zoo, where Kennedy had summer jobs cleaning cages and feeding rats to the raptors.

The seal had been a gift from his uncle Jimmy Skakel, one of his mother's older brothers, who kept exotic fish, including sharks, in giant aquariums at his home in Bel Air, where he used to dive in a wet suit. Jimmy was a self-styled adventurer who once harpooned a forty-two-ton whale from a thirty-eight-foot fishing boat for a *Life* magazine story spread over eight pages in the December 21, 1962, issue. For the magazine reporter, Jimmy was proof that "the American male was still cut from the same rugged cloth as his forebears had been." The article likened the challenge to a modern-day pursuit of Moby Dick, with a detailed description of Jimmy's battle with "a monstrous sperm whale." One photo showed him surfing on his giant catch in a pool of blood. "He comes from a wealthy daredevil family," noted the article about the geologist and businessman, who later kept the whale's jaws as a trophy in his home in Miami.

Another Skakel uncle, George, kept a pair of mountain lion cubs he had captured in western Canada at his home in Connecticut. But when they became a nuisance in his upscale neighborhood, he took matters into his own hands. He drugged the lions and stuffed them into his family's private plane en route to a ranch he owned in Canada. When the pilot refused to cross the border, George told him to land in Burlington, Vermont, where he rented a Cadillac and smuggled the lions in the trunk of the car. He later released them onto the family property. George, a big-game hunter, was killed in a plane crash in September 1966 while on his way to an elk hunt in Idaho with nineteen other members of the hunting party. The single-engine

Cessna "crashed into a wilderness canyon," according to a CIA report about the accident. A lack of radio and telephone communications prevented rescuers from reaching the crash site until two days later.

"Both families shared a love of nature that might have provided the genetic antecedents to my predilection for the outdoors, but while the Kennedys embraced the challenges of sea, river and wilderness, the Skakels glorified in capturing, collecting or subduing," wrote Kennedy, whose lifelong fascination with exotic birds and animals was likely informed by the Skakel brothers' adventures. Kennedy himself was obsessed with collecting animals from a young age. On a trip to Africa in 1964 with his cousin Bobby Shriver and his uncle Sargent Shriver, the first director of the Peace Corps, he returned home with a sixteen-pound leopard tortoise that he brought back in a Gucci suitcase that doubled as a diplomatic pouch and did not go through customs inspection. The tortoise, named Carruthers, lived at Hickory Hill for more than two decades.

Although Kennedy had much more contact with the Kennedy side of his family, he was certainly influenced by the legendary daring of his Skakel uncles and his mother, their younger sister. Ethel Skakel was an accomplished athlete and equestrienne. She was also highly competitive, and family legend has it that she had been determined to beat her mother-in-law and Kennedy family matriarch Rose Fitzgerald Kennedy at the baby game. Rose had nine children, and Ethel had eleven.

Like Kennedy's father, Ethel was the product of a big, boisterous wealthy family. She was the sixth of seven children born to George Skakel and Ann Brannack while they were still struggling to build their coal empire. The family was living in a Chicago tenement when Ethel was born on April 11, 1928, but their fortunes rapidly changed after George Skakel launched a successful coal and coke business, building up the company that would become the Great Lakes Carbon Corporation. The family struck it rich and eventually moved to a sprawling mansion on twelve acres in a wealthy enclave of

Greenwich, Connecticut, when Ethel was eight years old. She grew up riding horses and sailing on Long Island Sound. She was such an accomplished sailor by age eleven that she won the Larchmont Yacht Club championship "against a field of fifty boats, mostly piloted by older skippers," according to Kennedy, writing in his family memoir. "Winning made her happy."

Throughout her life she was fond of mischief and horses. She often skipped school to play the horses at Belmont Park during the season. She once burned a demerits book that recorded student absences so that she and a friend could attend the Harvard-Yale football game.

In 1944, she entered Manhattanville College of the Sacred Heart, a liberal arts all-girls school that was among the first in New York City to allow Black women students in 1938. During her first year at the school, her roommate was Jean Kennedy, Bobby and Jack Kennedy's younger sister. Ethel met her future husband for the first time on a ski vacation in Quebec in 1945 while he was on a home visit from the navy. At the time, she was seventeen and Bobby was nineteen. Although he dated her older sister Patricia "Pat" Sistine Skakel for two years, there was little doubt in Ethel's mind that she would marry him after that first meeting. "No maybe about it," she told *People* magazine in 2012.

The couple started dating after Bobby broke up with Pat, with Ethel, the daughter of staunch Republicans, plunging headlong with her friend Jean Kennedy into working on Jack's Democratic campaign for Congress.

Ethel's engagement to Bobby was announced in *The New York Times* in January 1950, and they were married at an elaborate society wedding in Greenwich in June. *The Boston Globe* called it "one of the prettiest of the year" in an article on its front page. The groom had twenty-six ushers, and all of the bridesmaids ended up in the pool, reported the newspaper. "The marriage unites two large American fortunes and was honored with a Papal blessing from Pope Pius XII," the newspaper noted. After spending their honeymoon in Hawaii, the couple moved to Charlottesville, Virginia, where Bobby was completing his degree at the University of Virginia Law School.

Bobby Kennedy was a good catch, even though his father had once referred to him, perhaps jokingly, as the "runt" of the Kennedy family because, unlike his older brothers and father, he measured under six feet tall. But like his brothers, he was an accomplished military veteran and scholar who despite his slight build played on the Harvard football team, earning a varsity letter, and was well known for his tenacity and determination. "He was smaller than his brothers," said Larry Tye, a Robert Kennedy biographer. "He was somebody who didn't seem to stand out, and yet . . . the most important thing in his life was having his dad realize that he had value."

Joe Kennedy was not an easy man to please and had high expectations for his sons. The Irish Catholic patriarch was a well-connected Boston-born Democrat with big ambitions. He graduated with an economics degree from Harvard in 1912 and cut his teeth in the banking industry, eventually becoming the youngest bank president in the United States at twenty-five, when he stepped in to head up the Columbia Trust Company, his father's bank, to block a takeover. He made a sizable fortune reorganizing Hollywood studios and began a torrid two-year affair with the silent film star Gloria Swanson in 1928 in Palm Beach, where he spent months at a time, eventually buying a mansion there in 1933. When her husband, Hollywood director Henry de La Falaise, threatened to get in the way, Joe Kennedy gave him a job at one of his studios.

The affair caused a rift in his marriage to Rose Fitzgerald, the eldest daughter of Boston's mayor, who temporarily moved back in with her family, and "began dealing with the disappointment in her marriage by leaving for extended periods," taking trips to Europe and other parts of the United States and leaving her children alone with Joe and the housekeepers.

In addition to banking and his interests in Hollywood, the Kennedy patriarch invested in the distribution rights for Scotch whisky and owned the largest commercial building in the world, the sprawling Chicago Merchandise Mart, which boasts 3.7 million square feet spread out over two city blocks and twenty-five stories.

A rising star within the Democratic Party, he was nakedly ambitious and dreamed of being the first Catholic president of the United States. With large homes in Bronxville, New York, Hyannis Port, and Palm Beach, he tooled around in a Bentley and was a major donor to Democratic campaigns. As a reward, he was appointed by Franklin D. Roosevelt to be the first chairman of the Securities and Exchange Commission in 1934 and later headed the Maritime Commission. Before Roosevelt announced that he would seek a third term in office, Joe was often cited in the papers as one of a handful of political rising stars who could win a Democratic nomination for president. But in 1938, the Irish Catholic patriarch was appointed President Roosevelt's ambassador to London, where his anti-Semitism, outspoken views on US isolationism, and appeasement of Adolf Hitler, whom he tried to meet with several times before the beginning of the war, eventually cost him his ambassadorship and his presidential ambitions. He was also seen as a coward by the British press, who dubbed him "Jittery Joe" for his decision to move his family of nine children to the countryside during the London Blitz. On October 6, 1940, he wrote a letter to Roosevelt asking to be recalled from the Court of St. James's.

With his presidential ambitions dashed after his disastrous tour in the United Kingdom, Joe Kennedy redoubled his efforts with his eldest son, Joe Jr., who had served as a delegate to the 1940 Democratic National Convention and had plans to run for Massachusetts's 11th Congressional District after his stint as a naval aviator during the war. But in 1944, he volunteered for a secret bombing campaign to fly over Normandy in a radio-controlled B-17 bomber to a German V-2 rocket–launching site, where he would arm the explosives and parachute to safety before the plane exploded over its German target. But Operation Aphrodite went horribly wrong when the explosives detonated prematurely, killing him and his copilot, Wilford John Willy.

The devastated Joe Kennedy transferred his political ambitions to his second-born son, Jack, who had been a frail child, suffering from a host of maladies that Joe had valiantly tried to nurse during his wife's frequent absences. "It was like being drafted," Jack later told a reporter. "My father wanted his oldest son in politics. 'Wanted' isn't the right word. He *demanded* it. You know my father."

Although he wasn't the hard-charging, accomplished athlete his brother Joe had been, Jack had other attributes that made his father proud. At twenty-three, he published his Harvard thesis as a book. His 1940 book, *Why England Slept*, was designed to contrast to Winston Churchill's bestseller *While England Slept*, published two years earlier. Jack was able to draw on primary research from the US Embassy in London for his central argument, which slammed Great Britain for not paying attention to Germany's massive military buildup. The book did not support Joe's isolationist or appeasement theories, but nonetheless Joe embraced the project with gusto, leaning on his friend Henry Luce, the publisher of *Time* and *Life* magazines, to write the foreword. The book became a bestseller, although many Kennedy observers have long suspected that Joe bought copies in bulk to bolster his son's ranking on the bestseller lists. Jack's future sister-in-law Ethel was so taken with the book that she wrote her college thesis on it, much to the chagrin of her Republican parents.

Like his older brother, Jack enlisted in the military, although it took two physical examinations before he was allowed to join the navy two months before the Japanese attack on Pearl Harbor in 1941. He was assigned to the Office of Naval Intelligence, but he was determined to see action, despite his physical frailties. By March 1943, he was on his way to the Solomon Islands as a patrol torpedo boat commander. He and his crew of twelve went missing a few months later, and his comrades were so sure that everyone was dead that they held a funeral service for them on the islands. In fact, two of the crew members had died when a Japanese destroyer had attacked their boat. Jack had swum for hours, pulling the body of one of his injured men to a nearby island, where he had scrawled "SOS" on a coconut and asked a group of islanders to deliver it to the US military base. The group was saved, and Jack was transformed into a war hero.

After returning to the United States, Jack Kennedy didn't waste any time. He took his older brother's place, running for Congress in Massachusetts' 11th District in 1946. His campaign focused on improved housing for veterans, better health care, support for organized labor and for world peace, and strong opposition to the Soviet Union. Six years later, he ran for the Senate, defeating the powerful incumbent and fellow war hero Henry Cabot Lodge Jr. In January 1960, he announced his candidacy for president, beating more experienced candidates such as Hubert Humphrey and Lyndon Johnson in the Democratic primary. In the presidential race, Johnson became his running mate. The shining era of Camelot began after they declared victory in November 1960. A year later, Joe suffered a stroke that left his right side paralyzed and greatly diminished his cognitive functions and ability to speak. Then in November 1963, he lost another son— this time to an assassin's bullet.

Bobby Kennedy Jr. was nine years old when his uncle was killed in Dallas on November 22, 1963, two days after his father's thirty-eighth birthday. Robert Kennedy heard the news that his brother had been shot while having lunch by the pool at Hickory Hill with US Attorney Robert Morgenthau and his aide Silvio Mollo when FBI Director J. Edgar Hoover called with the news. Morgenthau watched as Bobby put down the phone and turned away, clasping a hand to his mouth. Jack died thirty minutes later at Parkland Memorial Hospital. Bobby broke the news to his lunch guests after getting off the phone with Dallas. "There's so much bitterness," he said, pacing back and forth as Kennedy administration officials began arriving at Hickory Hill. "I thought they would get one of us. But Jack, after all he'd been through, never worried about it."

Ethel picked up Kennedy and his siblings Joe and Kathleen from school. Passing flags already at half-staff, she informed the children that "a bad man shot Uncle Jack," whom everyone in the family referred to as "the President." Still, she assured the children, he was already in Heaven.

His father was shattered and plunged into deep mourning. "He looked haunted," wrote Kennedy in his memoir, adding that he had begun wearing Jack's flight jacket with the presidential seal and had taken months to recover from his brother's death. "My mother said he was like a man who had lost both arms."

During the period of mourning, Bobby pondered his future in politics and continued to fulfill his duties as attorney general for the new president, Lyndon Johnson, a man he hated more than he did Roy Cohn. In one of his more daring acts, in the summer of 1964, he traveled on a goodwill mission to Europe, with a controversial stop in Communist Poland. During the four-day visit, he refused to follow any of the rules or protocols set out by the US embassy and the Polish government. He courted adoring crowds of thousands of Poles, riding on the roof of a Soviet-built sedan that the Polish government had loaned him for the visit with Ethel, his daughter Kathleen, and his sons Joe Jr. and Bobby Jr. Ethel and Bobby shook hands and signed autographs, with black-and-white newsreel footage showing even their children signing their names for the delirious spectators who swarmed city streets to get a glimpse of the family despite a news blackout on their visit ordered by authorities.

"Robert Kennedy, sensing he was among friends, responded like an Irish politician running for Mayor of Boston," wrote a reporter for *The New York Times* who followed the family throughout their tour.

He climbed onto the roof of the nearest automobile and spoke in simple, warm-spirited sentences of the friendship and Polish virtues and of historic ties between the two countries.

"You know, my brother would not have been elected if it weren't for the Polish vote," he would say, evoking delighted laughter every time. During each impromptu street rally Mr. Kennedy would summon his wife, and children onto the car roof and introduce them to the crowd.

Kennedy defied local authorities and demanded that embassy staff set up meetings at an orphanage and a visit with the head of the Catholic Church in the country, who was a sworn enemy of the state. "In three days he ripped to shreds the elaborate web of carefully articulated relationships that the United States and Poland have spun in the last eight years," wrote the *Times* reporter.

In Częstochowa, a city in southern Poland, the family visited Cardinal Stefan Wyszyński, an anti-Communist crusader who at the time was the biggest enemy of the Polish government. "Mr. Kennedy had lunch with the Pauline fathers in the monastery's refectory. Mrs. Kennedy, her daughter Kathleen, and the women in the party were admitted to the cloisters to have lunch separately—a concession said to have been previously made only to queens."

In a press release issued by the attorney general's office after the visit, Kennedy thanked the Polish government and remained firm in his anti-Communist position, invoking his dead brother's message of hope:

> Our objective is clear. It is to facilitate the reconciliation of Eastern and Western Europe in association with the United States. This is the only sure guarantee against nuclear war whether by design or by accident. It is the surest means of fostering our common prosperity. The task is not easy.
>
> But as President Kennedy said in his inaugural address:

"Let us begin." Just because we cannot see clearly the end of the road, that is no reason for not setting out on this most essential journey.

Shortly after the European trip, Robert Kennedy announced his decision to run for the US Senate to represent New York, where he had not lived for several years. He invoked his brother as well as President Johnson's success in passing the landmark Civil Rights Act, which outlawed discrimination based on race, color, religion, or sex, in his speech. The act passed Congress two days after Bobby returned from his European tour, on July 2, 1964. It was signed into law by Johnson on the same day. "All that President Kennedy stood for. All that President Johnson is trying to accomplish. All the progress that has been made is threatened by new and dangerous Republican assault," he said during the press conference announcing his Senate run. He resigned from his attorney general post in September to focus on his campaign against incumbent Senator Kenneth Keating, who had served one term in the Senate beginning in 1959. In his victory speech, Kennedy said that he had won an "overwhelming mandate" to continue the policies of his slain older brother.

And then, a few weeks after taking the oath of office, Bobby Kennedy found himself embarking on another challenge: climbing a mountain in Canada's remote north to honor his late brother. The nearly 14,000-foot-high Mount Kennedy, the highest unclimbed peak in North America, was located in the Yukon, more than 140 miles northwest of the provincial capital Whitehorse, and had been named to honor John F. Kennedy a year after his assassination in 1964. The mountain, in the Saint Elias range, had previously been known as East Hubbard. "I believe it is appropriate that Canada's memorial to him should be a mountain," said Lester B. Pearson, Canada's prime minister, in his speech christening the mountain after John F. Kennedy. "A mountain is solid and enduring. Mount Kennedy is a graceful, towering, unencumbered peak . . . a symbol of aspiration and upward reach." Months later, in January 1965, another Canadian mountain was named for JFK because it was discovered that Mount Logan, also in the Yukon, was, in fact, some 4,000 feet higher than East Hubbard.

Robert Kennedy, then thirty-nine, was flown by Royal Canadian Air Force helicopter to the first base camp at 9,000 feet along with a crew sponsored by *National Geographic*. The expedition was led by Jim Whittaker, the first American to climb Mount Everest in 1963. From the camp, he was to climb to the top, a 5,000-foot ascent. He took an American flag, two Canadian flags (the Union Jack and the newly adopted Maple Leaf), the Kennedy family crest, and a copy of his brother's inauguration address to leave at the top. Whittaker and another member of the climbing team unroped him near the mountain's peak, allowing him to climb the last fifty yards to the top on his own. It was a huge public relations coup for Bobby, as well as a personal memorial to his beloved brother.

When Bobby returned to base camp, crew members fed him steak, instant mashed potatoes, ice cream, and "the heel of a bottle of Madeira wine which someone had stashed in a pack sack," according to a Whitehorse newspaper, which ended its report with a description of the newly minted senator buying a round of drinks for locals at the Capital Hotel. Kennedy paid with a check, which Cal Miller, the owner of the hotel, refused to cash. "I told him I wanted to keep it as a souvenir of the next President of the United States," he said. Miller's comment proved prescient. Three years after climbing the mountain to honor his dead older brother, Bobby Kennedy would make his own ill-fated decision to run for president.

CHAPTER 3

"Everybody Takes Their Licks"

Robert Kennedy's children were dressed in their Sunday best as they sat with their mother on either side of the podium in the ornate Senate Caucus Room on Capitol Hill to await the arrival of their father, who was scheduled to announce his bid for the White House on March 16, 1968. The Kennedy boys were dressed in dark suits, stiff white shirts, and ties, carefully styled to match their father's outfit. The Kennedy girls wore dainty white gloves and their best dresses. Kathleen Kennedy, then sixteen, stood out in a brunette bob and Kelly green suit that was an almost exact match of the industrial broadloom carpet as a sea of dark-suited reporters and political supporters poured into the room. Many stood on tiptoe, straining with cameras held aloft to get a photo of Ethel and the Kennedy children. Ethel was resplendent in a bouffant hairdo and tailored suit, her tanned face and trim build a testament to her rugged Skakel forebears. She was pregnant with the couple's eleventh child, although no one had yet made a public announcement that she was expecting a baby.

Correspondent Roger Mudd, who was providing live commentary

from CBS's New York City studios, noted that the Senate Caucus Room, where John F. Kennedy had made his own campaign announcement on January 12, 1960, resembled "a gilded German nightclub" with its soaring ceilings, gold-covered eagles, and indirect lighting.

Supporters broke into applause as Robert Kennedy finally entered the room flanked by his press secretary, Frank Mankiewicz, whose signature pipe seemed to lead him through the surging crowd. Despite the wild applause, Mudd's commentary reminded the audience that the senator from New York had his work cut out for him: He faced "almost solid opposition" from his own party, with only three Democratic state chairmen—in Oregon, New York, and Tennessee—supporting his bid for the country's highest office.

As if to assuage his critics, he seemed to back into his historic speech when he announced, "I do not run for the presidency merely to oppose any man." In the same room where he had once so combatively presided over the Senate's hearings into organized crime, he warned that the country was on a "perilous course" and that he had "strong feelings about what must be done."

During the question period after the speech, he brushed off suggestions that he was an opportunist in announcing his run for the presidency on the heels of Democratic Senator Eugene McCarthy's stellar showing in the polls against President Johnson in the New Hampshire primary four days earlier. While McCarthy had lost that race with 42 percent of the vote to Johnson's 49 percent, the result had been critical because it had revealed Johnson's vulnerability within his own party. More important, as Bobby pointed out, New Hampshire highlighted the deep divisions within the party and the country itself, especially over the war in Vietnam. Years earlier, Johnson had considered McCarthy as a running mate before settling on his own vice president, Hubert Humphrey.

"I run for the presidency because I want the Democratic Party and the United States of America to stand for hope instead of despair, for reconciliation of men instead of the growing risk of world war," Bobby said.

Two weeks after Bobby entered the race, Johnson, whose approval rating had plummeted, largely as the result of the Vietnam War, announced his withdrawal. Less than a month later, Humphrey declared that he would run for president.

Like McCarthy, Bobby focused his campaign on the Vietnam War, but his emphasis was on uniting the country and helping the poor—his coalition of the "have-nots," as he liked to describe the people who came out in force during his campaign and treated him like a rock star.

And he was determined to exploit the memory of his older brother to win. It was no accident that he chose the Senate Caucus Room to jump-start his presidential campaign. His buttons and placards were nearly exact replicas of John F. Kennedy's campaign materials with a black-and-white portrait of the handsome candidate in a red, white, and blue setting urging supporters to "Vote for Our Next President, Robert F. Kennedy." Unable to summon the party leaders and the country's biggest unions to back his candidacy, his entourage leaned on Cesar Chavez's United Farm Workers and civil rights leaders, including John Lewis, a cofounder of the Student Nonviolent Coordinating Committee and speaker at the 1963 March on Washington alongside Martin Luther King Jr.

In fact, Bobby made his most impassioned speech extemporaneously in Indiana when he addressed a rally of mostly Black supporters on the day Martin Luther King had been shot. It fell to the former attorney general, who had once authorized wiretaps of the civil rights leader, to tell the crowd that he was dead, and in doing so he spoke publicly for the first time about his own grief after his brother's assassination nearly five years earlier. "Martin Luther King dedicated his life to love and to justice between fellow human beings," he said in the address in which he quoted the Greek poet Aeschylus. "He died in the cause of that effort. For those of you who are Black, and are tempted to be filled with hatred and mistrust of the injustice of such an act against all white people, I would only say that I can also feel in my own heart the same kind of feeling. I had a member of my family killed, but he was killed by a white man." Bobby would go on to travel through several states, shaking so many hands during a frenetic eighty-two-day campaign for president that his hands would be chafed and bleeding at the end of each day. "He identified with people who hurt," recalled his campaign manager, Fred Dutton. "Maybe it was because he hurt."

Bill Barry, his bodyguard, a former football player at Kent State, spent hours holding him around the waist to keep him from being lifted into the crowds that thronged the streets as adoring fans lurched perilously close to the open convertible where he stood to greet them. "The California crowds were much more exuberant and rough and bruising than any other crowds that we hit," said Barry, who on one occasion "hit face down on the pavement" when he tried to prevent Bobby from being pulled into the crowd.

One summer morning in San Francisco's Chinatown, Bobby's entourage, including Ethel, ducked at what sounded like eight gunshots. Only Bobby was left standing, according to reporter Jules Witcover, who covered the campaign. "It was as though he had prepared himself for just such a moment, and to endure through it," said Witcover.

That moment came a few days later when Robert Kennedy was shot along with several others in the kitchen of the Ambassador Hotel in Los Angeles while making his way from the podium in the ballroom where he had just made his victory speech. "Kennedy, you son of a bitch!" yelled Sirhan Bishara Sirhan, a twenty-four-year-old Palestinian Christian militant, who emptied all eight bullets from the chamber of his .22-caliber Iver Johnson Cadet revolver. In the melee of screaming aides, campaign reporters, and kitchen staff, Juan Romero, a seventeen-year-old busboy who had reached out to shake the candidate's hand as he walked through the kitchen, cradled the wounded candidate, who fell to the ground in a pool of blood.

"I kneeled down to him and I could see his lips moving, so I put my ear next to his lips and I heard him say, 'Is everybody OK?' I said, 'Yes, everybody's OK,'" recalled Romero, a Mexican immigrant, years after the shooting. "I put my hand between the cold concrete and his head just to make him comfortable." Romero remembered that he had had a rosary in his shirt pocket. "I took it out, thinking that he would need it a lot more than me," he said. "I wrapped it around his right hand and then they wheeled him away."

Bobby was rushed to Central Receiving Hospital about a mile away before being transferred to Good Samaritan Hospital, where doctors performed emergency neurosurgery to remove the bullets and bone fragments that had lodged in his brain. He had been hit at close range by three bullets. The fatal shot had entered behind his right ear. The other two shots had entered just below his right armpit.

Although some of Bobby's children were in Los Angeles during the primary, Hubert Humphrey sent Air Force Two to pick up Kennedy, his sister Kathleen, and his brother Joe, who were at different boarding schools on the East Coast. Kennedy was roused from his sleep at Georgetown Prep, a Jesuit high school in Bethesda, Maryland. A car was waiting to take him home. At Hickory Hill, Ethel's personal secretary, Jinx Hack, told him that his father had been shot. "But I was still thinking he'd be OK," wrote Kennedy in his family memoir. "He was, after all, indestructible." But when he heard that all the campaign offices were shutting down, "I knew my dad was going to die."

Outside Good Samaritan Hospital, thousands of supporters, some holding "Pray for Bobby" signs, stood, waiting for news. The hospital floor where Bobby was in surgery had been cleared except for close friends and family, including Martin Luther King's widow, Coretta Scott King, astronaut John Glenn, singer Andy Williams, and Olympic athlete and actor Rafer Johnson, as well as Kennedy's aunts Jackie, Pat, and Jean, uncle Ted, and Jean's husband, Steve Smith, he wrote. "My father lay on a gurney with his head bandaged and his face bruised, especially around the eyes. A priest had already administered last rites. My mother sat beside him, holding his hand. She stayed there all night. I sat down across the bed from her and took hold of his big wrestler's hand. I prayed and said goodbye to him, listening to the pumps that kept him breathing." Each of his ten children took turns sitting with their father and praying opposite Ethel.

Fifteen-year-old Joe Kennedy was deputized to tell his brothers and sisters assembled outside the operating room that their father was dead. At the hospital, Kennedy described a "hellish environment" as doctors and nurses who had been attending to Bobby wailed and screamed after he died. He was forty-two years old. Ethel, thirty-eight years old and pregnant, was the newest Kennedy widow.

When the body was taken back to New York City, more than a hundred thousand mourners lined up to pay their respects at St. Patrick's Cathedral. The coffin was placed in the nave of the church, and with their grandmother Rose the family held a private service. "Jackie broke down and wept as she hadn't allowed herself to when we buried Uncle Jack," wrote Kennedy in his memoir. On Friday, during the wake, the family took turns "standing honor guard" around the flag-draped casket while the mourners filed past.

Bobby's eldest sons, Joe, Robert Jr., and David, participated in the Mass at the historic church. Leonard Bernstein conducted the New York Philharmonic, and Williams, a friend of the family, sang "Battle Hymn of the Republic," Bobby's favorite song. The mourners who packed the church sang along. Williams and his wife had been in Los Angeles during the primary and had been on their way to meet Bobby and Ethel for a celebration at the Factory disco when he saw that Bobby had been shot on the TV in his hotel room.

The crowds that lined the train route as Bobby's casket traveled from New York's Penn Station to Washington's Union Station for his burial at Arlington National Cemetery were somber and stood at attention. The journey, normally four hours long, took double the amount of time because of the massive crowds; some two million people lined the route to pay their respects. Windows were removed from the the final train car—there were twenty-one cars in total with seven hundred campaign workers, family, and friends on board—and the casket was propped up on six chairs so that mourners would have a clear view as the train passed. Two people died in Elizabeth, New Jersey, when a train running on a parallel track struck a group of mourners at a crossing. One of them was cut in half—a scene witnessed by David, twelve years old, whose head was outside the train window during most of the trip. The train was delayed as organizers demanded that such an accident not happen again. Penn Central ended up canceling all northbound trains and provided a "pilot train" for security. At Union Station, Lyndon Johnson met the train with a hearse that drove the coffin to Arlington National Cemetery, where Bobby would be buried next to his older brother.

"No one came after him who could speak simultaneously for the unemployed black teenager and the white worker trapped in a dead-end job and feeling misunderstood," wrote reporter Jack Newfield, echoing what many of Bobby's supporters felt about his passing.

It was Joe Kennedy, a few months shy of his sixteenth birthday, who was allowed to sit in his father's chair at the dining room table days after the burial. Ethel had pronounced him "man of the house" on June 15, the same day the family assembled around the table at Hickory Hill to celebrate David's thirteenth birthday. For Ethel, Joe had surely earned the distinction for the very mature way he had carried himself after his father's death. On the train that had carried his father's body to Washington, it was Joe who had dressed up in one of his father's suits and made the rounds of the mourners with his mother, thanking them for their support.

Perhaps it was jealousy over Joe's new role in the family that drove Kennedy in his endless practical jokes, for during the lackluster celebration on David's birthday that year, he spiked everyone's drink with a laxative.

Of all the Kennedy children, David was likely the hardest hit by his father's death. On the final days of the campaign in California, he had had premonitions of his father dying, and on the day of his death he nearly drowned in the undertow at Malibu. The family was staying at the home of Hollywood director John Frankenheimer. It was Bobby who saved David when he saw him struggling in the surf.

On the night of the California primary, David Kennedy was alone in a room at the Beverly Hills Hotel watching his father's victory speech on television when he saw the news of the shooting. He watched the chaos on the screen and his father's head being cradled by the busboy, whose hands were covered in blood. In the confusion no one thought to check on him, assuming that he had gone to sleep. By the time astronaut John Glenn and the author Theodore White looked in on him several hours later, the twelve-year-old was still sitting in front of the television set, unable to speak.

"He was alone and supposed to be asleep, but the excitement of the day had kept him awake," wrote his older sister Kathleen Kennedy. "In the aftermath of the tragedy, it was some time before someone came to check on him. It was Presidential biographer Theodore White who found the boy 'devastated at the sight he had just seen.' Without stopping to rationalize why, White ordered a soothing hot chocolate from room service and cradled and comforted the shaken youngster."

In the period immediately following his father's death, as the children were home from school, Kennedy's practical jokes became a constant thorn in Ethel's side. At a memorial Mass for his father he played a trick on Phil Kirby, a Hyannis Port neighbor who had been asked to assist at the Mass. Kirby had asked the priest to let him know when he had to ring the bell at the Mass. The priest said he would tap him on the shoulder when it was time. At the beginning of the Mass, Kirby felt a tap and rang the bell; he was mortified when he realized he had done so at the wrong time and looked back at the smiling Kennedy.

Ethel, who had a short fuse when it came to her children, sank into anger and depression after her husband's death and ordered Bobby Jr. to leave the house more than once. When the family flew with Uncle Teddy to Connecticut to charter a boat to the family compound in Hyannis Port, Ethel was so angry with both Bobby Jr. and David that she hit them with a hairbrush and began to make plans to send them away. "Everyone takes their licks," she told her children, according to Kennedy's memoir, reminding them that there were children in Watts and Harlem who had lost their parents and didn't have the support they had.

During that difficult summer, Joe was sent to Spain to live with the Guardiolas, a family recommended to Teddy by the US Embassy in Madrid. The family raised bulls for matadors throughout Spain. David was sent to a tennis camp in Austria with his cousin Chris Lawford, where they both discovered sex. Kennedy seemed to score the greatest prize of all: He was sent to Africa with the man who had already inserted himself into his life as a surrogate father.

Kirk LeMoyne "Lem" Billings was a Kennedy family devotee who had first met John Kennedy when they had been students at Choate, an elite boarding school in Connecticut. Billings, who stood more than six feet tall and was the strongest member on the school's rowing team and a champion wrestler, formed a seemingly unlikely friendship with the frail Jack Kennedy. Lem was gay but kept his sex life hidden, especially as he got closer and closer to the Kennedy family. But the two became lifelong friends after meeting in the office of *The Brief*, the school's yearbook, in 1933. Lem spent Christmas that year in Palm Beach and summered at Hyannis Port, where he was burned in a defective shower and had to be hospitalized for three weeks. He met Bobby when he was an eight-year-old and Teddy when he was two and was such a constant presence that the family patriarch, Joe Kennedy, soon began referring to him as a son. Four years later, in

1937, Lem accompanied Jack on a tour of Europe the year before his father became ambassador to England. Joe Kennedy arranged for the young men to meet the pope.

Later, Lem was an usher at Jack's wedding in 1953 and worked on his political campaigns. He also participated in Jack's sister Jean Kennedy's wedding three years later to Stephen Smith, a financier and political strategist who worked on Jack's 1960 presidential campaign. Lem was so close to the entire family that he continued to spend holidays at Hyannis Port and had his own bedroom at the White House when Jack was president. He declined offers from Jack to become head of the Peace Corps and ambassador to Denmark but accompanied him and Jackie on many official trips abroad. An unofficial aide to Kennedy, it was Washington's best-kept open secret that he was homosexual.

Though Lem was not especially interested in children, he took an immediate liking to Kennedy. "That boy is just like Jack," he told Bobby. After Bobby's death, Lem stepped forward to be a mentor and a kind of surrogate father to Bobby Jr.

Lem volunteered to take Bobby Jr. to Africa, a trip that been arranged before the assassination. In 1966, Bobby and Ethel had traveled to South Africa at the invitation of the National Union of South African Students, a prominent anti-apartheid group, at the University of Cape Town, where Bobby delivered his "Ripple of Hope" speech in which he declared that individual action, no matter how small, could change the world for the better. They also traveled to Tanzania, where they told their host, John Owen, the director of the Tanzania National Parks, of their son's "deep interest" in animals and his summer jobs at the Washington Zoo. Owen invited them to send Bobby Jr. to spend time at one of the parks. He and his surrogate father, Lem, arrived in Nairobi on July 1, spending time at the home of the US ambassador before heading to Tanzania.

"Plans for the big trip had already been completed when the family—and the world—was plunged into grief by the senator's assassination in June," wrote a reporter for *Life*, which featured the story of his adventure months later. "It was his mother's decision that young Bobby should go."

Lem spent much of the trip speaking to Kennedy about public service, certain that he was the one who would continue the Kennedy legacy when he came of age. Lem encouraged him to keep a journal of their adventures and to take photographs to sell to a magazine once they returned. Lem, an erstwhile real estate developer and shrewd negotiator, managed to create a miniauction for the pictures and text, which were eventually sold to *Life*: an eight-page spread that paid the young Kennedy $25,000, a staggering sum that is equivalent to more than $200,000 today. Although the Kennedy children knew that they could easily profit off their famous last name, with many of them selling bags of "Kennedy sand" at Hyannis Port to tourists for $1, it was likely the first time Kennedy realized that he could make serious cash by trading on his last name.

"Bobby Jr. in Africa" opens with a photo of Kennedy wearing nothing more than a pair of surfer shorts and a St. Christopher medal around his neck climbing a tree in Samburu Park in Kenya. Skinny and disheveled, he grips the tree with his bare feet and hands, staring into the distance. He has the look of a feral animal, a kind of real-life Mowgli from *The Jungle Book* or the savage Jack Merridew in *Lord of the Flies*. He told the *Life* reporter that he had climbed the trees in order to get a a good angle to photograph the elephants. "I was in deadly danger," he joked. "If they sensed I was there, they might have pulled the tree or me down."

In another photo, taken amid the ruins of the Luxor temple in Egypt, a "somber Bobby" poses behind a headless statue, his expression distant and haunted. "Some animals are smarter than others, and the smartest ones are the most dangerous," said the young naturalist, who almost seemed to be describing himself rather than the wildlife he was encountering. "They always know what you're up to, and they go on the defensive."

Despite his grief, he clearly enjoyed the three weeks he spent with Lem in the wild and told everyone they met that he wanted to be a veterinarian. He fed the Pixy Stix he had brought for African children to the baboons they encountered and left a plate of fruit cocktail for a monkey in their cabin, leaving the doors wide open to invite it in. "I put Lem's fruit *inside*, held the door open, and when he ran in we ran out," he said. "We were safe and he had the house! He was furious at having been tricked, so he remained in residence until he had dirtied the entire cabin, including the beds and eaten everything in sight, including our toothpaste."

They also had "a gruesome and bloody battle" with bees. "Mommy thinks I am allergic to bees, which I am not," he said, adding that he was stung twice. "She had sent along about six containers of every medicine known to man."

In another adventure, he tossed a football—"Anywhere a Kennedy goes, a football seems to follow," the *Life* article noted—he had brought on the trip to a "torn-eared" lioness. "We had to do something with it," he said. "We saw this pride of lions—three females, one male, and about eight cubs. They all ran away when I first threw the ball, but one of the females came right back and picked it up in her mouth." The cubs then tore the pigskin to shreds, and Kennedy brought it back to show his new schoolmates at Millbrook School, an elite all-boys school in the Hudson Valley. "It was my cousin Bobby Shriver's football anyway," he said.

The *Life* reporter also described Lem having "a marvelously light-hearted and teasing relationship with his summer charge," with Kennedy saying, "I had to take care of him. He's afraid of animals, you know."

After their safari, the two traveled to Egypt at the invitation of Adel Younis, the country's minister of justice, who had befriended them in the Serengeti. They visited the pyramids, ruins, and museums before returning to the United States. In a fitting end to their adventure, the family friend and talk show host Jack Paar gave Kennedy a lion cub named Mtoto Mbaya, Swahili for "Bad Boy," which could have been a moniker applied to Kennedy and the downward spiral that would characterize the next several years of his life.

Like Bobby Jr., Bad Boy, who was one of Elsa's cubs from the 1966 film *Born Free*, boarded at Millbrook, which was modeled after a strict British boys' school, for a short time. Elsa was an orphaned lion cub who had been raised by a game warden and his wife in Kenya. After two years of training, she had been released back into the wild. Millbrook's on-site zoo and its natural history and ornithology programs were among the reasons that Kennedy wanted to attend the boarding school. Taking Mtoto Mbaya with him was surely a bonus, although he had promised to take the cub to join the Kennedy family menagerie at Hickory Hill as well.

Part of the students' required community service at the school was helping to bottle-feed Mtoto Mbaya at the zoo, which was run by the senior students.

Before he was kicked out of Millbrook for doing drugs, Bobby Jr. joined the school's informal falconry program, led by Peter Jenny, one of his fellow students. Jenny was the son of well-known veterinarians at the University of Pennsylvania, and he had been hawking since the age of seven. Jenny was two classes ahead of Kennedy at the school, but both were part of a small group of students who were passionate about falconry.

"When I first saw him, he was this skinny little kid who looked like he had gone through a great deal of trauma," said Jenny, who was the head of the Millbrook zoo while Bobby Jr. was at the school. "His father had just died, and he wore a black tie every day that he was at Millbrook. He was one of those kids who seemed so lost, so we sort of tucked him under our wing—pun intended."

The falconers went out with their trained birds of prey most days, on a few occasions taking them to a nearby pit filled with the carcasses of dead cows next to a dairy. The pit was full of rats. "It was kind of gross," said Jenny, describing how the group would train their birds on the "bazillion" rats in the pit. "We only did it a few times, but Bobby was never the ringleader. He was actually a very kind kid and very conscientious as a falconer. If he was some cruel weirdo, he wouldn't have been allowed in our group."

Years after their time at Millbrook, Kennedy sent Jenny a letter after his father died in 1971. "He wrote me a sweet note when he was in South America," he said. "I didn't expect it because we were not in touch."

For Kennedy, Millbrook was heaven—at least at first. "We talked about hawks every spare moment, at meals, between classes and after chapel," he wrote in his memoir. "At night, we fashioned ardor, hoods, jesses, gauntlets and befits out of tough, pliant kangaroo hide and marked in our memories the raptor nests we found during our daily hunting excursions in the winter months."

Hawks soon overtook his fascination with his lion cub, although he hadn't given up on taking him to visit his mother at Hickory Hill. "I'm going to take my lion home for vacations," he said. "Mommy will be delighted."

But Mommy was delighted with very little about her third-born child and soon threw him out of the house yet again. Jenny recalled visiting Hickory Hill with Bobby and their hawks in the last months of Ethel's pregnancy with Rory. "His mother was bedridden, and we were underfoot with our hawks," said Jenny.

For much of their childhood, Ethel had frequently been away from her children while she traveled with her husband on his various campaigns, sometimes leaving them for six weeks at a time in the care of volunteer aides and nannies. She had been keen to be first lady of the United States and likely figured that the children would survive the same way she had—in a rambunctious household with little adult supervision. "I plan to remain active in my husband's campaign," she had said. "We miss our children when we're away from home. Of course, I miss Robert when I'm home and not with him. It seems I'm caught in the middle."

After her husband was killed, she was suddenly confronted with the enormous task of being a full-time mother to eleven children. Rory, the couple's youngest, was born in December, six months after her father's death. In a photograph after the birth, Ethel wears a smart white coat, cradling her newborn daughter as her brother-in-law Teddy looks on.

Ethel, who had never been as prominent as her glamorous sister-in-law Jackie Kennedy, suddenly became big news when *Time* put her onto the cover of one of its spring 1969 issues and dubbed her "the country's most admired woman" and "the mini-skirted super mom who exemplified all the headlong, slightly manic 'vigah' of the Kennedys." The story went on to chronicle her infamous practical jokes at her parties at Hickory Hill when Kennedy historian Arthur Schlesinger Jr. had been pushed into one of the swimming pools and a raven had landed on "Mrs. Averell Harriman's head." Although Ethel was described as "a little harsh and sharp-tongued," she had managed to put her life back together after her husband's assassination just ten months before, the article said. "Yet those close to Ethel and to the life she has reconstructed regard her with something approaching awe. She has, they contend, emerged in many ways as the most remarkable member of her remarkable family. New York's Senator Jacob Javits describes her with absolute conviction as 'the greatest of the Kennedys, male or female.'"

Although she seems to have had a number of potential suitors, Ethel, the committed Catholic, decided early on that she would never remarry. "How could I possibly do that with Bobby looking down from heaven?" she asked *People* magazine in 1991. "That would be adultery."

"I'd wake up in the morning and think he was happy in heaven and he had Jack—and they were together as they had been together on earth," she said. "I didn't think how I would survive. I knew it would happen but I didn't know how."

The 1969 *Time* magazine profile contrasted her with her "regal" sister-in-law Jackie Kennedy, who had "traced an esthetic arc of grief, ending with a stylish whirl into another world." Months after Bobby's assassination, Jackie had married the Greek shipping magnate Aristotle Onassis, a union that was frowned upon by most of the Kennedy family. According to the magazine, "Ethel's special triumph has been to maintain normalcy. She has simply carried on, as best she could, the kind of existence that Bobby would have pursued had he lived."

But life at Hickory Hill following Bobby's death was the very antithesis of "normalcy," according to the magazine. It bordered on chaos, which mirrored the way Ethel had grown up in Connecticut with her older Skakel brothers. Despite a staff of nine, including both paid and volunteer aides,

> Ethel is up every morning at 7 for breakfast with the children. Before attending Mass, she shuttles youngsters back and forth to school in one of the several car pools her large brood involves her in. Eight children are at Hickory Hill with her now. She sits down to every meal with them, says the rosary and reads the Bible with them every night. She comforts, counsels and disciplines quite strictly sometimes.
>
> "Once in a while she gets sore as hell at them," says a family intimate. "Bobby never struck any of the kids. Ethel, I think, has."

At Hickory Hill, a long retinue of baby sisters and assistants resigned, unable to rein in Ethel's unruly brood, who lacked discipline and were left to their own devices. The estate was dubbed "Horror Hill" by many who had worked there. For Kennedy, life at home soon proved to be untenable. "I cultivated a troubled relationship with my mother from the moment I could talk back, and the conflict mushroomed into an uninterrupted parade of skirmishes during my adolescence," he wrote in *American Values*, adding that things had been so bad for him at Hickory Hill a year before his father had been killed that he had asked his parents to send him to boarding school when he was thirteen. Georgetown Prep became the first of three schools that he attended in high school before he was suspended. He repeated the tenth grade twice.

When he was at Millbrook, he returned to Hickory Hill only sporadically. Ethel did not visit him. Only Lem arrived for regular outings with his new charge. "Lem used to take us to lunch a couple of times a month, which when you're in boarding school is such a rare treat," said Jenny. But the lunches with Lem could be annoying, with Lem constantly telling Bobby Jr. that he needed to live up to the Kennedy family legacy. "He was a second father to Bobby, but he was a strange guy," said Jenny. "But what he was doing was cruel. Nobody should be saddled with that burden."

Jenny said he had felt the same kind of pressure in his life when he was expected to continue the legacy of his parents, who were both leading veterinary scientists. His Swiss-born father, Jacques Jenny, was a prominent professor at the University of Pennsylvania, known as "the father of equine orthopedics" because he had developed an innovative way to treat fractures in large animals, Jenny said. His mother, Mary Elinor Butt Jenny, had been among the first women to earn a veterinary degree in the United States, in 1949. Instead of following in his parents' footsteps, Jenny said, he had broken from family tradition and helped establish a nonprofit dedicated to preserving the peregrine falcon, which was in danger of becoming extinct in the late 1960s. Years later, in 1999, the bird was removed from the US Endangered Species list, largely thanks to Jenny and the Peregrine Fund's efforts. "I knew how Bobby felt," he said. "It was a lot to live up to. I didn't want to follow my parents. I wanted to work with birds of prey."

Bobby Jr. remained at Millbrook for a little more than a year, Jenny said. He was suspended for doing drugs at a time when if you were caught smoking a cigarette, "you were out," Jenny said.

It was Lem who found him yet another boarding school: Pomfret School in Connecticut. At the elite prep school, Kennedy insisted upon living in the all-Black dormitory and sneaking in Kim Kelley, his girlfriend from Hyannis Port. He hid her in his room during the day and then sneaked her into the basement, where he had set up a hot plate for meals. He refused to do any schoolwork, spending his days reading Eldridge Cleaver, Frantz Fanon, and other Black writers. By the end of the year, he was expelled.

That summer in Hyannis Port, Kennedy was arrested for the second time. The first time had been a year earlier, when he had been caught selling a joint to an undercover cop near the summer compound. Ethel had thrown him out of the house again, prompting Kennedy to buy a used Ford and drive across the country to Los Angeles, hopping freight trains and doing drugs with the hobos he met.

During his second brush with the law in Hyannis Port, he allegedly spat out an ice cream cone in a police officer's face. He was arrested on the spot and taken to court, where he faced charges of "sauntering and loitering." His response was to say that the officer was lying. In fact, in his memoir *American Values* he took great pains to "set the record straight." He said he had come out of an ice cream parlor on Main Street in Hyannis Port to find a police officer yelling at his girlfriend, Kim, for sitting on the hood of a car. When he had explained that it was his car and that he didn't mind if she sat there, the police officer had handcuffed him and taken him to jail. He claimed he had never spat ice cream in the police officer's face. He had spent the night in prison and the next day had left Hyannis Port with his girlfriend and moved into Lem's apartment in New York City, where they stayed for the rest of the summer.

In addition to Kennedy's run-ins with the law, the summer of 1969 would prove a calamitous year for the entire clan. On July 18, Mary

Jo Kopechne, who had worked on Bobby Kennedy's 1968 campaign as part of the so-called boiler room girls, died inside the car driven by Teddy Kennedy, a rising star in the Democratic Party who had been named majority whip in the Senate a few months earlier. The vehicle veered off a narrow bridge on Chappaquiddick Island, a wealthy enclave located off the eastern part of Martha's Vineyard, as they were driving back from a party. Teddy's car skidded off the bridge into Poucha Pond. Although he was able to get out of the vehicle and swim to safety, Kopechne drowned. Teddy did not report the accident until 10:00 a.m. the next day, after a diver had retrieved Kopechne's body from the pond. He later pled guilty to leaving the scene of an accident and in a televised address called his conduct "indefensible." He received a suspended sentence, and his driver's license was suspended for sixteen months. His reckless and entitled conduct at Chappaquiddick ended up dashing his plans to run in the Democratic primary for the presidency in 1972.

Four months after Kopechne's death, the Kennedy family patriarch, Joe Kennedy, suffered a series of heart attacks at the family compound in Hyannis Port. Following his 1961 stroke, he had been an invalid confined to a wheelchair, attended by a full-time nurse and shuttled between his homes in Palm Beach and Hyannis Port. Deeply depressed after the assassination of a second son, he feared that his last living son, Teddy, had also died as he watched the funeral of President Eisenhower on television in March 1969. He died on November 18, surrounded by his family, including his sons' widows, Jackie and Ethel Kennedy.

In Ethel's *Time* magazine profile, she said she had promised to bring up the children the way Bobby would have wanted. "They all have a special obligation," she said. "They've all been given so much; they must try to give that again." It was an oft-repeated

Kennedy refrain, and it would dog Bobby Kennedy Jr. for the rest of his life.

Kennedy had difficulty concentrating in school and had little interest in academics. He was described as "the most disorganized student in the history of Georgetown Prep," where he was in ninth grade. When he was forced to repeat the tenth grade and expelled from Millbrook, it was Lem who went to his aid, not his mother, who refused to help him. Ethel was "like an ostrich," said Lem, "always with her head deep in the sand." Lem arranged for Kennedy to spend his summers away from Hickory Hill in Colombia on a large ranch owned by Lem's nephew Sandy Fisher, a former Peace Corps volunteer.

"For two dollars per week, I worked from dawn clearing fields with machetes and fire, branding the skeletal Brahmin steers in a rough plank corral, and riding fence lines to check for breaks in the wire or for squatters," wrote Kennedy in his family memoir. "We ate yams and potatoes and fried plantains and only occasionally beef or capybara—a giant rodent." At night, he slept in bunkhouse hammocks with the other workers, and he spent his free time roaming the rainforest.

In addition to Lem Billings, the other adult who Kennedy felt loved him unconditionally was the Kennedy children's nanny, Ena Bernard, a descendant of slaves, who had fled her native Costa Rica and a violent husband when she was nineteen and had eventually gotten a job at the Costa Rican Embassy in Washington. She went to live with the family at their Georgetown house in 1951 and moved with the clan to Hickory Hill a few years later. Kennedy credited both Lem and Ena for enabling him to forge lasting relationships despite what he described as his "waxing jihad" with his mother, which had forced him to leave home at a young age. "For forty-four years, Ena was a serene island in a tempestuous sea," he wrote. "She cooked for and fed all eleven of us, wiped tears, bandaged wounds, changed diapers, read bedtime stories, tended us in illness, and if love is not boundless, then she loved us to its human limit." Jack Kennedy was fond of calling Ena a "saint," he said. "Daddy called her a wonder."

Ena kept in touch with many of her charges into adulthood, at one point calling Kennedy to reminisce about how his father had used to take his youngest brother, Douglas, to work with the family dog and send them both home in a government car. She also recalled one of the last conversations Kennedy had had with his father, when Bobby Sr. had called the house and promised that Bobby Jr. could choose any animal from the local pet store.

Ena was fearless. "She once straddled an alligator's back and another time fled a threatening tortoise," Kennedy wrote, adding that she had once grabbed a Masai spear hanging in his room in order to threaten a man who had broken into Hickory Hill and made it as far as Rory's room. "She disoriented the intruder with a hammer blow, then cornered him in my mother's bedroom and kept him at bay with some keen spear prodding until the police arrived." Ena lived to be 105. Kennedy dedicated a children's book he wrote about Saint Francis to her.

Beginning in the summer of 1969, the fifteen-year-old prankster Bobby Jr. founded the Hyannis Port Terrors, with local boys from the summer enclave, including his younger brother David and John Kelley, Kim's brother. Their sister Pam Kelley was David's girlfriend at the time. The gang would roam the area with walkie-talkies and listen to police frequencies while they vandalized cars, untied boats from their moorings so that they would float away, and experimented with drugs, mostly amphetamine tablets called "black beauties," as well as LSD. Kennedy would routinely throw himself in front of cars while the others yelled "You've killed a Kennedy!"

When Kennedy insisted upon arranging trysts with Kim at the "president's house" in the compound, his mother kicked him out of their own house. He set up a tent in a neighbor's yard, cooking his meals on a camp stove and raiding their refrigerators for food.

Bobby Jr., David, and their cousin Christopher Kennedy Lawford spent their summers together. "We taught each other how to shoot drugs—acid, meth and dope, and listened to Traffic, Buffalo Springfield . . . Eric Clapton, Steppenwolf and Dave Mason, etc.," Kennedy wrote in his diary years later, adding that he preferred to hang out with the Kelleys because the matriarch, Peggy, allowed him and Kim to sleep together at their home, beginning when he was fourteen. "She was like a mother, but more understanding and let Kim and me sleep together in that house where I spent much of my youth," he wrote, noting that he had dated Kim until he was twenty-one.

"We were with them all summer long. If we weren't dating them, we had crushes on them," said Pam Kelley, the middle child of the Kelley clan of four sisters and a brother. "We knew them. They weren't 'famous' to us."

The Kelleys' association with the Kennedys would turn dark after Pam was hurt in a jeep accident in Nantucket in the summer of 1973. The eighteen-year-old, who had just graduated from Barnstable High School, was thrown from the jeep driven by twenty-year-old Joe Kennedy, who flipped the vehicle on a sandy road. Besides the driver, there were five other passengers in the jeep, all of them standing up as Joe drove in circles. Pam was paralyzed from the waist down and never walked again. Joe, who would be heading to the University of Massachusetts in the fall, appeared before District Court Judge George Anastos, a Nantucket judge who had gone to Harvard with Kennedy's dead uncle Joseph Kennedy Jr. and worked with Bobby Kennedy on Senator Joe McCarthy's committee investigating Communist infiltration in the United States in the 1950s. Accompanied by his uncle Ted Kennedy and mother, Ethel, Joe pled not guilty. "You had a great father and you have a great mother," Anastos told Kennedy. "Use your illustrious name as an asset instead of coming into court like this." Kennedy was found guilty of negligence, although Judge Anastos let him off with a $100 speeding ticket.

At the hospital, Ethel visited Pam and David every day, taking them cookies and flowers, and arranged to screen a film in Pam's room practically every night—a series of bribes contrived to prevent her from suing. David had also been thrown from the jeep and was in the hospital with a fractured vertebra. In the end, Pam decided not to sue and received nearly $700,000 from an insurance settlement as well as a total of $50,000 from Joe over the years. She broke her silence about the accident in 2005 to say that Joe had treated her "like trash" and had stopped helping her financially, claiming that he was broke. She devoted her life to fighting for the disabled and died in 2020.

Throughout the early 1970s, the Kennedy pranks grew darker, and members of the extended family, including the Shrivers and the Smiths, began keeping their children away from him and his brothers. "Don't pretend to understand me if you haven't taken acid," he would say to them. And then he'd walk away.

At one point, Kennedy threatened a local police officer with a falcon when they caught his cousin Bobby Shriver putting a potato into a car's tailpipe in order to make it backfire. "I have a hawk and he's trained to kill cops," he said.

On July 4, after attending a goodbye party for one of his friends who had been drafted to Vietnam, Kennedy swallowed LSD for the first time. "Buildings melted like wax candles; trees bowed and swayed on a windless night; bright lights with long comet tails lent Hyannis Port the cheery aura of Christmas in July," he wrote.

It was only his commitment to falconry that likely prevented him from becoming a full-blown drug addict in his teens. By then he was a committed falconer, following Holy Roman Emperor Frederick II's thirteenth-century treatise *On the Art of Hunting with Birds*, which stipulated that drugs and alcohol were strictly forbidden. "I had resolved never to use drugs or alcohol," he said, beginning a lifelong struggle at self-discipline that he recorded repeatedly in his diaries. For him, the precepts enshrined in the holy Roman emperor's rules for falconry—"He must avoid inebriation. Laziness in falconers is prohibited"—became "my blueprints for living." A good falconer "must possess a retentive memory, and be impervious to hunger, heat and cold," wrote Frederick. "He should be a light sleeper so as to hear his falcon bells, and have an even temper." Kennedy had followed those rules since he was a child, committed to the red-tailed hawk that his father had bought him from a pet store to cheer him up after an accident had required him to use crutches for months in 1965. And while his father was still alive, he had found a local falconer in Virginia, an aviation engineer and aircraft acquisitions specialist for the Defense Department. "I know them and I think they know me," he said in an interview years later. ". . . I can fly any bird, any bird."

Yet not even his obsession with falconry and the strict rules set out by Emperor Frederick could curb his drug habit once he discovered heroin. Kennedy, his brother David, and the Kelleys began using heroin, and their problems multiplied. David later told a Kennedy biographer that it was Kennedy who had introduced him to heroin. "It was Bobby who got him involved with drugs," said David Horowitz. "Bobby held him down when David was thirteen and shot him with heroin. Bobby was the ringleader."

After Kennedy was kicked out of Pomfret, Lem went to work to find him yet another school for his senior year of high school. He enrolled Kennedy at the Palfrey Street School in Watertown, Massachusetts. The small, experimental school did not focus on exams or IQs, nor was classroom instruction divided by grades. Instead, students were taught in seminar settings and encouraged to do community work in Cambridge and Watertown.

Unlike at his previous schools, there was no boarding at Palfrey, which meant that Lem had to find him a place to live. During the year he spent at Palfrey, Kennedy lived with the Brode family. According to Joanne Brode, the first time she met Kennedy, she offered him a piece of the coffee cake she had just made. Kennedy ate the whole cake. "When Bobby came to the door that first time, he looked like a bird with a broken wing," she said. "He was terribly thin and there was something not coordinated about him—quite handsome, but at the same time flapping, too tall and skinny." Still, she was impressed that Lem took such a huge interest in his well-being, calling him every day and paying for his food and lodging. Ethel had never called her son, she said.

It was at Palfrey that Kennedy finally began to get excited about his studies—at least in biology. "The teacher who had the most influence on me was my Palfrey School biology teacher, Skip Lazell," he wrote in his diary on June 11, 2001.

James D. "Skip" Lazell was an expert on amphibians, specifically lizards of the West Indies. Born in New York City, he had grown up in Philadelphia and earned graduate degrees from the University of Illinois and Harvard University. For Kennedy, he was a true kindred spirit, who had worked at the Philadelphia Zoo. The zoo's directors had paid him to go to the West Indies when he was seventeen to collect lizard specimens. In 1957, *The Philadelphia Inquirer* magazine had featured him in an article, describing how he had captured crocodiles in Jamaica. His doctoral research at the University of Rhode Island focused on a genus of iguanian lizards, and he eventually discovered thirty new species and wrote *This Broken Archipelago: Cape Cod and the Islands, Amphibians and Reptiles*, which was published in 1976.

"He was contrary by nature and was an outspoken supporter of the Vietnam war at a liberal progressive school, an active member of the YAF [Young America's Foundation] and firm supporter of the John Birch Society," wrote Kennedy in his diary on June 11, 2001, referring to the far-right groups that his father would likely have been against. "He always wore shorts even in the frigid Boston winters."

Established in secret in 1958 by a retired candy manufacturer, Robert W. Welch Jr., whose company made Junior Mints and Sugar Babies, the John Birch Society was active until the 1970s. Its members opposed the United Nations and believed that Communists in the United States were behind putting fluoride in the water supply and teaching sex education in schools. The YAF was founded in 1960 with the help of William F. Buckley Jr., the founder of *National Review*. Two years later, the actor Ronald Reagan, a former

Screen Actors Guild president, joined the conservative nonprofit's advisory board.

Lazell was not shy about his extremist views and was open about his personal life with his pupils. He told his class that he had gotten a vasectomy in 1960, when he had been twenty-one years old, wrote Kennedy in his diary. "Skip believed that the vigor of the human race was being destabilized by radical technology that makes genetic defects proliferate and he had himself fixed to spare future generations the burden of the diabetes genes that he carries," wrote Kennedy.

Lazell, who was telling his students about the dangers of global warming and desertification as early as the 1970s, hadn't changed his mind years later. "Population has been a hot topic of mine for some time, but there's very little we can do about it," he said in an interview in 2017.

> The economic system is a Ponzi scheme that requires growth, growth, growth to sell more and more products. More consumers are needed year after year. Overpopulation is the root cause of all of our problems, from excess carbon dioxide to global warming.
>
> Sea-level rise, desertification and ocean acidification are linked to overpopulation. Human-induced climate change is going to wipe out entire species and ecosystems. It's likely going to end with catastrophic population decline.

Every spring, Lazell took "all his adoring students" on a weeklong camping trip to Cape Hatteras on South Carolina's Outer Banks to document wildlife. Kennedy described in his diary how he would drive with a can of beer in a plastic cup holder near the steering wheel. "He always had a girlfriend from his classes and stayed with her in a private tent," wrote Kennedy, who went on the trip during his senior year. "He taught us how to catch skunks without being sprayed" as well as rattlesnakes and all manner of lizards, he wrote.

Palfrey Street School closed down shortly after Kennedy graduated in 1972. Lazell died in 2023.

Kennedy, who had a spotty academic career at best, was off to Harvard thanks to his mother's entreaties to the university that seemed his birthright, the alma mater of his grandfather, uncles, and father. The elite university did little to temper his growing addictions, not only to dangerous drugs such as cocaine and heroin but to women. "My adolescence went on until I was 29," he said.

CHAPTER 4

"I Bought the Ticket; I Took the Ride"

Lem Billings was determined to mold the next President Kennedy, and he worked diligently on Bobby Jr. in spite all of his shortcomings. "I have watched him over assert himself with that raw strength that young men so often [possess] . . . and I have watched him learn to restrain himself," he wrote in a letter to one of the US committees judging applicants for the Rhodes Scholarship at Oxford University. "Since I have known him he has become a man and an impressive one. . . . I am almost sixty years old and I have watched a few great ones come along. I've fought in a war and I've been active in politics and business, and I know what qualities are the ones that shape strong men into strong leaders. Bobby has those qualities."

But Lem might have been too optimistic about his charge. Bobby Jr. was ultimately rejected by the Rhodes Scholarship panel even as he gained entry to Harvard University, thanks to his family's legacy and relationship with the Ivy League school. During his freshman year, he became a full-blown drug user, as well as a drug dealer. "I was so angry in my early life," he wrote in his diary years later. "But I was out of touch with the feeling. . . . Those violent fantasies I entertained all those years as I sat in the back of 1,000 classes during my interminable education . . . were rooted in anger." At Harvard he was known by his cohort to do "speedballs," a mixture of heroin and cocaine.

The journalist Kurt Andersen, who was also a freshman at Harvard in 1972, bought cocaine from Bobby Jr., who was selling it out of his dorm room at Hurlbut Hall. "The dealer was Bobby Kennedy. I'd never met him. I got in touch; he said sure, come over to his room in Hurlbut, his dorm, where I'd never been, a five-minute walk," wrote Andersen. "His roommate, whom I knew, was the future journalist Peter Kaplan—with whom I, like Kennedy, remained friends for the rest of his life. He left as I arrived. I wondered whether he always did that when Bobby had customers." Another kid, "tall, lanky and handsome" was in the room; he turned out to be Bobby Jr.'s older brother, Joe Kennedy III.

Bobby Jr. poured out a line for Andersen to sample with a bit of a plastic straw and sold him a gram of cocaine for $40. "It was a lot of money, the equivalent of $300 today," Andersen wrote. "But *cocaine* bought from a *Kennedy* accompanied by a *Kennedy brother*—the moment of glamour seemed worth it."

Ten minutes after he left, Andersen received a call in his dorm room from Kennedy demanding the broken plastic straw back. "You took my *straw!*"

"I realized that I had indeed, and had thought nothing of it. Because . . . it was a crummy piece of plastic straw, but Bobby was pissed."

For Kennedy's roommate, Kaplan, a Jewish intellectual from New Jersey, Kennedy adopted a "swashbuckling Douglas Fairbanks defiance." He was fond of showing off his various pets and his derring-do. He kept a defanged rattlesnake in his room, feeding it by hand and allowing it to wrap itself around a ski pole. During Visit Week at the school, he climbed a tree to get into his third-story window rather than going up the stairs, Kaplan said.

Among Kennedy's most daring feats at the school was what later came to be known as the "Bhutto leap," a bet he made with Murtaza Bhutto, a son of Pakistani President Zulfikar Ali Bhutto, to jump between Hurlbut Hall and Pennypacker Hall, which was six stories high and a distance of ten to twelve feet away. "People heard about it and gathered below, a large crowd shading their eyes and looking up as if waiting for Superman," Kaplan said. "The distance wasn't that great, but it looked twice as big as it was; if he missed he'd probably die. Suddenly Bobby just soars across. Everybody down on the ground gasped and shook their heads in disbelief."

In another stunt worthy of Fairbanks, Bobby Jr. went skiing in the Andes during a period of political upheaval in the region in the summer of his freshman year. Weeks before the military coup that would result in the overthrow and murder of Salvador Allende in Chile, Kennedy went skiing with his friend Blake Fleetwood on the country's border with Argentina and came under gunfire. "I write about events of our trek today not because this is the right season for skiing in Chile (it isn't) and certainly not to recommend a visit to this tortured country at the present time, but rather to report on the thrilling skiing that may be experienced in the Andes," wrote Fleetwood in an article published in *The New York Times* nearly a year later.

In some ways, the trip to Chile may have been an effort to outdo his older brother, Joe. In February 1972, he landed on the front page of the newspaper after being aboard a hijacked Boeing 747. Joe had accompanied his uncle Ted Kennedy and Ted's wife, Joan, on a trip to Bangladesh and was returning to the United States on his own after spending time in India. The five Arab hijackers struck an hour after the Lufthansa jet took off from New Delhi en route to Frankfurt with 175 passengers and 14 crew on board. Initial reports said that the hijackers had ordered the pilot to fly to the Jordanian capital, Amman, where two years earlier guerrillas had hijacked two jetliners, demanding the release of Robert Kennedy's assassin, Sirhan Sirhan, who was in a high-security prison in California, in exchange for the passengers. A spokesman for the guerrillas later denied the claim.

The hijackers, who were part of the Popular Front for the Liberation of Palestine, demanded $5 million to be delivered to a location in Lebanon. When the plane landed in Aden, about 2,500 miles from New Delhi, the hijackers freed the women and children and held on to the male passengers and crew. They threatened to blow up the plane and kill the men unless the ransom was paid. Lufthansa decided to comply with their demands. A few months later, at the September Summer Olympics in Munich, a Palestinian terrorist group attacked the Israeli Olympic team, killing two athletes and taking nine hostages. All of the hostages were killed, in addition to five terrorists and a German police officer.

"It's great to be out," said Joe Kennedy, dressed in a blue blazer and white shirt, after landing in Frankfurt on February 24, two days after the hijacking. He said he had been struck on the shoulder with a pistol because he had been slow to raise his hands after the plane was hijacked. "I just didn't raise my hands," said the nineteen-year-old, adding that he had been "treated like anyone else." Asked if he knew anything of the hijackers' motives, he said, "Their English was very bad. It wasn't clear what their position was."

Bobby Jr. was determined to ski to *Christ of the Andes*, a statue forged from melted-down cannon barrels, in the remote Uspallata Pass between Chile and Argentina. The statue, which depicts Christ with a cross in one hand and holding up the other in a blessing, had been built in 1904 to commemorate the end of a border dispute between the two countries but was rarely visited because of its remote location, some 13,000 feet above sea level. Accompanied by Fleetwood and three other friends, he had already faced avalanches and twenty-foot walls of snow as he skied through perilous mountain passes, perhaps recalling the famous trek that his father had undertaken to climb Mount Kennedy in the Yukon after it had been named for his slain brother. Fleetwood, writing in *The New York Times*, insisted that Bobby Jr. was no daredevil, although he recounted that he had once lowered himself over a rock cliff to capture a young condor on a recent trip to Peru and was "anxious to make the climb to the Christ statue."

As they embarked on the final slope, they heard "an incomprehensible yell from off to our left," wrote Fleetwood. "About 600 yards away we see a Chilean alpine trooper who suddenly, without further warning, raises his machine gun," he continued. When Bobby Jr. suddenly dropped, "his face shoved in the snow," Fleetwood thought he had been shot. "I am wondering what that soldier would do if he knew he'd nearly killed Robert Kennedy's son, President Kennedy's nephew," he wrote. ". . . I shudder to think what was going on inside Bobby's head . . . while these shots zipped over his head."

Fleetwood noted that his friend had been a child when his uncle had been killed and fourteen years old when his own father had been assassinated, admitting that the deaths had "had a traumatic effect" on his life. But when he looked over at Bobby Jr., he noted, "Strangely, he seems calmer than the rest of us right now."

Still, the shooting incident made its way into the press, which "had him dead or wounded." Kennedy later called his mother to tell her he was all right.

During the skiing excursion, Fleetwood engaged in "a succession of skiing races, swimming contests, snowball fights, diving matches and other competitions." Although Fleetwood won a few, "overall [Kennedy] demolished me. He simply took more chances than I and he refused to be beaten."

The adrenaline rush continued into the following year as Kennedy sought out even more dangerous pursuits to prove his mettle and reach a thrill-seeking high. Lem, who had started doing heroin and other drugs with Kennedy, was even more convinced that he could be president and searched for another challenge that could compare with his uncle's heroics on the Solomon Islands during the Second World War and his father's climb up Mount Kennedy.

They settled on a rafting trip on the Apurímac River in Peru, a far-flung tributary of the Amazon. In Quechua, "Apurímac" translates as "the great speaker," likely because of the noise of its thundering rapids. Known for its treacherous waters and wild currents, the river had barely been explored at the time Kennedy and Billings decided it was a challenge they needed to tackle. At twenty, Kennedy was determined to become the first to explore the uncharted river, engaging in his own Kennedy mythmaking to catapult himself onto the national stage and establish himself as the true heir of Camelot. "I can't do it the way they did," he said, referring to his father and uncle. "The conditions aren't the same. I've got to take shortcuts." He didn't hedge about his ambitions at the time. "I feel it is my destiny," he said.

Despite the dangers of the journey—in addition to the wild currents, the alligators, and the poisonous snakes, the region was home to terrorists and drug traffickers—Kennedy and Billings assembled a group of eager adventurers, including Kennedy's cousin Chris Kennedy Lawford and his younger brother David, as well as his friend Doug Spooner and Billings's friend Morris Stroud. Fleetwood was also invited, chosen by Kennedy to act as the official chronicler. As if to remind everyone of the importance of the journey, David took along *The Making of the President 1968* by Theodore H. White as reading material.

The bare-bones white-water rafting expedition couldn't have been more different from the river trips organized by Robert Kennedy for the Kennedy clan. "The trips with Uncle Bobby were exciting, but cushy," wrote Chris Kennedy Lawford, the son of actor Peter Lawford and Patricia Kennedy. "We were well taken care of by Hatch River Expeditions. Tents were set up, meals were as good as anything one is likely to get in the great outdoors, and real danger to life and limb was minimized. River rafting in South America was different. It's not cushy and your life and limbs are always in danger."

There was little surprise when Kennedy appointed himself the leader of the expedition. Ever since they had been children, "Bobby Jr. was the king," wrote Lawford. "He was cool, dangerous, daring and had charisma, which drew people to him."

The trip had a shaky start, with most of the group getting dysentery by their second day and Billings falling into a ravine. The gash on his leg was so bad that he needed twelve stitches, administered by the twenty-year-old Kennedy, who had acquired the skill during the days when he still aspired to be a veterinarian. In a diary that Fleetwood kept of the trip, he noted, "Bobby sick, Lem's wounds infected, David strep throat."

With Kennedy in the lead, the group was at his mercy, as Lawford noted in his memoir. After arriving in Lima, they got onto a plane to Cuzco and from there drove in a dump truck the 150 miles to San Francisco, which was on the banks of the Apurímac. They set up their tents and "spent the entire night evacuating our bowels all over the field we had set up camp on," wrote Lawford, noting that the thirty inhabitants of the town "were confused and a little angry at the visitors who were camped and had shit all over their soccer field."

They soon hired Epifinio, the "town drunk," who rubbed urine all over his body in order to ward off mosquitoes—a habit that irritated the straightlaced Lem Billings. "Whenever he did this, Lem would shout to Bobby, 'Make him stop now. Please make him *stop*!'" recalled Lawford.

The misfit crew had brought live chickens and canned goods for their three-hundred-mile river crossing, a journey that ended up taking ten days. They killed one chicken a day "by putting its neck between two fingers and snapping." Bobby was the most efficient killer, Lawford said.

They had also brought a bag of drugs that Fleetwood's physician mother had assembled. Kennedy appointed himself the custodian of the bag, much to the indignation of both David and Lawford, who were also addicts. Once they broke into the bag, however, they noticed that most of the stash was missing. "Someone had figured out how to get the cookies without opening the cookie jar," wrote Kennedy Lawford. "David and I were pissed."

At one point, Lawford said, they came under attack by a group of drunken Quechua Indians on the river. "We floated by Indian villages, once having to avoid the arrows being shot in our direction by a drunken tribe on the shore," he wrote.

The attack is portrayed as a deadlier encounter in *The Kennedys: An American Drama* by Peter Collier and David Horowitz. "They had tied up along the bank to try to dig the roots of a yucca-like plant they thought might be edible when a band of Indians began shooting arrows at them," they wrote, based on interviews with some of the participants. "One penetrated the canteen near Lem's leg. As Lem began to yell, Bobby rummaged for the bow and arrows he had earlier obtained in a trade. He hadn't brought them. Chris found a stick of dynamite and held it up." Kennedy told the writers that Lawford had held up the stick of dynamite, which he had lit and then thrown into the river, scattering the attackers.

But the Indian attack described by both Lawford and Kennedy seemed to be just more Camelot mythmaking. After Collier and Horowitz's book was published in 1984, Fleetwood pierced the bubble when he told *The Washington Post* that the Indian attack had never taken place.

The ragtag group finally made it to Atalaya, where they convinced the owner of a small plane to fly them to San Ramón. From there they took an eleven-hour bus ride to Lima. In the Peruvian capital, Lawford claimed, they had awakened to tanks in the street and realized that a coup had taken place overnight. It's unclear if he was referring to the coup d'état, the "Tacnazo," so called because it had originated among military officers in the city of Tacna. That coup, in which the military replaced President Juan Velasco Alvarado with General Francisco Morales Bermúdez, took place on August 29, 1975, several days after the group had left the country. In any event, whatever military unrest and maneuvers were taking place in Lima when they arrived in the city seemed not to get in the way of their return to New York.

They arrived in Manhattan in time to make an entrance into the annual Robert F. Kennedy Memorial Tennis Tournament Dinner at the Plaza Hotel, where the entire family had assembled along with sports heroes, politicians, and various celebrities. The tournament, which had begun in 1971, featured Ted Kennedy and Ethel Kennedy, among other members of the clan squaring off on the court against other well-known names to raise funds for the Robert F. Kennedy Foundation.

"Nobody in the family had heard from us for close to three weeks and there was great concern as to whether we were still alive," wrote Lawford. "We loved creating this sort of drama. Bobby, David, Lem and I made our entrance into the Grand Ballroom like the conquering heroes we felt we were. It was quite dramatic, and for the moment we were adored. But only for a moment."

Upon his return to the fall semester at Harvard, Bobby Jr. embarked on yet another life-changing trip, this time with fellow classmate Peter Kaplan, to the deep South. They were determined to research their senior theses in American history, "well aware of the important role the South played in forming American political and social institutions." In October 1975, the pair drove to Alabama, the scene of the tense standoff in 1963 between his father and Governor George Wallace to allow two Black students to attend the University of Alabama. "We came to the South loaded with our standard Yankee preconceptions—with visions of small-town ignorance, bigotry and senseless brutality, burly white sheriffs, wielding bullwhips and spitting tobacco, men in sheets, burn crosses and dignified Black elders addressed as 'boy,'" Kennedy wrote in his thesis.

But upon their arrival in the town of Hayneville in Lowndes County, those assumptions were seriously challenged. For one thing, the sheriff, John Hulett, was Black, and the white probate judge, Harrell Hammond, knew he needed Black votes to stay in office in a county where 60 percent of the voting population was Black. But there were, as Kennedy noted in his diary years later, "still plenty of residues of racism in the South." The racism was always under the surface, he noted, recounting Hammond sizing up Kaplan when he first met him. "'I never met a Jew before,'" said the judge, "looking at Peter up and down like someone was trying to sell him a fur coat in the summer," wrote Kennedy in his diary. "By the time Peter left, Harrell felt close enough to him to say 'When you get ready to kill all them n—s up there, you give me a holler.'"

Kaplan left Hayneville after a few months, while Bobby Jr. stayed nearly a year, living with John "Sweet Pea" Russell Jr., a local businessman who lived in an imposing antebellum mansion near the courthouse. He also managed to hook up with people who grew marijuana and sold cocaine, "but not very good cocaine," he wrote in his diary years later. Looking back on his adventures in Alabama, where he had begun using chewing tobacco and wearing cowboy boots, Kennedy recalled blast fishing with dynamite, hunting for squirrels, losing his hawk and his dog, the scent of wild mint growing next to streams, tar-paper shacks, and endless cotton fields. The images are listed in point form in his 2001 diary—notes for a book that he planned to write about his time in the Deep South. "For the most part, I found people who were sentimental about our country, enshrined its best values and recognized the years of segregation as a perversion of that conservatism—a blind mindless fearful climax to an immoral past— torn apart . . . by violence," he wrote in his diary years later.

But most of all he remembered his encounters with Wallace, who was in his second term as governor when Kennedy and Kaplan arrived. "Tears filled his eyes when he spoke about my father," Kennedy noted in his diary more than twenty-five years later. "'Those were good boys,'" he said, recalling both John and Robert Kennedy. "I spent a lot of time with Governor Wallace visiting him at his office in the Alabama statehouse over which the Confederate flag still flew, in defiance of federal laws. Wallace welcomed me in my first meeting with words that surprised me, 'Your daddy was a good man,' he said. 'I loved the Kennedy boys. They was good for America. . . . I could never figure out how to get to them.'"

Wallace was confined to a wheelchair, paralyzed from the waist down and in constant pain, after he had been shot while campaigning in the Democratic primary for president in suburban Maryland in 1972. After the assassination attempt, Ethel had visited him at Holy Cross Hospital in Silver Spring, where a photographer had captured the governor sitting by his bed, clutching Ethel's wrist. Three years later, another black-and-white press photo showed Wallace seated at his desk in the governor's office in Montgomery with Kennedy and Kaplan standing like sentries on either side of him. "There were many people, including the governor himself, who believed that if it had not been for the 1972 tragedy . . . he might well have been president," wrote Kennedy in his senior thesis. "There is no doubt that he would have had a decisive influence on the final outcome of the race."

When they arrived, Wallace was preparing for the 1976 Democratic presidential primary campaign. Amazingly, he had accumulated more money in small contributions than any other Democratic contender, noted Kennedy. "None of us was surprised when he carried Boston in the Massachusetts Democratic primary, although just twelve months earlier no one would have believed Wallace could make that kind of impact in South Boston." Both Kaplan and Kennedy were determined to find out why the country's most notorious segregationist was having so much success: "This frightening hold over 'our people,' the good Irish citizens of South Boston."

But almost as soon as they arrived in Alabama, they started hearing a great deal about Frank Minis Johnson Jr., the civil rights judge who had abolished the corrupt justice of the peace system and whose rulings had been instrumental in abolishing segregation in the state. As a result of meeting Johnson and hanging out in his courtroom, Kennedy decided to switch the focus of his thesis to telling Johnson's story. "I went down South to write about Mr. Wallace but I found out that, basically, it was Frank Johnson who was running the State of Alabama," he told a reporter in 1977. "I realized after doing preliminary research that Johnson was the real subject and the more influential and exciting personality."

While Kennedy was completing his thesis at his grandmother's home in Palm Beach—working between midnight and dawn, his "best working time"—Johnson was chosen by President Carter to be the director of the FBI. But in November 1977, after undergoing surgery, Johnson asked Carter to withdraw his name. For years, Johnson, a Republican appointee to the federal bench, had been Wallace's biggest enemy, even though the two had been good friends when they both attended the University of Alabama Law School, with Wallace often relying on Johnson's meticulous study notes to get him through his classes. "Every major issue that has confronted Alabama in the last two decades has been embodied in repeated clashes between Wallace and Johnson," Kennedy wrote in his thesis. "Much is known about one of them, little about the other."

Johnson's historic rulings were critical to the civil rights movement and the dismantling of Jim Crow laws in the South. He ruled on the 1955 bus boycott after the arrest of activist Rosa Parks in Montgomery, deeming segregation on public buses unconstitutional. Ten years later, he forced Wallace to allow Martin Luther King Jr.'s march from Selma to Montgomery to protest segregation.

When he returned for visits to New York, Kennedy discussed his research with Lem, who decided that the thesis should be published—in the same manner as John Kennedy's Harvard thesis on England's appeasement at Munich had been published in the years before the Second World War.

It's not clear who contacted the legendary editor Phyllis Grann, then at G. P. Putnam's Sons, about publishing the book, but in his acknowledgments Kennedy thanks both Grann and Arthur Schlesinger Jr., a Harvard classmate of John Kennedy and Pulitzer Prize–winning historian who had written books about Jack Kennedy and Kennedy's own father after his assassination. It was Schlesinger "who encouraged me to complete and publish my work," wrote Kennedy in his acknowledgments, even though it was his aunt Jean Kennedy Smith who had mentioned the book to Grann, according to a report. But Smith is not thanked in the acknowledgments. Instead, Kennedy thanked his siblings and his girlfriend, Duff Pacifico, and dedicated the book "To my mother and father."

The acknowledgments read like a who's who of his father's advisers. In addition to Schlesinger, Kennedy thanked Robert Coles, a professor of psychiatry at Harvard, who "first sparked my interest in the South." Coles had met his father in 1965 during his testimony before a Senate committee investigating racism in the United States. Coles had accompanied Bobby Sr. on trips to Appalachia and Mississippi and acted as an adviser to him on civil rights in the South. He had later profiled him in his book *Lives of Moral Leadership*.

In addition to the high-powered help, Kennedy's family connections went a long way to convincing John Doar, a lawyer from Wisconsin who was instrumental to helping the federal government end segregation in the South, to write the foreword. Doar had worked under Robert Kennedy as deputy attorney general for civil rights between 1961 and 1965 and had been promoted to director of the Department of Justice's Civil Rights Division between 1965 and 1967. He had worked with Bobby Sr. on the legal challenge to the segregated University of Mississippi when administrators had refused to allow James Meredith to register at the school. In 1973, he had been appointed lead special counsel on the House Judiciary Committee's inquiry into Richard Nixon's impeachment.

Doar described Alabama as a "caste system" where "almost every human activity was affected by considerations of race" and "the principal means used to enforce second-class citizenship on an entire race of American citizens was official corruption and unofficial intimidation designed to deprive Black citizens of the right to vote." For him, "Judge Johnson's career as a federal district judge marked the period of our history when this country became an honest constitutional system of self-government." Johnson's "command of the courtroom was exceptional," and he believed that it was his duty "to require a state to regulate its citizens within a constitutional framework."

After extolling the virtues of the courageous jurist for six pages in his introduction, Doar devoted only a few sentences to Kennedy's work. "Robert Kennedy Jr. writes about this decent, this honorable, this superior man," he wrote. "He sees Judge Johnson not only as I saw him, as a reserved lonely Federal District Judge, but also a friend and companion. He describes the human qualities of Judge Johnson."

Despite the high-powered endorsement, the book never made the bestseller lists and was savaged by *New York Times* national correspondent Howell Raines, who described it as "a plodding, disjointed analysis that clouds rather than clarifies Johnson's achievements as a jurist." Raines, who had grown up in Birmingham and would go on to become executive editor of the newspaper years later, admonished Kennedy for never mentioning the constant death threats and intimidation directed against Johnson. At one point, Johnson had been known as "the most hated man in Alabama." His mother's home had been bombed in 1967, and the threats against him had been so numerous that federal marshals had been assigned to protect him round the clock for more than twenty years.

Kennedy earned a "cum plus" for his thesis, a Harvard expression for an A with honors. Years later there was speculation that it was his Harvard classmate Peter Kaplan, who went on to become a journalist and editor, who had written his paper. Perhaps Kennedy did get some help, but the choppy and meandering prose of the narrative would suggest that he didn't benefit from the aid of a professional writer or even his Harvard roommate, who would go on to be one of New York City's leading newsmen.

The year he spent in Alabama was important for other reasons. By the end of his sojourn, he seemed more confident and to be coming into his own as a politician, noted Kaplan. On a visit to the state legislature in Montgomery, he was treated like a rock star. "There was an air of business being carried on with slight boredom," said Kaplan. "But when Bobby entered, there was a sudden electricity. A couple of the more liberal members came over and then suddenly everyone was mobbing him, grabbing his hands and slapping him on the back. It was like something had clicked." Suddenly Kennedy started "flashing the Kennedy smile and pumping hands in a way I'd never seen him do before. He was a candidate."

Bobby Jr. had flashed that Kennedy smile when he had helped Peter Shapiro in his campaign for New Jersey State assemblyman. On the eve of the election in 1975, he had campaigned in the heavily Irish Vailsburg section of Newark, going door to door with Shapiro. At twenty-three, Shapiro became the youngest person ever elected to the Assembly, defeating incumbent Rocco Neri. He served in the Assembly for two terms, and in 1978, he helped change the Essex County charter, creating a new position of county executive. He ran for the newly created office, a move "that set off seismic shifts, causing realignments and rifts that partly exist more than 40 years after the election" in New Jersey politics.

Following his work on his thesis, Kennedy continued to follow in his uncle's footsteps. At Lem's urging, he enrolled at the London School of Economics, although he lasted only a few weeks at the school before taking off for Ireland to get stoned.

While in the United Kingdom, he started dating Rebecca Fraser, the daughter of his uncle's friend Hugh Fraser, a Conservative member of Parliament, whom Jack Kennedy had met in the late 1930s while his father had been ambassador in London. Kennedy met Fraser through his cousin Caroline, who was staying at the Fraser home in Kensington while she was an intern at Sotheby's Institute of Art in London in the fall of 1975. In October, Caroline, then seventeen, was staying with the couple when the Irish Republican Army placed a bomb under the front wheel of the conservative MP's red Jaguar, parked outside the Fraser home. Caroline had planned to ride with

Fraser to her course at Sotheby's but was saved from getting into the vehicle when Fraser had to answer a phone call. The bomb detonated before they left the house, killing Gordon Hamilton Fairley, a professor known for his research into leukemia, who was walking by with his dog. Fairley's legs were blown off, and his body was thrown across the sidewalk into the Frasers' garden.

Duff Pacifico, Kennedy's girlfriend, the woman he had thanked so profusely in his book, learned about the relationship from the New York newspapers and was so upset that she called Kennedy in London. He denied the tryst and later traveled with her and Lem to Haiti, but when the trio returned to New York City, Kennedy resumed his relationship with Rebecca. She was his date at his sister Courtney's wedding to ABC-TV producer Jeffrey Ruhe in June 1980. The couple are pictured in photos at the rehearsal dinner at the Georgetown Club.

By that time, most of the Kennedy siblings had been tapped to help Ted Kennedy's presidential campaign. After seventeen years in the Senate, Ted had decided to follow his older brothers' footsteps and run against the incumbent Democrat, Jimmy Carter. On the day Iranian students stormed the US Embassy in Iran and took sixty-six Americans hostage, he gave an interview to CBS-TV that practically sealed his fate in the upcoming race. Although he had not yet announced his candidacy, it was pretty much an open secret that he would run, and he sat down for an exclusive one-hour interview. When Roger Mudd, who had provided live commentary during Robert Kennedy's announcement that he would run for president in 1968, asked him why he wanted to run for president, Ted fumbled and gave a rambling answer. Mudd also took him to task on Chappaquiddick. Nonetheless, three days after the interview, Ted announced his candidacy for the 1980 election.

During the campaign, Bobby Jr. dropped out of law school to help his uncle. He was assigned to Alabama by the campaign and returned to his old stomping grounds. In between speeches at Black churches in the area, he raced cars and continued to date Rebecca

Fraser. He continued to do drugs. He lived in Montgomery, this time with Harris McGough, whose family owned the Capitol Motor Company. Harris had been involved in the dealership since returning in 1970 from Vietnam, where he claimed to have killed twenty-four Viet Cong singlehandedly.

Carter would go on to win twenty-four primary contests, with Ted taking only ten. Ted conceded defeat on August 11, 1980, during the Democratic National Convention in New York City despite having many of his brothers' campaign strategists and advisers in his corner, including Arthur Schlesinger Jr. But one person who was perhaps glaringly absent was Lem Billings, an enthusiastic supporter of so many Kennedy campaigns. In failing health because of all the drugs he was using—Bobby Jr. had also introduced him to heroin—Lem didn't have the energy to get involved. He regularly suffered from heart palpitations and used an asthma inhaler. The former champion wrestler was increasingly stoned out of his mind. He felt that Ted Kennedy's womanizing, his alcoholism, his failing marriage, and the events at Chappaquiddick would just drag the rest of the family through the mud. "I don't know about everybody else, but I'm just going to sit this one out," he said, later adding that the campaign had seemed like "a half-assed effort."

He might have used the same phrase for his protégé, who had again followed in his father's footsteps by enrolling at the University of Virginia School of Law but seemed no closer to political stardom. In his elegant apartment on East 88th Street in Manhattan, a veritable shrine to the Kennedys, with photos and campaign posters crowding every wall, Lem began making his will. The faithful servant and friend of the Kennedys, who had acted as an usher at Kennedy weddings and a pallbearer at so many funerals, headed the committee that oversaw the construction of the John F. Kennedy Center for the Performing Arts, worked as a trustee of the Kennedy Library at Harvard, and, perhaps most important, served as a surrogate father to a generation of Kennedy children, was no longer interested in promoting the clan. At least on the political stage. In later years, many of them would call him for advice or end up at his apartment to do drugs. Lem was one of the few in the Kennedy orbit who regaled the new generation of Kennedys with the stories of their crusading forebears.

"Lem's house was more than a fun house; it was a museum, a library, a classroom. Books lined the walls throughout," said Kennedy. "They were all histories, biographies and art books. Whenever I felt lonely, or sad, or left out, I would call Lem and laugh."

Lem bequeathed his apartment to Bobby Jr. in his will. He died of a heart attack in his sleep on May 28, 1981, a day before what would have been his best friend Jack Kennedy's sixty-fourth birthday. Lem was sixty-five years old. "He felt pain for every one of us—pain that no one else could have the courage to feel," said Bobby Jr. at Lem's funeral. "I don't know how we will carry on without him. In many ways, Lem was like a father to me and he was the best friend I will ever have."

"Everyone, a friend has observed, is given something to overcome," wrote Kennedy in a memoir. "My biggest battle was with addiction to drugs. Soon after my father's death I made a series of choices involving drugs that started me down a road from which I had to struggle to return." But initially anyway, he blamed others for his inability to seek help. "My life experience with public scrutiny and an aggressive and nosy press made me wary of attending public twelve-step programs, where I might have otherwise found recovery," he wrote.

Yet on the surface his life seemed to be going well. Less than a year after Lem's death, he married a law school classmate, Emily Black, in April 1982 in Bloomington, Indiana, the bride's hometown. Although Kennedy had wanted to marry at St. Patrick's Cathedral in New York, the bride had insisted on a Protestant church wedding in Bloomington, where she had been baptized. Moreover, the couple could not afford a New York City wedding, according to reports. Nonetheless, she agreed to have a Catholic priest preside at the ceremony alongside a Protestant minister. A Kennedy family spokesman declared that she was receiving instruction in Catholicism and would likely convert by Easter.

"She is lovely," said Peter Kaplan in an interview in *The New York Times* in a story about the announcement of their engagement. "She is beautiful, a very intelligent young woman, really serious and quiet, a fantastic student and very Midwestern. There's no doubt that she's from Indiana."

Days before the wedding and a few months from graduating law school, Kennedy had already landed a job through his family connections as assistant district attorney in the Manhattan District Attorney's Office. The office was run by Robert Morgenthau, a Kennedy family friend who had grown up with Robert and John Kennedy. He had worked on John Kennedy's presidential campaign and been appointed US attorney in New York's Southern District by Attorney General Bobby Kennedy in 1961. When Jack Kennedy was assassinated, Morgenthau was at Hickory Hill having lunch by the pool with Bobby Kennedy and Ethel when Bobby received the call from FBI Director J. Edgar Hoover. In 1975, he became Manhattan district attorney. He retired in 2009 at the age of ninety.

"After law school I went to the Manhattan District Attorney's Office where I spent a year prosecuting misdemeanor cases, assaults, prostitutes and fare beaters," Kennedy wrote in one of his memoirs. He had already worked in Morgenthau's office as a law student in 1979. As a prosecutor, his starting salary was $20,000 a year.

His cousin John F. Kennedy Jr. would follow in his footsteps, becoming an assistant district attorney in Morgenthau's office in 1989 even after he had failed to pass the New York bar twice, passing on his third attempt. Declared *People* magazine's "Hunk of the Year" in 1988, John Jr. had paid off $2,000 in fines for outstanding parking tickets and made headlines when he had been pulled over on his way to Kennedy Airport by Port Authority police, who said he was speeding, and driving an unregistered, uninsured vehicle. He had been issued four summonses, and his car had ben impounded.

Meanwhile, Emily had secured a position as a legal aid attorney with the New York Legal Aid Society. Following Kennedy's graduation in June, the couple moved into Lem's apartment on the Upper East Side. Emily had graduated the year before. "She's interested in keeping people out of jail, and I'm interested in putting them in," Kennedy said.

Kennedy continued using drugs, frequenting dealers in Harlem at night as well as Manhattan's Xenon disco, where he partied with his brothers David and Michael and his cousin John Jr.—all while trying to work for Manhattan's top cop during the day.

Still, Bobby Jr. and Emily were committed to being a modern couple, they said in a joint interview with *People* magazine days before their April 3, 1982, nuptials. Bobby Jr., then twenty-eight, called himself "a women's lib advocate" who was committed to sharing the housework and "raising around five" children. Emily agreed to add "Kennedy" to her last name. "I never considered not changing my name, just out of tradition," she said. Kennedy added rather imperiously that "a name can be helpful in a lot of situations, and Kennedy is better than Black."

In November of that year, Emily made headlines when she became the victim of a robbery near Lem's apartment. Although a passing cab driver chased down the teenage muggers after the robbery and caught them, Emily steadfastly refused to press charges because the suspects were all under sixteen. She changed her mind following police appeals.

Perhaps the mugging foreshadowed Kennedy's downfall several months later. Not only had he failed the bar exam that year (he would pass it in 1983 and be admitted to the New York State Bar in 1985), he resigned from his position at the District Attorney's Office in July and was arrested for heroin possession after he was found strung out in the bathroom of a Republic Airlines airplane en route to Rapid City, South Dakota, in September. He was on his way to the Black Hills to meet with Bill Walsh, a former Catholic priest whom he had befriended while both were campaigning for Ted Kennedy in the state in 1980 and who was known for his work with drug addicts.

One of the passengers on the turboprop plane from Minnesota heard someone crying for help in the bathroom. Bill Waeckerle, a school administrator and amateur boxing referee, went to investigate. The bathroom door was open, and Kennedy was asking for a stewardess. "He wanted assistance," Waeckerle said. "He was in his white socks, without his boots, sitting a little bit off balance on the toilet with the seat down, slipping a little bit as the plane bounced along. He was nervous, almost overactive, jumpy and chatty and incoherent. He appeared very ill." Waeckerle and another passenger tried to convince Kennedy to return to his seat, but he refused. They finally settled him on a seat next to the bathroom, covering him with blankets and administering oxygen, according to news reports. "The stewardess had asked me to get his name," said Waeckerle. "He told me his name was Bobby Francis. He spelled it out for me."

The airplane crew called ahead for medical help in Rapid City. Kennedy was much improved by the time the plane landed, Waeckerle said. He was escorted off the plane by police officers, who held on to his flight bag, and was forced to divulge his full name. Two days later, the police obtained a search warrant. Kennedy was charged when police found a small amount of heroin in his bag. It was Walsh whom Kennedy called after the arrest, and it was Walsh who found him a lawyer right away.

Two days after the arrest, Kennedy checked into a drug rehabilitation facility in New Jersey and was discharged on the eve of his court appearance in South Dakota. The Kennedys issued a statement from his uncle Ted Kennedy's Senate office in which he admitted to his drug addiction and said he would seek help. Several days later, he was admitted to a rehab facility at Summit Oaks Hospital in Summit, New Jersey. "I have admitted myself to the hospital for the treatment of a drug problem," the statement said. "With the best medical help I can find I am determined to beat this problem. I deeply regret the pain which this situation will bring to my family and to so many Americans who admire my parents and the Kennedy family. I am grateful for the support of my wife, Emily, the other members of my family, and my friends during this very difficult time." Kennedy remained at Summit Oaks for five months.

With his hands shaking and accompanied by his older brother, Joe, and his wife, Kennedy pled guilty to the felony charge. He faced two years in prison, but in typical Kennedy fashion, he got off easy. When he returned to court on March 16, Circuit Court Judge Marshall Young made a point of saying that he had not been influenced by the Kennedy family name when he gave Kennedy a suspended sentence. He ordered Kennedy to submit to a drug treatment program with regular urine tests and ordered him to perform 1,500 hours of community service. "You're the only one who can choose between drug dependence or sobriety and either road you choose the treatment is difficult," he said, adding that he had been impressed with Kennedy's "candor and honesty" during his trial.

If Kennedy felt any sort of relief, it quickly dissipated about a month later, when *Playboy* magazine featured a bombshell cover story about his family. "The Fall of the Young Kennedys: Inside a Troubled American Dynasty" was a book excerpt from Peter Collier and Howard Horowitz's upcoming book, *The Kennedys: An American Drama*. The two journalists had interviewed several Kennedy family members, including Kennedy's troubled younger brother David.

David died of a drug overdose soon after the *Playboy* excerpt was published. He had gone to Florida when his uncle Ted had issued a call to the family because Rose Kennedy was sick. David was thrown out of the Kennedys' Palm Beach compound for being drunk even though Ted himself was an alcoholic. He then checked into a nearby hotel room, where he was found dead on April 25. Ted was quick to blame the journalists for his death, slamming their work through a spokesman as "absolutely inaccurate, the lowest form of journalism, except to call it journalism dignifies it."

But in an interview a few years after *The Kennedys* was released, Horowitz said that the Kennedys had turned against David a long time before, starting when they had forgotten that he had been alone in a Beverly Hills hotel room watching the news of his father's death on television. "The minute he gave the interview they started to abuse him, and they didn't let up until he was dead," Horowitz said, adding that when his older brother Bobby Jr. had checked into a rehab facility, the entire family, including Ethel, had gone to visit him. By contrast, when David had been sent away to California to seek treatment, nobody had gone to visit. "I knew from his girlfriend that when the mother went to see Bobby in the hospital, David was in tears," he said. "He said, 'nobody ever came to see me.'" He blamed Bobby Jr. and the entire Kennedy family for abandoning David. "He died after his brother, Bobby, who had introduced him to hard drugs and who taunted him his entire life, even though he was a bigger drug user or at least as big a drug user as David. David couldn't buy love in that family. He was excluded. They said he dragged his family's name through the mud."

The family was so desperate to rein David in that they had pressured him into seeing a "prominent Boston attorney" to find out if he could retract the conversations he had had with Collier and Horowitz—interviews that had stretched over several months. "David was bitterly criticized for breaching the family faith," wrote the authors. "The word used in condemning him was 'treason,' a word with political even more than personal implications."

Despite his addiction, David may have been one of the most prescient members of the Kennedy family when he said about his older brother after his arrest in South Dakota, "He was the best and the brightest, no doubt about that. Bobby was our last illusion."

CHAPTER 5

The Riverkeeper

Bobby Kennedy's life changed dramatically after his heroin addiction was made public. "My arrest generated tremendous publicity and, ironically, neutralized my fear of scandal, allowing me to get help," he wrote.

He began attending Alcoholics Anonymous meetings regularly and keeping a journal to chronicle his progress. In September 1984, Emily gave birth to their first child, Robert "Bobby" Francis Kennedy III. Perhaps it was the experience of becoming a father months after the loss of his younger brother David that led Kennedy back to Catholicism and his childhood habit of daily prayers. He prayed for enlightenment, for guidance, and for helping him stay on the right path, even as his addiction to drugs gave way to an even more intense addiction to women, according to several entries in his diaries.

But in the early days of struggling to stay sober, his focus was on trying to overcome his temptation to shoot up. "Sobriety is about long term commitment," he wrote in his diary years later. "I had to learn to go through the meetings and walk through life no matter how I felt, just because I'd made the commitment and for no other reason."

Among his new challenges was becoming a better person and

devoting himself to what he felt was his calling: cracking down on polluters and cleaning up the environment. "The purpose of life is to act well in my personal relationships," he continued in his diary. "That's the most important thing. I love my purpose which is saving the planet. But saving the planet is ultimately in God's hands."

It was the punishment for being caught with heroin in South Dakota that led to his environmental activism and his commitment to finally taking seriously his career as a lawyer. "Following my arrest and my recovery, I began to rethink my life," he wrote in one of his memoirs, referring to the beginning of his community service working on a project for the Natural Resources Defense Council, an environmental nonprofit made up mostly of scientists and lawyers. "My decision to work on environmental issues was consistent with my other efforts to retrace my steps to that point where I had started off on the wrong path."

It was clear to him that getting onto the right path would require a major pivot in his own behavior: leaving aside the Kennedy sense of entitlement and superiority. "The only thing I can control is how I behave in my successes and failures," he wrote in his diary. "How I treat the people who work with me, and the people with whom I have personal contact." But judging by the sometimes very callous ways he treated fellow activists and environmental lawyers in the early days of his activism, he had a long way to go.

At the beginning of his professional environmental activism, Kennedy teamed up with John Cronin, a former house painter and roofer who had grown up along the Hudson River. "I was in the first generation that was taught the river was unsafe—not because of tides that might pull you down but because of water quality," Cronin said in an interview with *Time*. "As a young adult, I found a legacy I had been kept from inheriting. The lives of my family had swirled around the river;

my grandfather was a fisherman; that's where families gathered. I discovered that connection."

Later, the folk singer Pete Seeger encouraged Cronin to become a volunteer in the effort to clean up the Hudson River in 1973. Seeger was passionate about the Hudson River, founding the Clearwater Initiative in 1966 and commissioning the construction of a Hudson River sloop, *Clearwater*, a replica of the boats that had used to sail the river in the eighteenth and nineteenth centuries. In the late 1960s and early 1970s, Seeger sailed on the majestic wooden 106-foot sloop, playing dockside concerts and passing around a guitar case to collect donations for the river cleanup.

In October 1973, *Clearwater* pulled up to the ferry dock in Beacon to deliver a load of pumpkins for the town's annual "Pumpkin Sail." Cronin, a fan of the folk singer since high school, attended the event and later answered a call for volunteers to rebuild the town's dock. Working side by side with his idol for a few days replacing dock timbers convinced him to commit to the Clearwater Initiative. In the early days, his focus was on Beacon, where he collected water samples to make sure that the Tuck Tape company was abiding by the federal Clean Water Act of 1972. "At the Tuck factory we found barrels of thick, white waste adhesive that had been poured out the back doors," he wrote. "The company had a permit for only two discharges. We discovered twenty-three that poured hot solvents, adhesives, sewage, latex, and titanium dioxide." Cronin and another volunteer took their samples to the Manhattan District Attorney's Office, where prosecutors built a successful case against the firm, charging it with twenty-four violations of the Clean Water Act and Federal Refuse Act.

In other parts of the river, the amount of pollution was staggering, he said. Near the General Motors assembly plant in Tarrytown, fishermen could tell what color the cars were being painted on a given day by looking at the river, wrote Cronin. At the Diamond Candle Company near Newburgh, the ground surrounding the factory was covered in wax.

After he left Clearwater, Cronin continued his environmental advocacy, working as a lobbyist and then as a commercial fisherman, trawling for shad and blue crabs on the Hudson. In the early 1980s, the journalist and environmentalist Robert Hamilton Boyle Jr. hired him to be a "riverkeeper" for the Hudson River Fishermen's Association (HRFA), a group of commercial and sports fishermen who "operated like a lightweight cavalry unit in enemy territory, relying on mobility and offensive tactics against larger, better equipped forces," wrote Kennedy. "The fishermen patrolled the river, sailing its waterways and nailing polluters on the spot."

Boyle, a former marine in the Atlantic Fleet during the Korean War and a onetime professional baseball player, was a hard-nosed advocate for the Hudson River. A graduate of Yale University and magazine journalist, he had grown up fishing on the Hudson River when he attended boarding school in Highland Falls, New York. He was among the first to raise the alarm about global warming in his articles, three decades before the issue became an environmental rallying cry. He was also among the first journalists to report that North American fish were contaminated with toxic polychlorinated biphenyls, or PCBs. Shocked by the industrial pollution he found when he moved back to Croton-on-Hudson from the West Coast in 1960, he became an unofficial guardian of the river when he joined the Scenic Hudson Preservation Conference, a coalition of nonprofits dedicated to cleaning up the river. The group launched a lawsuit against the Federal Power Commission in order to prevent the construction of a Consolidated Edison power plant on Storm King Mountain in the Hudson Highlands, near Cornwall. They argued that the project would result in lasting environmental damage and kill fish in the surrounding waters. Con Edison wanted to establish a hydroelectric power plant on the river in order to provide more power to New York City. According to scientists hired by the utility, the new hydroelectric plant would have no damaging effects on fish or contribute to any other ecological hazards—false assertions that were successfully challenged by Boyle and others who were among the guardians of the Hudson. For if anyone knew about the dangers that faced the river, it was Boyle, who had just finished an article on the subject for *Sports Illustrated*. He had learned from local fishermen that a nearby Con Edison facility at Indian Point was using millions of gallons of Hudson River water per day to cool its reactors, killing tens of thousands of fish in the process.

The Storm King litigation, which began in 1963, went on for seventeen years, with the Storm King group launching a statewide grassroots campaign to educate the public about the hazards of the hydroelectric plant. Soon, local residents, including boaters and sports fishermen, signed petitions, launched letter-writing campaigns, and lobbied their local and national elected representatives to prevent the construction of the power plant. The campaign was successful, and in 1980, Con Edison agreed to drop the plan for the Storm King facility. Moreover, the landmark federal lawsuit became a model for the environmental movement, establishing important legal precedents. Most of all, it demonstrated how community engagement could be used as an effective weapon in the battle to save the environment at a time when there were growing concerns about the future of the planet.

The nuclear accident at Three Mile Island in Pennsylvania in 1979—the worst nuclear accident in US history—had also contributed to concerns about the environment as the partial meltdown of one of the nuclear reactors at the power plant spread dangerous levels of radiation, contaminating nearby waterways and fields. Pregnant women and children were advised to leave if they lived within a five-mile radius of the reactors, sowing panic and confusion that sensitized a generation to the dangers of nuclear power and helped bolster the burgeoning environmental movement.

In the midst of the long-running Storm King litigation, Boyle met with a group of concerned residents at an American Legion hall in Crotonville to launch HRFA. Boyle, who had done his homework, told the group that they could bring federal lawsuits against polluters by using the Federal Refuse Act of 1899, which prohibits the discharge of pollutants into navigable waterways. The legislation became the fishermen's most lethal weapon. Combined with Boyle's bold publicity stunts, the nonprofit, later named Riverkeeper became an important force for change on the Hudson.

"From the outset Boyle's style was combative," wrote Cronin and Kennedy. "He provoked Consolidated Edison to cancel its advertising in a Hudson Valley paper when he compared the company in an editorial to Genghis Khan. He once clapped a giant striped bass on a congressman's desk during a hearing on the Indian Point fish kills, and he dismissed Lyndon and Lady Bird Johnson's popular American Beautification program as 'rouge on a cancer patient.'"

On his inaugural sail as the Hudson Riverkeeper, Cronin came face-to-face with a 750-foot Exxon oil tanker, rinsing its tanks and discharging 14,000 tons of seawater into the river. The oil tankers, which originated in Aruba, regularly dumped their chemicals into the Hudson and then loaded up with fresh river water for the company's Caribbean refinery, Cronin soon found. He collected samples of the water, which was laden with petrochemicals, and under Boyle's leadership the group took their case to the Manhattan District Attorney's Office. The $16 million lawsuit against Exxon for dumping petrochemicals into the Hudson and stealing fresh water from it was front-page news around the world. The lawsuit, which was heard in New York Supreme Court in Ulster County, accused Exxon of having removed 3 million tons of water from the Hudson River without paying for it for use in its Aruba refinery and for sale on the island. "This is the most flagrant example of environmental crime," said Henry G. Williams, the state's environmental conservation commissioner, in April 1984 in reference to the lawsuit. In a settlement negotiated by the oil giant, the US attorney, and the fishermen, Exxon agreed to pay $1.5 million to the state of New York and $500,000 to Boyle's group, half of which was to fund the Riverkeeper program.

Kennedy came on board the program just as the Fishermen's

Association was preparing to sue Exxon. "He showed up wearing shit-kicker boots, ragged chinos and spitting tobacco," said a former friend, reflecting on Kennedy's deep appreciation of the South. "Bobby loved the rednecks in the South and he looked more like he belonged at a truck stop."

Kennedy, now thirty-one, believed that he was finally firmly following in his father's footsteps, working for social justice. His two-year probation was over—in fact, it had been ended a year early—and he had finally been sworn in to the New York State Bar Association following a standard review by the Committee on Character and Fitness of the Appellate Division of the State Supreme Court. "He impressed me as a person of considerable integrity, a person who is intellectually acute and unusually modest," said Harold J. Reynolds, the committee's interviewer. "I unreservedly approved him."

For Kennedy, the newly minted attorney, the experience marked the beginning of his career in environmental law, a subject he confessed he knew little about. "Prior to that time, I knew little about civil litigation, and next to nothing about environmental law," he wrote.

His first big case involved litigation over the cleanup of Quassaick Creek, a seven-mile tributary of the Hudson River that flows into the town and city of Newburgh. The creek was a "conveyance for industrial and municipal waste," he wrote. When Kennedy and Cronin began their investigation of the toxic and refuse-choked creek, they found "so many pipes and drains emptying into the mouth [of the creek] that I wondered whether there was anything alive in this part of the creek. I found long strings of toilet paper and what we euphemistically called 'brown trout' or 'river pickles': human fecal material," wrote Kennedy. "After a short time cuts on my hand began to fester."

Both riverkeepers went undercover, carrying backpacks filled with vials, maps, and flashlights as well as fishing poles, enabling them to pose as local anglers out for a day trip on the river. They donned wet suits and dived into waters laced with raw sewage and naphthalene, a cancer-causing toxin found in coal tar and gasoline, to collect samples from illegally discharging pipes. They walked every inch of the seven-mile-long creek, sneaking into shoreline companies under cover of darkness to document pipes that were illegally pouring toxins into the water.

The two riverkeepers appealed to local authorities, who they quickly found were more interested in getting rich than in providing clean water for their constituents. When they found that the city of Newburgh planned to sell a boat ramp and three acres of public parkland to an acquaintance of the mayor at a low price in order to develop a floating restaurant, they were even more committed to do battle. The restaurant and a new boat ramp, which would benefit from a state government grant to stabilize the shoreline, would cut off access to the creek for residents. For many of the local lawmakers, barring locals from enjoying the creek seemed to be the point. One local developer, cited by Kennedy in his environmental memoir, noted, "We are not going to have spades drinking and screwing and swimming around our *new* boat ramp, if that's what you mean by the public." For Kennedy, the racist comments were an epiphany. "At that moment I knew I wanted to be an environmental lawyer. Any ambivalence I'd felt about having abandoned the battle for social justice when I took up arms for a clean environment was gone," he wrote in *The Riverkeepers*. "In fact, the battle for the environment was the ultimate civil rights and human rights contest, a struggle to maintain public control over publicly owned resources against special interests that would monopolize, segregate and liquidate them for cash."

Kennedy and his partner began researching the boat launch property as well as the Newburgh City Charter's rules on selling city-owned land. Reading through the minutes of various city council meetings, they learned that the city had blatantly ignored the rules. The charter required a vote of four to five council members on all sales of city-owned property. The council vote had been three to five. The charter had also made provisions for competitive bidding, which had also been ignored, he wrote.

Kennedy called the city's corporation counsel, letting him know that the city was not in compliance with its own rules. Newburgh's lawyer agreed to retake the vote. In the meantime, Kennedy told him that Riverkeeper would be bidding on the boat launch property even though the group didn't have the cash. "Our offer put the city government in a temporary quandary," he wrote. "... We were able to stall the vote in city council, giving ourselves time to devise a strategy to save the boat ramp."

Cronin and Kennedy eventually identified twenty-four sources of pollution of the creek and brought lawsuits against sixteen companies under the federal Clean Water Act, which became front-page news in New York. The companies settled before trial and paid hundreds of thousands of dollars to help Riverkeeper clean up the Quassaick, wrote Kennedy. Among the defendants was the city of Newburgh. Although the activists had demanded financial penalties from the industrialists polluting the Quassaick, they knew that Newburgh was "so impoverished, and the poverty of its citizenry so stark," that they decided to offer a compromise. In lieu of monetary penalties, the fishermen asked that the city permanently abandon its plan to sell the boat ramp, which it readily accepted. Newburgh also granted the fishermen's group a "conservation easement" that perpetually protected the ramp from being sold to any private developer, said Kennedy, adding that the city had agreed to maintain the property as a public space. "The results of the Quassaick Creek cases were particularly gratifying because they were my first successes as an environmental lawyer," he wrote. "I'd discovered powerful tools for making polluters clean up after themselves."

The two militant environmentalists continued to work together on projects for the Fishermen's Association and began to establish an important national presence. The group opened a clinic at Pace University law school, where Kennedy soon found himself teaching environmental law and working with his students to identify and sue companies that continued to pollute the Hudson River.

In their working relationship, Cronin spent a great deal of time "managing Bobby," said a government official who worked with both of them on the New York City Watershed, a vital water source encompassing 2,000 square miles in upstate New York. "It was John who kept Bobby in line and made sure he didn't do anything crazy."

Kennedy's life was looking up. In 1985, he and Emily bought a sprawling white clapboard farmhouse on ten acres on South Bedford Road in Bedford, New York, for $745,000. Three years later, in 1988, he and Emily celebrated another milestone with the birth of their daughter, Kathleen "Kick" Kennedy. Kick was named for her great-aunt, the lively, outgoing second daughter of Joe and Rose Kennedy, who in 1944 had married the British politician and aristocrat William Cavendish, Marquess of Hartington, who had a tragic end. "Billy," as he was known in British society circles, was among the wealthiest and most eligible bachelors in London. Kathleen's older brother Joe Kennedy, who was in London on the eve of his secret mission for the US Navy, was the only Kennedy family member to attend her wedding.

The couple spent only a few weeks together before Cavendish was called up for military duty in France and Belgium, where he died four months later in September 1944, killed by a sniper bullet while leading forces to capture the town of Heppen in Belgium. His death followed on the heels of Joe Kennedy's fiery accident when his plane exploded during Operation Aphrodite. Later, Kathleen began a romantic relationship with Peter Wentworth-Fitzwilliam, Eighth Earl Fitzwilliam, a well-known married gambler and Protestant who was even wealthier than Cavendish. Her parents were furious at the relationship, even though Peter had promised to leave his wife and marry her. In May 1948, Kathleen had planned to meet her father in Paris to appeal for his help in marrying Peter. Days before the meeting, the couple took off for a vacation in the south of France. They died when their plane crashed during a storm.

In order to memorialize Kathleen within the family, Robert and Ethel Kennedy had named their first child, born in 1951, Kathleen.

More than thirty years later, Kennedy sought to do the same thing by naming his daughter Kathleen.

By the late 1980s, as he solidified his environmental bona fides, Kennedy found himself surrounded by some powerful family members whom he could call upon to help him in his crusade to save the planet. Kathleen, Kennedy's older sister, worked in the Maryland state government and would serve as lieutenant governor of the state from 1995 to 2003. His uncle Teddy continued in his role as "the lion of the Senate," and his older brother, Joe, was elected to Congress for Massachusetts in 1987. "I have enough friends and family who are in the House and Senate, so if I want legislation, I have the access," Kennedy told a reporter.

In June 1990, another powerful ally emerged when his younger sister Kerry married Andrew Cuomo, the politically ambitious son of New York Governor Mario Cuomo. In fact, it was at Andrew Cuomo's bachelor party that Kennedy buttonholed the governor, who was sitting alone at the bar, to lobby him on his environmental crusades. "Nobody else was talking to him," Kennedy recalled. "So I made him sit and listen to me." Years later, he would rely on the elder Cuomo for legal representation after he was charged with trespassing on Vieques.

Andrew was his father's closest adviser and the manager of his political campaigns. When he married into the Kennedy dynasty, he was the chair of the New York City Homeless Commission under Mayor David Dinkins. He would go on to be federal secretary of housing and urban development in the Clinton administration and launched his first run for governor of New York in 2000. At that time, Kennedy confessed his true feelings about his brother-in-law in his diary when he wrote, "Andrew could win because he is totally focused and energetic. He could lose because he lacks humanity and doesn't love people. He is not a retail politician."

For his part, Kennedy was emerging as a power player in environmental circles. He began openly criticizing the city of New York for "stalling" in its commitment to clean up its water supply and later took credit for helping to establish an important environmental agreement.

"We tried cases in every court in New York and helped orchestrate a watershed agreement that garnered $1.5 billion from New York City to buy land and otherwise restore and protect the Catskill and Westchester streams that feed the Hudson," he said.

But Kennedy greatly exaggerated his role in the protracted negotiations among the New York City government, the state of New York, and the communities along the Hudson that hammered out the agreement for New York's drinking water that has stood the test of time. "Bobby was never part of the negotiations," said Daniel Ruzow, the environmental attorney who represented and continues to represent the Catskill Watershed Corporation. "Bobby was more of a visitor at the negotiations."

Ruzow said that Riverkeeper and Kennedy had been brought in only toward the end of the eighteen months of negotiations, which had begun in the spring of 1995 although the entire project had started in 1990. New York Governor George Pataki believed that consulting local environmental groups would make for good optics, but none of them was ever profoundly involved in the process, said Ruzow, adding that of the hundreds of meetings that had taken place, Kennedy and Cronin had been part of two or three. "Bobby was a flake," he said. "He would say things he was not prepared for then. He would come with a script to the meetings but had little understanding of what he was talking about."

The federal Environmental Protection Agency wanted New York City to come up with a better way to keep the upstate reservoirs that are the source of the city's drinking water clean. The choices were to build a huge filtration plant that could cost the city between $4 billion and $8 billion or to buy up land near the reservoirs and restrict development within the 2,000-square-mile watershed. The land would act as a buffer around the reservoirs.

To spur the city to buy up the properties, Kennedy said, his team at Riverkeeper had come up with a public service campaign in the spring of 1993 that speculated about how much of Amy Fisher's urine was seeping into a city reservoir from the sewage of the nearby Bedford Hills Correctional Facility for Women, where she was an inmate. The campaign drew on the notoriety of Fisher, who had been on the front pages of newspapers across the city in the spring of 1992, known by her tabloid moniker "Long Island Lolita." Fisher was convicted in December of that year in the shooting of her neighbor Mary Jo Buttafuoco on the front porch of her home in Massapequa. Fisher, who was seventeen at the time of the shooting, was having an affair with Mary Jo's husband, Joey Buttafuoco, who was thirty-eight years old. Mary Jo survived the shooting but was left with a bullet lodged in her head. After Fisher pled guilty, she was convicted of assault and sentenced to five to fifteen years in prison, which she served in New Hampshire State Prison for Women and the higher-security Bedford Hills Correctional Facility for Women near the Kennedy farmhouse.

The ploy seemed to work on David Dinkins, who was mayor of New York at the time. He agreed to meet with Kennedy to discuss the water issue if his group would refrain from running the ads. Kennedy agreed and later boasted about having spent two hours speaking with Dinkins in his office.

Kennedy could be very persuasive in his environmental crusades, but he could also be arrogant and nasty when he was involved in negotiations, according to a key government bureaucrat who was at the forefront of the watershed negotiations. "He was very ambitious, and I was eager to meet him because I admired the Kennedys, but in our first meeting he threatened to have me fired," said Marilyn Gelber, New York's commissioner of environmental protection, the first woman to be appointed to the position in 1994. Gelber had dealt with the myriad lawsuits that Kennedy launched against the city, and it was she who had negotiated with Pataki after he had come into office the following year, about the watershed program. Following "very hard" negotiations with state officials, community leaders in the Catskills, and later environmental groups, including Riverkeeper and especially the NRDC, the city reached a landmark agreement to protect New York City's water supply. "We were successful," she said. "And thirty years later, the agreement has held."

At the time, though, she said, she had been concerned that displacing residents in the Catskills to create the watershed would be too disruptive and wanted to set up a fund to help them resettle in other parts of the state. "Bobby was very critical, and just wanted people out and the government to acquire more land, even though statistics showed that there was a high poverty rate in the Catskills," she said. "Most people found him to be very aggressive and questioned his character and truthfulness. Both Bobby and Riverkeeper didn't really do anything in the negotiations except to tell us we weren't doing enough."

In addition to alienating the city authorities and other environmental attorneys negotiating the watershed, Kennedy was treated with suspicion by the local leaders in the western part of the watershed, most of whom were Republican, Ruzow said. "They all thought Bobby was a lunatic. I was disappointed. I had worked on his father's campaign in Yonkers when he ran for senator. I could never reconcile what I remembered of Bobby Kennedy with his son."

For his part, Kennedy said he had launched some forty lawsuits against nursing homes, schools, and hospitals within the watershed, claiming that they were illegally pumping untreated sewage into the reservoirs without penalty from New York City.

Before their contretemps, Gelber had asked Kennedy to speak to a community group in Brooklyn on Martin Luther King Jr. Day. He was "a very gifted person" and a great public speaker, she said, although he had few qualms about "creating scapegoats and victims" to win an argument. Still, after New York City Mayor Rudolph Giuliani had fired her in 1996 because she had tried to protect the commission from political appointees, she said, Kennedy had sent her a bouquet of flowers and a nice note. "Bobby thought I'd done a good job, and sent me the most beautiful narcissus bulbs," she said. "Our relationship ended on that note."

As Kennedy's environmental activism grew, he found himself increasingly in demand to speak to nonprofits and conventions across the country and around the world. Democratic politicians, including former Vice President Al Gore, reached out to him when they wanted to emphasize their own environmental bona fides. Gore wrote the introduction to *The Riverkeepers*. As his outside influence rose, Kennedy soon began to demand a greater profile at Riverkeeper, and it wasn't long before he began butting heads with Bob Boyle, the head of the group. "Kennedy saw Riverkeeper as a way to get out of his pariah status," said Alex Boyle, an art dealer and filmmaker as well as Bob Boyle's son. "He saw this as a stepping-stone to prominence and was a bit reckless. One thing about him is that he always bragged about taking shortcuts, and his recklessness made him look quite shallow."

Boyle continued to keep Kennedy on the board because his last name brought in millions of dollars in donations and celebrity endorsements, said Alex. During Kennedy's involvement with the group, Riverkeeper grew from a single nonprofit to chapters across the country, protecting various rivers.

While Kennedy continued his high-profile environmental activism, the Kennedy family was back in the gossip columns and on the front pages for more of their entitled behavior. His uncle Ted Kennedy had married for the second time in July 1992, which was a fairly positive story after his decade of womanizing and heavy drinking before and after his divorce from his first wife, the socialite Joan Bennett. His new wife, Victoria Reggie, was a lawyer who specialized in banking law and divorced mother of two, who is credited with revitalizing his political career. Reggie was also his most important confidante and a key political adviser as well as a formidable campaigner during his 1994 Senate campaign—his seventh. During the campaign, his first wife tried to reopen the financial settlement from her divorce from the senator.

"People used to choose the Kennedys because they represented youth, energy and good looks," said the historian Doris Kearns Goodwin, who had written *The Fitzgeralds and the Kennedys: An American Saga* and had remained close to the Kennedy family. "In this race, given that Mitt Romney is young, with a beautiful wife and a perfect looking family, and that Teddy is older, it helps that Vicki can play the role of the Kennedyesque figure—young, beautiful, energetic." Reggie appeared in campaign commercials in which she was seen listening intently to the sixty-two-year-old lawmaker and nestling her head on his shoulder.

But it was Joe Kennedy who became even worse tabloid fodder when he used the Kennedy legacy and his family's connections to get an annulment from the Catholic Archdiocese of Boston to end the marriage to his first wife, Sheila Brewster Rauch. Joe Kennedy was in love with his congressional aide Beth Kelly, with whom he had been having an affair, and in order to maintain his good standing to remarry in the Catholic faith, he needed the Church to declare that his twelve-year marriage to Rauch, a city planner and the mother of his two sons, had no meaning and had technically never taken place.

"In 1993 my former husband asked the Catholic Church to annul our marriage," wrote Rauch in her memoir *Shattered Faith*. "We had been divorced for over two years, and he wanted to remarry. Since the only way he could do so and remain in good standing within the Church was to have our marriage declared invalid, he was prepared to testify before a church court that in the eyes of God our marriage had never existed."

Rauch, an Episcopalian, was expected to stand by and not get in the way of the annulment, she said. To make matters worse, Joe blamed her, seeking the annulment because of her "lack of discretion of judgment." In other words, he was trying to maintain that his former wife had not been in her right mind when she had agreed to marry him in 1979. "We had a true and valid marriage," she said. "While the marriage failed, I think we need to accept responsibility for that and not say, 'You know, God didn't bless the union from the beginning and it's really out of our hands.'"

The Boston Archdiocese granted the annulment, which Rauch said she had found out about in 1996, after Kennedy had been married to his new wife for three years. The Church hierarchy in Boston was so committed to working for the Kennedys that it had never informed Rauch that she could appeal its decision. She figured it out on her own. She refused to accept the annulment and appealed to the Vatican, which ruled in her favor. She learned about the favorable ruling in 2007.

While Kennedy's older brother was trying to rewrite his marital history, Kennedy was facing the end of his marriage to Emily Black. It's not clear why the marriage ended. By 1993, he was having an affair with Mary Richardson, a svelte brunette who had been his sister Kerry's schoolmate and best friend.

Kennedy had known Mary, an erstwhile fashion model who studied architecture, since she was fourteen years old. Raised in Hoboken, New Jersey, she came from a large Irish American family. She had four sisters and two brothers. Her father, John F. Richardson, was a lawyer and law professor who died when Mary was twelve years old. Her mother, née Nancy Higgins, worked as a public school English teacher. Although they were not wealthy, they managed to send Mary to the elite Putney School in Vermont, where she was Kerry Kennedy's roommate. As a result, she grew up in very close proximity to the Kennedys, spending time at Hyannis Port and Hickory Hill during school vacations. Later, both young women went on to study at Brown University, where they were also roommates. Mary, an A student, went on to the Rhode Island School of Design. But the friends remained close, sharing apartments in Boston and New York, and in June 1990, Mary was the maid of honor at Kerry's wedding to Andrew Cuomo. "Mary was as talented with the left side of the brain as the right," Kerry said years later. "She was the kindest person I've ever met. And she was that way to everybody, not just celebrities but fishermen, cabdrivers, and the guy who installed her floors."

Another school friend, Jen Just, remembered Mary as a detail-oriented, immensely kind person. "Mary never did anything half-way whether you were her friend or her classmate," she wrote in a post on an online memorial page. "In fact, she did it fully and then added her own twist. When we shared birthday cake duty, Mary insisted on tossing aside the cake mix and making not just chocolate cakes but German chocolate cakes! When Easter came around, we made Easter baskets out of papier mache, painted them, stuffed them with candy and put them at the end of our friends' beds in the middle of the night."

While they were at Brown, Just and Mary often held a Valentine's Day treasure hunt across the campus, writing a poem for each of their friends. "She, and we, did this not just because it was fun to go the extra mile—and it was!—but because she could do no less when it came to showing the people she cared about how much they mattered to her."

Another friend, Diana Kellogg, described Mary's trying to prevent a domestic abuse incident that was playing out in front of her family home in Rhode Island, where Mary was visiting. "Outside we heard a car screech to a stop, car doors slam and raised voices of a man and a woman screaming at each other," Kellogg wrote. "While my siblings, my mother and myself crouched below the windows and reached for the phone to call 911, Mary moved in an instant. As we looked outside we saw Mary, still in her nightgown in the middle of the street, where she had positioned herself between the man and woman fighting. She was gently asking the man to stop yelling and abusing the woman. She was persuasively saying to the woman that there was help available to her. She quickly wrote down on a piece of paper a number for an abused women's hotline and tried to get them to calm down, which they gradually did, and then she came inside."

Despite her cheerful disposition, Mary suffered from anorexia. It was serious enough that she had to be hospitalized for her condition as a teenager. Later, she enrolled in twelve-step programs to deal with her addictive behavior.

Following her studies, Mary moved to Manhattan and, beginning in 1979, briefly worked as an assistant to *Interview* magazine editor Bob Colacello. Fred Hughes, Andy Warhol's business manager, took Mary to the Factory, the artist's studio, which at the time was located at 860 Broadway, overlooking Union Square Park.

"Fred thought Mary would be a good assistant for me," said Colacello, who was a close friend of Warhol and collaborated with the pop artist on his books. "It was hard to get assistants who actually wanted to do secretarial work. Most of them were really good at selling art but not good at playing secretary. Mary was an exception because she wasn't from a fancy family and she was willing to work." She was, he said, also "ravishingly beautiful" and had what he described as "an ethereal quality."

As with all the young women he hired, Colacello warned Mary not to go through Union Square Park, which was full of heroin addicts. "I remember every time we hired a new girl, I always said, 'Whatever you do don't take shortcuts through the park,'" he said, adding that the photo lab used by Warhol was located on the other side of the park. "Like most of downtown at that time, it wasn't safe. She said, 'Oh, Bob, don't worry about me. I know how to handle myself, I was raped three times.'" At the Factory, the comment, delivered with deadpan humor, was treated with some skepticism, coming from a young woman who was a staunch Catholic.

Colacello recalled that Mary was obsessed with the Kennedys and extremely close to her former classmate Kerry. "She was like a lady-in-waiting to Kerry," he said. "They were constantly together. Her head wasn't turned by celebrities, only the Kennedys."

One day when he walked into the magazine's offices, he found her with a pile of Cartier stationery and a calligraphy pen. She said that she was writing wedding invitations as a favor to Ethel Kennedy, likely for the wedding of Courtney Kennedy to Jeffrey Robert Ruhe, which was to take place in the summer of 1980. When Colacello complained to Hughes about Mary working for Ethel during *Interview* work hours, Hughes admonished him. "Ethel can help us," said Hughes, who, unlike Colacello, was a lifelong Democrat and another Kennedy family acolyte. Hughes convinced Warhol to create a screen print of Ted Kennedy to raise funds for his 1980 presidential campaign, said Colacello, who left *Interview* in 1983 and later became a contributing writer for *Vanity Fair*. He also wrote biographies of Ronald and Nancy Reagan as well as Warhol.

In addition to Warhol, Mary helped solicit donations of art from other prominent artists for Ted's unsuccessful presidential run. Like most of the young Kennedys, she frequented Xenon, a popular disco founded by the Swiss restaurateur Peppo Vanini. After her stint at *Interview*, she worked as a fashion model for New York designer Bill Blass. She also worked at the prestigious design firm Parish-Hadley Associates, where she was among the architects collaborating on a green renovation of the US Naval Observatory, the official Washington residence of then Vice President Al Gore.

Tall and striking with long, flowing brown hair, she was active on the dating scene. At one point, she was involved with Carlos Mavroleon, an Eton- and Harvard-educated journalist and scion of a wealthy Greek shipping family, who had converted to Islam, joined the Mujahedeen in their fight against the Soviets in Afghanistan, and worked as a bodyguard for an Afghan tribal chief. According to his friends, Mavroleon was deeply in love with Mary. "His one true love" was how one friend described her. While he was away on the front lines, it was Mary who was entrusted with delivering the film he sent to news outlets, the friend said. "Mary was a formidable angel, one who moved mountains effortlessly, for joy, for love, for loyalty and for good," the friend said in a remembrance of Mary, who always figured in Mavroleon's stories in quiet moments when he was on the front lines. "Mary would become the topic of his quietest conversations at the end of many nights, a persistent turn into Sufi style refrain on love and desire."

Mavroleon had also been a Wall Street broker and was working as a war correspondent before his mysterious death from a heroin overdose while on assignment in Pakistan in 1998. A former addict, he had gone through rehabilitation and had been sober when he went to Pakistan, according to his friends. A few days before he was found dead in his hotel room in Peshawar, he left phone messages for a *60 Minutes* producer saying that he was "in terrible trouble" while researching training camps run by al-Qaeda leader Osama bin Laden, according to the Committee to Protect Journalists, which maintains that he was murdered.

Mary kept in touch with the Mavroleon family after his death, visiting Carlos's brother Nicholas "Nicky," who was married to the actress Barbara Carrera, in Millbrook, the same Hudson Valley town where Kennedy had first gone to boarding school following the death of his father. "She was always so kind, thoughtful and giving," wrote Nicholas. "She was also very funny, fun and such great company. We spent a lot of time in Greece and London, but mostly New York."

Like Kennedy, Mary was a devout Catholic, although she seemed to have no problem with having an affair with the father of two young children. "She was a contrarian," said a source who knew the family. "She struck me as a person who didn't show off her religion but abided by the best version of being Catholic."

Kennedy "fell deeply in love" with Mary in 1993, the year, he says, he became estranged from his first wife, Emily Black. On a trip to Ireland that same year, he proposed to Mary. "She was stunningly beautiful, with pitch-perfect taste, electric charm and a genius for friendship that had won her an army of loyal and loving friends," he said in an affidavit. "Mary had a subtle humor, a photographic memory, and an enthusiasm for life. She was blessed with a profound spirituality that had emerged from her struggles with her eating disorders that had, in her youth, caused her hospitalization and nearly killed her. I loved the way she blossomed in crowds, the thirst for adventure that brought her alive during our frequent white water and wilderness camping trips."

On top of that, Mary had been born on October 4, the feast day of Saint Francis, for whom Kennedy and his father had been named. For the deeply religious environmentalist, marrying Mary might have seemed like something that was preordained and certainly blessed.

Kennedy started appearing at public events with Mary even though he was still married to Emily. Photos show them at an event at the Pierre Hotel in Manhattan with the billionaire pedophile Jeffrey Epstein in March 1994, years before Epstein was convicted of soliciting underage girls in Florida for sex. Kennedy also said that the year before, he had flown with his "wife" on Epstein's private jet to Palm Beach to visit his mother. Kennedy was referring to Mary, even though at the time he was still married to his first wife. He later admitted to having flown on the so-called Lolita Express to South Dakota to go fossil hunting with his children and Mary. He later admitted that it was through Mary's friendship with Ghislaine Maxwell, Epstein's girlfriend and madam, that they had secured the free flights on the private jet.

Kennedy was close enough to Epstein that the financier had a long entry for "Kennedy, Bobby & Mary" in his "little black book," which included the contact information of socialites and politicians as well as the young girls he employed as masseuses and used for sex. Epstein also loaned Kennedy an office at his headquarters on Madison Avenue, according to Christina Oxenberg, a member of the Serbian royal family, whom Kennedy employed to help set up an event for former New York City Mayor David Dinkins in 1993.

When Mary became pregnant with their first child, Kennedy arranged for a quick divorce from Emily in the Dominican Republic. Unlike his older brother, he didn't have the time nor the inclination to petition the Catholic Church for an annulment. In many ways, he was far more practical, perhaps because his girlfriend was six months pregnant. Kennedy flew to Santo Domingo on Thursday, March 24, 1994—days before his and Emily's twelfth wedding anniversary—for the hearing. He flew out the next day. News reports said that he and Emily had been separated since 1992.

Less than a month after obtaining the divorce, Kennedy married Mary in a civil ceremony aboard the *Shannon*, a Riverkeeper research boat, on the Hudson River near Stony Point. The ceremony, which included Bobby III, then nine years old, and his six-year-old sister, Kick, followed a Roman Catholic Mass. Under the divorce agreement with Emily, the children were scheduled to spend two weekends every month with Kennedy and Mary—a situation that quickly became unbearable for everyone concerned.

Three months later, in July, Mary gave birth to their first child, Conor. The young family moved into Kennedy's mansion in Bedford, and Mary spent the next few years having more children. A year after Conor's birth, in August 1995, their daughter, Kyra, was born, and two years after that, William Finbar was born.

"This is my fifth and, God willing, last," Kennedy said about the child they would nickname Finn, adding that the baby's middle name had been inspired by St. Finbar, a sixth-century Irish monk from County Wexford, the ancestral home of the Kennedy clan. "Actually, there were two sixth-century St. Finbars. The other one founded Cork and is credited with building a river there and a monastery on the river. I'm very fond of him." But the couple wasn't quite done. Their last child, Aidan, was born in 2001.

To an outside observer, Kennedy's life after his second marriage might have seemed idyllic. He was a rising star in the environmental movement, courted by powerful Democratic politicians and celebrities. He had a beautiful wife and a gaggle of healthy children. But, as he confessed to his diary, something was missing. "I've been given everything that any person could wish for: A beautiful wife and kids and loving family, wealth, education and good health and job I love. And yet I'm always on the lookout for something I can't have to wreck it all." In his diary he mused on the Garden of Eden, noting that Adam and Eve had been given everything—"Love, good company, beauty, freedom from disease and death, abundance of food, etc." Yet it wasn't enough. "They wanted the things they are not supposed to have," he wrote. "And they are ready to wreck the house for it." He recognized the same tragic flaw in himself: a relentless pursuit of something more that he could not define—restlessness, ambition, addiction.

In a moment of intense self-reflection, he wrote about wanting that undefined "more," the word thickly underlined in his diary and followed by an exclamation point: "No matter how much I have, I want more!" That unbridled desire, his obsession with "more" would become all-consuming and the catalyst for tragedy.

CHAPTER 6

"The Sirens Were on Every Rock"

Robert Kennedy Jr. settled into his role as an environmental activist star. He had timed his foray perfectly, at a moment when the movement to save the planet was gaining greater urgency around the world. Suddenly, after the launch of *Riverkeepers*, the memoir he had written with Cronin, the former heroin addict was in demand to make speeches across the country. Trading on the Kennedy legacy, he demanded tens of thousands of dollars for his appearances as well as free travel for his family, which in some cases allowed him to turn what were largely work events into mini all-expenses-paid vacations to exotic destinations. The grift worked well at a time when he was cash-strapped and raising five children.

Riverkeepers was his ticket. Billed as "a modern-day David and Goliath tale," the book chronicled Kennedy and Cronin's battles on the front lines of the war against big corporations and corrupt local authorities to save the Hudson River. The book featured a foreword by Vice President Al Gore, who was in the midst of negotiating the Kyoto Protocol, an international treaty to reduce greenhouse gases, when the book was published at the end of 1997. Although the book brought national attention to the Riverkeeper nonprofit, it was panned by *The New York Times* in a scathing review that may have reminded Kennedy of the newspaper's earlier takedown of his first book, the biography of Judge Frank Johnson in 1978.

"Someone should have edited this book," wrote James Gorman, the newspaper's deputy science editor. "Someone should have sat the authors down and said, 'Look, the subject of importance here is the Hudson River, not you.'" The review went on to criticize the authors for boasting about the press attention they were getting for their efforts to save the Hudson River. "They point out that the battle for public opinion requires the news media," Gorman wrote. "But it is still tedious to read a list of Kennedy's Op-Ed pieces, to be given accounts of calls from CBS and NBC and front-page articles in *The New York Times*. No doubt gaining press coverage is an important tactic, but it is treated almost as an achievement in itself, and of course the heroes, again, are the authors."

Less than a month after the book was published, the Kennedy clan suffered another tragedy that made headlines across the country. On December 31, 1997, Kennedy's younger brother Michael died after crashing into a tree while playing football on skis in Aspen. Michael, thirty-nine, was an expert skier and had been team captain during the game but lost control of one of his skis as he hit a patch of ice, likely distracted by the football, according to press accounts. Those who had witnessed the accident said that his head had been covered in blood when his younger sister Rory had skied over to him and begun giving him mouth-to-mouth resuscitation. "Michael, now is the time to fight," she had said as she bent over her brother, pounding his chest, surrounded by his three children ages ten, thirteen, and fourteen, who had gathered around him to try to help. "Don't leave us." At one point, Rory turned her brother on his side and spat out the blood in her mouth, then wiped her face with snow. Michael's children knelt down in the snow and began to pray, according to witnesses. Paramedics arrived, and one of them took over the CPR, while the others worked to fit Michael with a cervical collar. Rory told the children to think positive thoughts.

Michael was still breathing when he was taken to Aspen Valley Hospital but slipped into a coma and was pronounced dead soon after. The cause of death was "massive head and neck trauma," according to deputy coroner Tom Walsh, who found no trace of drugs or alcohol in the body. Michael's estranged wife, Vicki, who was spending the Christmas holidays with her father sportscaster, Frank Gifford, in Vail, flew to Aspen to pick up the children. Michael's body was flown home to Hyannis Port on Kevin Costner's private jet.

Perhaps there were other issues distracting Michael as he skied into the tree. Months before the accident, *The Boston Globe* had revealed that he had had an affair with his children's babysitter, beginning when she was as young as fourteen years old and he was in his midthirties. The babysitter, who was identified by the newspaper, had broken off the relationship in the fall of 1996 when she had gone to college. As a result of the newspaper report, the Norfolk District Attorney's Office had begun "a preliminary review" of the allegations. Sex with a minor under sixteen is a criminal offense in Massachusetts. The investigation was later dropped when the babysitter refused to cooperate with the authorities. "A protracted investigation and trial, accompanied by unrelenting media coverage, would cause potentially irreparable harm to the victim of this outrageous conduct," said the family of the young woman, who was a student at Boston University when the story surfaced. Her father was a prominent businessman and important donor to the Democratic Party. News of the affair ended Michael's sixteen-year marriage.

At the time the story broke, Michael, a father of three and the head of an energy nonprofit that provided low-cost heating oil to poor families, had been managing his uncle Ted's tough 1994 reelection campaign for the Senate and was also helping his older brother Joe in his bid for governor of Massachusetts. The scandal, coupled with Sheila Rauch Kennedy's book about the end of her marriage and her battle against the Catholic Church, would end Joe Kennedy's political career. He not only dropped out of the governor's race but also decided not to pursue reelection to Congress. It was he who had organized the football game on skis that had ended his brother's life, according to press reports.

Kennedy, taking on the mantle of family spokesman, seemed to have the last word on the sordid state of affairs that had ruined his older brother's career and devastated Michael's wife, Vicki, and their children. "A lot of people's lives have been ruined," Kennedy told *The New York Times*. "I feel most concern about the children. I think it's a tragedy for everyone who is involved."

Still, Michael was redeemed in death. More than 450 guests, many of them politicians and celebrities, including John F. Kennedy Jr., Mario Cuomo, Maria Shriver and her husband, Arnold Schwarzenegger, Ted Kennedy, and Senator John Kerry crowded into Our Lady of Victory Church in Centerville, the scene of so many Kennedy weddings and baptisms, for his funeral on January 3, 1998. The Mass opened with the reading of letters of condolence from President Clinton, Nelson Mandela, and the archbishop of Angola. Michael's son Michael Jr. helped carry his father's casket. Family friend Andy Williams sang "Ave Maria," as he had done at Robert Kennedy's funeral nearly thirty years before. "I ask now only that we look at Michael truly—not in the glare of a moment, but in the wholeness of his life," said Joe Kennedy in his eulogy. "It was a life cut short, a life not without pain and imperfection—but full of hope and high achievement."

Michael's death was hard on his entire family, but it was Rory, the youngest of Robert and Ethel Kennedy's children, who likely suffered the most. Rory, who had been born six months after her father's assassination, had been very close to her brother. Ethel had assigned him to be her "godfather," the brother who looked after her within the chaotic family. Rory, who had been the other team's captain in the football game on skis, had spoken to her brother every day.

A year after the family buried Michael, Rory's life seemed to be filled with joy. Her documentary about Appalachia was released, and the clan headed to the cape for her wedding to writer Mark Bailey. Little did they know that they were coming together not for a celebration but for an unthinkable tragedy that would plunge them all back into a deep state of mourning.

Despite the news of Michael's death and the scandal that had ended his eldest brother's political career, Kennedy was riding high—cashing in on his family name and becoming increasingly important in the world of environmental activists. He was invited to address large audiences across the country and around the world. It didn't matter that the reviews of *Riverkeepers* were mediocre at best; he used the book as a calling card to launch himself on the increasingly important environmental stage, court lucrative speaking fees for himself, and solicit donations to Riverkeeper and the NRDC. For his part, Cronin seemed to be out of the picture, with Kennedy questioning his coauthor's commitment to the movement that had once bound them together. "I feel bad for John because he has so thoroughly wrecked his life," wrote Kennedy in his diary after a fraught board meeting of the organization in May 1999. In addition to losing his father to cancer that year, Cronin had "destroyed his friendship with me and dramatically changed his credibility and relationships to virtually all the members of the board," he continued. Cronin eventually left Riverkeeper for "family reasons," according to former members of the group's board.

By the time they were honored together as Heroes of the Planet by *Time* magazine in August 1999, they were no longer speaking to each other even as the article announcing the award described them as the best of friends and partners in the crusade to save the Hudson River—"A partnership based on vigilance and the law." The *Time* magazine reporter, who had gone out on the Hudson with the environmentalists in May, described them as "two serious and good-humored men in their late 40s who look like kids, think like politicians and talk like poets." But by that time, the two were already headed down separate paths. Kennedy blamed both the Riverkeeper board and Cronin for not doing enough to support the movement. During the planning of an annual fundraising dinner for the group, he had noted that "Cronin and the board are doing nothing. They haven't sold a single ticket." At the time, some of the stalwart members of the board, including Boyle, were growing frustrated with Kennedy, who was heading up an initiative to sell bottled water using the group's logo to bring in money for Riverkeeper. "My father considered it a huge conflict of interest for an advocacy group like Riverkeeper to market water for money," said Boyle's son, Alex. "Everyone, including Cronin, just got sick of Bobby's game."

Kennedy seemed unfazed by the growing tensions on the board and began to fashion himself as a peripatetic hero. On his own, he traveled to Hollywood, where he met with some of the biggest stars involved with the Natural Resources Defense Council and Riverkeeper, including the actor and director Robert Redford, Leonardo DiCaprio, and Laurie David, a committed environmentalist who would go on to produce *An Inconvenient Truth*, an Oscar-winning documentary about Al Gore's environmental activism. Laurie David was married to the comedian and writer Larry David, and Kennedy appears to have started his friendship with the couple just as Larry launched the first episode of *Curb Your Enthusiasm*, which went on to be a big hit for HBO.

On February 25, 1999, Kennedy wrote about having dinner at the couple's Pacific Palisades home, where he had given a half-hour speech on the environment in front of celebrities and "movie big shots" such as Billy Crystal, as well as his cousin Chris Kennedy Lawford. "I am crazy about these guys," he wrote about the Davids and Julia Louis-Dreyfus, who was also at the dinner and was among the stars of the long-running *Seinfeld* series, on which Larry David had been a writer.

Kennedy had flown in the day before for a NRDC board meeting. He had hit the ground running, dining at Giorgio in Santa Monica with Nancy Stephens, an actress whose most famous role was as Nurse Marion Chambers in the *Halloween* films, directed by her husband, Rick Rosenthal, who was also at the dinner.

Earlier in the day, he'd gone to meet Rob Reiner at Culver Studios and bumped into Michelle Pfeiffer and Bruce Willis. "I was struck by how small Willis was, almost slight," he wrote. "He looks buff and tough in the movies. Reiner was great fun and was helpful as usual. He said he never talked politics with Willis who is a Libertarian and was a Republican."

The stars were filming *The Story of Us*, a romantic drama about a couple who are forced to face their marital difficulties after their two children go away to summer camp. Katie and Ben Jordan's marital troubles in the film might have reminded Kennedy of his own difficult union, but if he made the connection, he didn't write about it in his diary that day. For Kennedy, Los Angeles was always a challenge in terms of staying away from women, but on that trip he managed to restrain himself. Before leaving the city, he noted, "I stayed out of trouble which always dogs me in LA."

He then headed to Hawaii for more environmental talks but also to meet up with Mary, who was joining him there for a romantic getaway. "We have a honeymoon weekend together at the Halekulani Hotel in Waikiki," he wrote on February 26, on his way to give a speech to the National Association of Consumer Advocates, which was likely footing the bill for his trip.

But before Mary arrived, Kennedy hit the beach with his friend John Wilbur, a legendary former offensive lineman for the Dallas Cowboys, the Los Angeles Rams, and the Washington Redskins, who lived in Hawaii. The two men rented an outrigger canoe and paddled across Waikiki Bay, past the pink stucco Royal Hawaiian hotel, "where Mommy and Daddy spent much of their honeymoon," he wrote in his diary. During their outing, Kennedy marveled that his friend had managed to "pick up two pretty girls" in their own single outrigger canoes. "It always amazes me," he wrote about Wilbur, who was good friends with the gonzo journalist Hunter S. Thompson, a Kennedy family friend. "His head is shaped like a football and his ears like wings on a blimp but he is . . . always successful. He calls it his 'hot bod.'"

Mary arrived later that afternoon, and other than a reference to paddling in Waikiki Bay with his wife and watching *Meet Joe Black* on their hotel room TV, much of his "romantic weekend" in Hawaii was spent with Wilbur or diving with Henry Keawe Ayau Jr., one of the island's great free divers, who was known for plunging into ninety feet of water, where he was able to hold his breath for so long that, he confessed to Kennedy, he sometimes fell asleep under water. During one of their dives Kennedy caught two octopuses and later tried his hand at surfing. "I rode 12 to 15 waves all the way standing on the board and did it until I was exhausted and it was getting dark," he wrote.

The next day Mary went back home with a sunburn, and Kennedy was off to San Diego to take part in a whale-watching expedition with the biologist Roger Payne, an expert on whales who was the first to document whale song among humpback whales and was committed to ending commercial whaling. Also along for the ride were Payne's wife, Lisa, Lauren Hutton, and a group of Japanese tourists. Joel Reynolds, an attorney and senior member of the NRDC, was also on the whaling expedition, according to Kennedy's diary. "Roger and I gave lectures to a group of young high school and college students who came by the camp," he wrote. "They are on a one year special program studying whales. I was impressed with their intelligence and maturity."

Like one of his favorite heroes, Odysseus, Kennedy traveled the world on his crusade to save the planet one speech at a time. He left Mary to manage the household and care for their three children, all of them under the age of five. And like the Greek king of Ithaca, he faced temptations everywhere along the way. "I made it through a difficult week without acting out," he wrote during a trip to the Hamptons to promote Riverkeeper in the summer of 1999. "I am proud of myself because the Sirens were on every rock out there."

Kennedy might have been sober and abiding by his twelve-step program, but he couldn't resist the random sexual encounters with women that he referred to as "mugging" in his journal. The term implied that he was the hapless victim and, as with Odysseus, who'd had his sailors tie him to the mast of his ship so that he could hear the sirens' song without giving in to their charms, it was a huge effort of will to resist them.

But he seemed to have other motives for seeking out his own sirens. After only five years of marriage, life with his second wife was proving to be difficult. "Mary is full of anger as usual," he wrote on May 7, 1999. "The kids arrived, and by the time I got home . . . she was seething." Kennedy's children with Emily—Bobby Jr. and Kick—spent two weekends a month with him, Mary, and their three young children. On that particular day, Mary had interrupted his time with his older children "and bludgeoned me with Conor's schedule for tomorrow (soccer)," he wrote. The day before, a Thursday, Mary had "started bludgeoning me with the schedule for the next week as I tried to use the exercise bike."

He worried that his wife was "out of control" and was upset to hear from Bobby III that she was angry at him all the time. "She is filled with venom, retribution and vituperation," he wrote, on May 7, adding in a passage at the end of the month, "This is how she gets in the summer when she knows Bobby and Kick are coming."

On a boat trip to Cruger Island in the Catskills with the children and fellow Riverkeeper environmentalists on May 30, Mary was "spoiling for a fight" and admonished her husband in front of some of the group after Conor had an allergic reaction after eating a chocolate bar. Hives broke out on his stomach, according to Kennedy. Mary insisted that they take him to the hospital, even though Kennedy felt that the attack was mild, adding that he had tried to calm his wife down and told her he was feeling blamed. "That's because you're probably feeling guilty, which you ought to be feeling," she said. Then she insisted upon taking both Conor and Kyra, who had just recovered from a bout of Lyme disease, back home to Bedford. "She did it to embarrass and hurt me," he wrote. "Mary can be vicious. She knows just how to hurt me the worst, and she said the reason she was taking Kyra is because I couldn't be trusted with any of her children."

At one point, he confessed to his diary that he wished he wasn't married because he felt that the marriage contract gave Mary license to attack him. "If we weren't married, she might feel like she had to put some effort into the relationship and perhaps she would take some responsibility for her unhappiness rather than blaming it all on others," he wrote.

Mary's mood swings and depression likely stemmed from her own addiction to alcohol and drugs. Like Kennedy, she was enrolled in a twelve-step program, and during the early years of their marriage, she went on frequent "retreats" to expensive rehab centers. During the latest contretemps, she had been on her way to a rehab center in Minnesota, according to Kennedy's diary. "Our bed is an unfriendly place," he wrote. "If I move at night, she becomes furious. She hates it when I go to bed with her, and will never have sex at night. She rarely speaks to me of anything but scheduling. . . . She never enjoys my company."

On Mother's Day, May 9, Mary left for one of the Hazelden addiction treatment centers in Minnesota, a facility popular with celebrities such as Robin Williams, Eric Clapton, and Liza Minnelli, among others. But before she left, she woke up in a rage, blaming Kennedy for having left a box of cookies in the bedroom and telling everyone she was headed for an addiction treatment facility.

Kennedy breathed a sigh of relief after she left for the airport and noted that he had taken his children to Mass at St. Francis of Assisi Church in Mount Kisco—"We were on time for the first time ever"—and spent the rest of Mother's Day without Mary, canoeing and fishing. They caught a fifteen-pound pickerel and ended the afternoon in typical Kennedy fashion, with a "massive" capture-the-flag game.

Despite their bickering, there still seemed to be hope for the relationship, especially after Mary returned from Hazelden the following week. On May 15, Kennedy recorded in his diary that "I feel so grateful" after Mary seemed to have returned with a renewed faith in God and commitment to their relationship. Often after their arguments, the couple "prayed about it and heard God calling, and it was lovely," he wrote.

Kennedy never took responsibility for Mary's growing depression, at least not in the pages of his diaries. For him, Mary's biggest problem seemed to be her inability to have a good time and her insistence upon operating what he called "a control patrol" to make sure no one else had fun when she was around. But according to interviews with close friends, much of Mary's depression stemmed from Kennedy's increasing philandering. "He definitely gaslit her and told her that she was crazy and that her accusations about other women were fantasies," said a source in an interview who was close to Mary. "She was innocent and naive, but she drank, which was classic in the sense of being in pain a lot of the time."

It's not clear when Mary became aware that Kennedy was a serial cheater, but she clearly resented his behavior even as she was determined to be a good Kennedy wife. There was nothing she wanted more than to be part of the storied clan and spend summers at their compound in Hyannis Port, according to her friends. "She was just 200 percent invested in being his wife and his helpmate and living the Kennedy lifestyle," said a source who had treated Mary for depression during her marriage to Kennedy. "She was sick about his cheating, and she felt Bobby was a real star fucker. Mary was a bit of one as well, but she looked down on that aspect of Bobby's character, but was also jealous when she was no longer part of it."

Another source who was close to Mary agreed. "She loved being a Kennedy, and the notion that she would stop being a Kennedy was scary to her," they said.

The couple were invited to film premieres and celebrity parties, and in 1999 Kennedy's diary included a loose ticket to the Metropolitan Museum's Costume Institute Benefit, an annual fundraiser organized by *Vogue* magazine's legendary editor Anna Wintour. But Mary, who had spent much of her twenties hanging out at Andy Warhol's Factory and partying with artists and celebrities at Xenon and Studio 54, was now largely stuck at home, without her architecture job, attending yoga classes in suburban Westchester and coordinating her children's schedules and dealing with their illnesses.

In 1999, their youngest child, Finn, was diagnosed with asthma. "Finny still has bad asthma," wrote the worried Kennedy on May 20, 1999. "Ten days on steroids. Conor used to improve instantly. Finny is sick all the time. He must be allergic to something in the house. We need to move."

As a result of Finn's health struggles, Mary insisted upon keeping him back from what she considered strenuous sporting outings with his older brothers and sisters. She soon became a volunteer for the Food Allergy Initiative (now known as Food Allergy Research & Education), a nonprofit that helps sponsor research and legislation for those suffering from severe allergies. Mary worked to help the group organize its annual fundraising event, the Food Allergy Ball. Despite her work for the group, it was her husband who occupied a place on the nonprofit's board of directors.

Kennedy returned to Hawaii later that year for a series of speeches at Honolulu City Hall, this time with his sister Kerry. The entire family took advantage of the paid vacation. Kennedy took along Mary and their children, as well as Bobby and Kick. "Kerry and I did three swell speeches and a press conference at city hall," he reported on June 21. The occasion was the inaugural Asia-Pacific Environmental Summit, which brought together four hundred environmental leaders from around the world. Kennedy and his younger sister also spoke at a gala dinner hosted by Honolulu Mayor Jeremy Harris. John Wilbur, the former football player, attended all of their events and left the dinner "with a couple of girls" to head to a hot tub, Kennedy reported.

In between snorkeling with Prince Alfred of Liechtenstein and his wife, who were in Hawaii for the conference, Kennedy spent much of that long weekend playing with his children. He took Conor, then almost five years old, diving off Makena Beach in Maui, where they came face to face with a nearly seven-foot-long shark. "Conor saw him the same time I did and froze," wrote Kennedy. "The shark passed under us as Conor scrambled onto my back. It was a great experience."

At one point, he set off with his children and Kerry's three daughters on a lizard hunting expedition, returning with six green snakes in a pillowcase. He was thrilled about Finn's fearlessness in the water. Five months shy of his second birthday, Finn "sinks and rises and can usually get one breath in before you have to rescue him." He also noted that he was proud of Conor's ability to handle a boogie board and that Bobby would soon get his diving certification. He noted that Kyra, then almost four years old, was still afraid to swim.

But the marital problems persisted. "Mary is being impossible," he wrote on June 25. "She refuses to do anything fun with me, like snorkeling or surfing and is resentful after I do it by myself. She . . . simmers with anger . . . using any opportunity to erupt and constantly assigning me make-work projects which is her way of venting her anger."

Kennedy might have been forging a career as an environmentalist, but to Democratic politicians running for office, his value lay in his last name. When Hillary Clinton took the first step toward her run for the Senate in the summer of 1999, her exploratory campaign called upon Kennedy for help. Clinton, the first first lady to run for political office, asked Kennedy and other supporters to write an opinion piece for *The New York Times* endorsing her campaign. Kennedy wrote it while in hospital undergoing a liver biopsy, he noted on July 9. "Demerol refused. It was nothing."

Like Kennedy's father years before, Clinton was accused of being a carpetbagger—a political opportunist—when she ran for the seat left vacant after Daniel Patrick Moynihan's retirement. The epithet was a favorite talking point of her opponent, Rick Lazio, a Republican congressman from Long Island. Clinton had moved to New York in January to establish residency for her Senate run while Bill Clinton remained in the White House to serve out the rest of his second term.

"The passions against my father were equal to or exceeded what I have seen," read Kennedy's opinion piece in the newspaper. He noted in his diary that he was proud that the editor at the *Times* had praised his piece, calling it "beautifully written" and much better than those by the other writers whom Clinton had called upon to back her campaign. "This is the question that was asked about my father," continued Kennedy, who had been ten years old when Robert Kennedy had run for senator from New York in 1964. "Is somebody who is not born in this state capable of putting in or offering leadership to this state? And my answer to that is resoundingly, yes, they are. New Yorkers come from everywhere. We have the most cosmopolitan community in North America and maybe one of the most cosmopolitan in the world." Kennedy criticized Lazio for not being tough enough on polluters. "You can't point—and Rick Lazio can't point—to a single instance in which he has ever demonstrated environmental leadership on any environmental issue."

Clinton's Senate run promised to be a Kennedy family affair. Shortly after announcing her intentions, Kennedy noted that President Clinton was with his sister Kerry and brother-in-law Andrew Cuomo in Pound Ridge, New York, and that his youngest sister, Rory, was "starting a film on Hillary which everyone envied."

It was already turning out to be a big year for thirty-year-old Rory. Her first documentary feature film, *American Hollow*, had its premiere in May at Manhattan's Film Forum and would be shown on HBO later in the year. She had taken inspiration from her father's visit to Appalachia in February 1968, before he had announced his run for the presidency. On a visit to a one-room schoolhouse in Barwick, a hardscrabble coal town in eastern Kentucky, the children had been so traumatized by his entrance, followed by an entourage of aides and journalists, that they had hidden their heads on their desks. Instead of making a speech to the press, Kennedy had gone from child to child asking what they had eaten that day and reassuring them that everything would be fine.

Rory followed in her father's footsteps to eastern Kentucky, where she focused on the extended Bowling family. She practically moved into their modest home in Mudlick Hollow over the course of a year to get close to them. In interviews to promote the movie, she spoke about how she had seen many similarities between the dirt-poor clan and her own family. "It's a way to access a culture that otherwise feels different and feels 'other,'" she said. "Then you identify and you think, 'Wow, I've been through those—everybody I know has gone through those—exact same emotions, the exact same things. They're just like you and me.'"

Like the Kennedys, the Bowlings go to church and organize Easter egg hunts and family picnics. The family's matriarch is the mother of thirteen and has thirty grandchildren, and the film hints at the family's problems with drug abuse, depression, and domestic violence. *New York Times* film critic Stephen Holden called it a "fine" film and said that it "does a good job of showing us how difficult it is for the poor to transcend their backgrounds and move up the social ladder."

For the Kennedys, the links to the past and the assassinations seemed to follow them everywhere, even decades later. In May 1999, Kennedy family spokeswoman Melody Miller called Kennedy to let him know that the National Archives was poised to release documents regarding John F. Kennedy's original casket. Following his autopsy at Bethesda Naval Hospital in Maryland in November 1963, the four-hundred-pound bronze casket that had carried his remains from Dallas to Washington had been so bloodied that it was unusable for any public viewing of the body and had been stored in the basement at the National Archives. Vernon B. O'Neal of O'Neal's Funeral Home in Dallas wanted it returned to him, largely because he had received offers to sell the casket for more than $100,000 (more than $1 million today). "When Daddy heard that the funeral home in Dallas wanted it back for macabre display, he asked [Nick] Katzenbach for a legal memo which determined the family ownership," wrote Kennedy, referring to his father's deputy attorney general in the Kennedy administration.

"I think it belongs to the family [and] we can get rid of it any way we want to," Robert Kennedy told Lawson Knott Jr., the director of the General Services Administration, according to one of the memos released by the National Archives of their telephone conversation in 1966. "What I would like to have done is take it to sea. I don't think anybody will be upset about the fact that we disposed of it."

Robert Kennedy sought the advice of the Department of Defense over the best way to drop the casket at sea. The heavy casket was filled with 240 pounds of sandbags and drilled with holes before it was dropped by a military airplane near the Outer Banks off the coast of North Carolina. In his diary, Kennedy made a note not to forget to mention the imminent declassification of the documents to his mother. The documents were made public a couple of weeks later.

"This has been a difficult year for our family and everyone is feeling so stressed and angry," wrote Kennedy on Thursday, July 15, the day he drove to Hyannis Port for Rory's wedding. He took along thirty cases of his new water, Keeper Springs, for taste testing during the wedding. Little did he know that within a matter of hours, the year was about to get even more difficult.

Among those feeling particularly stressed were John F. Kennedy Jr. and his wife of three years, Carolyn Bessette. Although John Jr.'s mother, Jackie Kennedy Onassis, had died in May 1994, he and his sister, Caroline, were still fighting about her estate, specifically the furniture at Red Gate Farm. John Jr. had purchased his sister's half of the Martha's Vineyard estate, which took up 340 acres and had more than a mile of beachfront. Jackie had left all her assets, including her New York City apartment and two homes in Martha's Vineyard, to her children. "John confided in me how hurt he was by Caroline's actions," wrote Kennedy in his diary. "It's like a divorce."

John Jr., who had been dubbed the "sexiest man alive" by *People* magazine in 1988, was also stung by criticisms leveled against him by his uncle Ted Kennedy, who hammered him for seating *Hustler* magazine publisher Larry Flynt at his table during the White House Correspondents' Dinner. "John was hurt by that because his family is important," wrote Kennedy. The staff of *George*, the glossy magazine he had founded with a partner in 1995, had reserved six tables, according to Kennedy. At the May dinner, Flynt had sat in his trademark gold wheelchair, wearing a green satin dinner jacket. John Jr. had invited the actors Sean Penn and Claire Danes to the dinner as his guests. "This event, and the culture of our magazine, is about melding extremes," said John Jr. at the event.

Caroline Kennedy's husband, Edwin Schlossberg, was horrified and wrote his brother-in-law "a long disappointed letter," wrote Kennedy, who noted that John Jr. was also dealing with the news that "his best friend" and cousin Anthony Radziwill was dying of cancer. In September 1996, Radziwill, the son of Jackie's sister, Caroline Lee Bouvier Radziwill, had been best man at John Jr.'s wedding on Cumberland Island in Georgia.

On top of the infighting with his closest family, John Jr. was having serious financial troubles at *George*, billed as a "fun" read about the intersection of politics and popular culture. The inaugural issue had been unveiled in the fall of 1995 with great fanfare at Manhattan's Federal Hall, where George Washington had taken his presidential oath of office. The first issue's cover had featured a photo of supermodel Cindy Crawford as a sexy powdered-wigged George Washington, with exposed midriff and pancake makeup. Another cover had featured Barbra Streisand as Betsy Ross. Unlike other startups, the magazine had seemed to do well with its first two issues and was later backed by David Pecker, then the CEO of Hachette Filipacchi Media. But by the time Pecker had left the company in 1998, *George* had been pretty much in free fall. The new Hachette CEO, Jack Kliger, had told John Jr. in June 1999 that the company was going to pull the plug on the magazine. A month before Rory's wedding, John Jr. had been prepared to put his own money behind the failing magazine and take the whole venture digital. "He has trouble refinancing and whenever he asks for money it gets in the press with predictions he's failing and advertisers all get jumpy," wrote Kennedy, noting that the circulation was 400,000—half that of *Newsweek*—and was widely circulated at every airport and newsstand in America. "But they still predict his demise."

Kennedy and Mary planned to seek out the young couple during the weekend festivities in Hyannis Port. "Mary and I resolved we will go see them this weekend and spend a lot of time with them," wrote Kennedy. Mary had visited them in Manhattan a week earlier and reported that Carolyn had told her that her husband was "so depressed."

The couple stopped by John Jr.'s house in Hyannis Port shortly before Rory's rehearsal dinner at 6:00 p.m. the following day, but the couple had not shown up yet. John Jr., Carolyn, and Carolyn's sister Lauren Bessette were scheduled to arrive on the small plane piloted by John Jr.

"We had the most wonderful rehearsal dinner," Kennedy wrote on July 16. "Everyone made loving toasts. Kerry recited a clever, clever poem." Family members sang an ode to Rory and her fiancé to the tune of "Angel from Montgomery." "Mark and Rory were so happy and I've never met two people who inspire so much love and good will. Everyone is crazy about them," he wrote.

After dinner, the couple returned to John Jr.'s home, but they still hadn't arrived. John Jr. was flying his Piper PA-32R-301 Saratoga II HP, a small plane he'd bought just three months before. Although he had been taking flying lessons since the early 1980s, he lacked experience flying at night, using only the plane's instruments to guide him. He had started training for his private pilot's license in 1997 and passed the exam in April 1998 but had logged only a handful of hours of nighttime flying. Nevertheless, he took off with his wife and her sister, Lauren, from Essex County Airport in Caldwell, New Jersey, at 8:38 p.m. for Martha's Vineyard Airport. There was little cloud cover that night, but a summer haze reduced visibility over Long Island Sound, according to reports. "Other pilots flying similar routes on the night of the accident reported no visual horizon while flying over the water because of haze," according to the National Transportation Safety Board.

Kennedy and his wife returned to John's house at 10:00 and 11:30 that night, Kennedy wrote. John Jr.'s friend Pinky and the housekeeper were at the house, and they were expecting to eat dinner when John and Carolyn arrived. "I wasn't worried at all because anything can happen with John," wrote Kennedy. But Pinky was worried enough to call Carole Radziwill, Anthony's wife, who called the Coast Guard. Kennedy had wanted to send someone over to John's apartment in Manhattan to check if he was still there.

But at 3:00 a.m., Kennedy was awakened by his sister Kerry, who said that their cousin's plane was missing. "I knew then that John was dead," he wrote. "I looked out the window of Carolyn's house from which I could see the lights on in John's front porch and I felt empty, sad." Then he wrote a half-remembered quote from *King Lear*: "We are to the Gods as flies to wanton boys," he wrote, mangling the line spoken by Gloucester. "They kill us for their sport."

In the morning, Ted Kennedy assembled his public relations team and announced to the Associated Press that Rory's wedding had been postponed. The large white tent that had been erected for the festivities had just been completed and the caterers were standing around in shock, Kennedy wrote. Hundreds of reporters began to pull up outside the gates of the compound, and satellite trucks began to set up for live broadcasts. Kennedy noted that the water was 68 degrees F., and some of the family members had hope that they might still be alive. "But I had none," he wrote.

That afternoon, emergency teams found the nose of John's plane near Gay Head. The priests who had been set to preside at Rory's wedding instead said a Mass for the plane's tragic passengers in the morning and again at 6:00 p.m. In the evening, the cousins gathered for dinner at Ethel's house to eat Rory's wedding dinner. Kennedy spent most of his time in a nearby carriage house watching the news, which "was all about John." He was also on the phone with Carole and Anthony Radziwill as well as John Jr.'s secretary, RoseMarie Terenzio, who was at the couple's home in Manhattan.

The NTSB later determined that the probable cause of the accident had been John Jr.'s inexperience flying at night: "The pilot's failure to maintain control of the airplane during a descent over water at night, which was a result of spatial disorientation. Factors in the accident were haze, and the dark night."

John Jr. had also fractured his left ankle during a paragliding accident on Memorial Day. He had undergone surgery, and the cast had been taken off just a day before he flew from New Jersey. The injury likely still caused pain and might have made it difficult for him to use the rudder pedals, which are foot-operated, on the plane.

The bickering over the bodies began the following day even though they hadn't yet been recovered. Carolyn's mother, Ann Freeman, was "very upset" about where the bodies would be buried. She wanted the trio to be buried in Greenwich, Connecticut, which Kennedy said would be an impossibility. "John Kennedy couldn't be buried in Greenwich because he had no connection and for all the other reasons," he wrote on July 18. Ann wanted her daughters close and "is terrified that they will try to spirit her [Carolyn] to Brookline or Martha's Vineyard . . . because both of them loved it there."

Kennedy helped arrange a meeting between the Bessette family and John's sister, Caroline, in New York the following day. Caroline didn't show up and instead sent her husband, Edwin Schlossberg, who hated John Jr.'s wife. Vicki Reggie, Ted Kennedy's second wife, was also at the meeting. According to Kennedy, Schlossberg "did everything in his power to make her life miserable" and then proceeded to bully the "shattered" grieving mother, who had just lost two of her three daughters.

The bodies were finally recovered on July 21, all of them still wearing their seat belts. "Coast Guard found John's body and fuselage at 2:30 a.m. and found the girls soon after," Kennedy wrote, adding that his uncle Ted and his sons Teddy Jr. and Patrick had taken a helicopter to be present at the recovery. "Teddy was shaken afterwards. The bodies were in bad shape, and the autopsy would find they'd been killed on impact," he wrote.

The bodies were cremated and the ashes placed in three Tiffany blue boxes for burial at sea. The next day, July 22, Kennedy and other family members, including his uncle Ted, Carole and Anthony Radziwill, Maria Shriver, and Caroline and Edwin Schlossberg, among others, met at Otis Air Force Base on Cape Cod. There they got into three vans, with a police escort, for the trip to Woods Hole, Massachusetts, where they boarded a navy cutter and rendezvoused with the destroyer USS *Briscoe* a mile off the coast. The ship took them out twenty miles off Gay Head, about a mile from the crash site.

A Kennedy family friend, the Roman Catholic priest Charles O'Byrne, who had married Carolyn and John Jr. just three years before in 1996, presided at the funeral at sea. Ann and her second husband, Richard Freeman, "climbed over the landing and scattered the girls' ashes one at a time," Kennedy wrote, adding that Caroline and Edwin had then spread John Jr.'s ashes over the sea.

"The water had more jellyfish in it than anyone had ever seen," he later wrote in his diary. "When they let go of the ashes, the plume erupted and settled in the water and passed by in the green current like a ghost. We tossed flowers onto the ghosts. Some of the girls tossed letters from a packet they'd assembled from John's and Carolyn's friends. It was a civil violation but the Coast Guard let it go." He added that a navy band had played "mournful music and we all cried like babies."

Kennedy and his cousin William Kennedy Smith took turns carrying Anthony Radziwill up the steps of the ship when the ceremony moved from the lower deck to the upper one.

The memorial services continued the next day, but not before protracted negotiations about who would do the eulogies for the dead. In a tense conference call, the families decided that Ted Kennedy would eulogize John Jr. and that Hamilton South, a good friend of Carolyn, would do her eulogy. When Lisa Bessette, Lauren's twin sister, suggested that Kennedy should eulogize the couple together since he had known them both very well, Schlossberg shot down the idea, even after Kennedy had accepted to do it. "Kennedys do not eulogize non-Kennedys," he said, according to Kennedy's diary.

Lisa, disgusted by Schlossberg's reaction, asked him if he made up his rules on the spot and slammed down the phone. Schlossberg's behavior also angered other members of the extended family with Carole Radziwill calling Kennedy to complain that he had flown into a tantrum because she hadn't said hello to him. "I know you've always hated me," he told her, according to Kennedy's diary. Carole suggested that the family start an "I hate Ed club." Kennedy agreed that there would be many members and that John Jr. and Carolyn would certainly have applied. Through it all, Kennedy resolved to be "a good soldier" and have only positive thoughts and make positive comments about Schlossberg.

It was a difficult undertaking, since Schlossberg had annoyed many of the Kennedys with his imperious behavior. Kennedy was still angry over Schlossberg's alleged pressure on the clan to sell patriarch Joe Kennedy's Merchandise Mart in Chicago in 1998. "Our family should never have sold it," he wrote in his diary. "But Ed Schlossberg forced the sale. He brought in a top real estate lawyer . . . to force the family to sell. He considers himself a financial genius."

Ted Kennedy delivered a "wrenching" eulogy for his nephew at the funeral at the small St. Thomas More Church on the Upper East Side, where "the streets were packed and the press were piled on each other like a wedding cake," Kennedy wrote. More than 350 people attended the private service for the couple, passing through strict security measures at the church. Sharpshooters were positioned in the tower of the church and on top of nearby buildings, likely due to the presence of President Clinton and his family, according to press reports. John Jr.'s hero Muhammad Ali was among the celebrity guests. The hip hop artist Wyclef Jean, a favorite of John Jr., sang Jimmy Cliff's "Many Rivers to Cross." A gospel choir sang "Amazing Grace."

"We dared to think, in that other Irish phrase, that this John Kennedy would live to comb gray hair, with his beloved Carolyn by his side," said Ted Kennedy, paraphrasing the William Butler Yeats poem "In Memory of Major Robert Gregory" in the eulogy, which was released to the public by his Senate office. "But like his father, he had every gift but length of years." John Jr. was thirty-eight when he died; Carolyn Bessette was thirty-three.

Ted also made sure to thank the Clintons for their presence and told of how, when they had once asked John Jr. what he would do if he were ever elected president, he had replied, "I guess the first thing is to call up Uncle Teddy and gloat." "I loved that," said Ted. "It was so like his father."

At the reception afterward, which took place at the Convent of the Sacred Heart two blocks away from the church, where Caroline had gone to school, the senator led a choir in three songs "and danced his silly Teddy dances and sang loudly and beautifully and made everyone . . . love him," Kennedy wrote. But when the choir sang a mournful song to conclude, the senator scolded them and said a livelier number was needed. They closed with "Happy Days," the anthem of John F. Kennedy's presidential campaign in 1960.

Kennedy did a brief reading for John Jr. at a service for Lauren Bessette in Greenwich, Connecticut, on July 24. Mary was an usher at the ceremony at Christ Episcopal Church. It was Melody Miller, a Kennedy family aide who had begun her career by answering the thousands of condolence letters that had poured in after the assassination of John Kennedy and had gone on to work for his brothers Robert and Ted, who gave Kennedy the idea for his short eulogy to John Jr. "Your cause of sorrow must not be measured by his worth, for then it hath no end" was from *Macbeth*, spoken by Ross to Old Siward in the play after he informs him that his son has just died in battle. Kennedy pronounced it perfect for John. "The service couldn't have been better and I think Mary and I were able to be of some comfort to both families, so I am grateful," he wrote.

On Sunday, Kennedy received more bad news after he found out that Judge Johnson had died in Alabama. He didn't hesitate; the next day he boarded a plane for Montgomery, showing up on time for a service in the judge's courtroom. "Judge Johnson, really through his courage and integrity, helped make this country a true constitutional democracy," he said after the service. "He is as much an American hero as the leaders of the Revolutionary War and the Civil War."

Kennedy might have been entitled and arrogant, but he rarely missed a funeral. "Bobby takes death very seriously," said a former friend who has known Kennedy for nearly twenty years. "He wasn't scoring any political points by showing up for my father's funeral."

Nor was he trying to score political points when he sent his Millbrook classmate Peter Jenny "a sweet note" in 1971 after he'd read that his father had died. Perhaps his thoughtfulness around death stemmed from his deep-seated conviction that he wanted to be a better person.

"I always wanted to be useful, to meet the expectation of the gifts I'd been given," he wrote in his diary on May 27, 1999, under a thickly underlined heading reading "Service." But he recognized that he was largely a failure because everything he did revolved around "vanity that proceeded from ego. I've seen people in my sobriety attend funerals and face crisis and make themselves the centerpiece—the crisis is about them and their suffering. They shout and create drama to call attention to themselves. They show up at the funeral and make a scene or don't show up at all to make their absence a controversy. I recognize similar kinds of behavior in myself. At the dinner table, my brother will tell a story and I will tell a better one to top his. I will want the attention of someone and I will show off."

He willed himself to "sit back and wait for God" to tell him to act, he wrote. "I must sit still and get in touch with God, praying for the ability to be useful. . . . I need to look for opportunities to quietly help rather than looking for opportunities to shine brightly." But sitting still would prove to be almost impossible for Robert Kennedy Jr., the crusading lawyer and environmental activist. Perhaps it was his unchecked ambition to "shine brightly" that would lead to one of the worst tragedies in his family.

CHAPTER 7

"Things Fall Apart"

Death continued to haunt the Kennedy family in the summer of 1999. Shortly after they had attended the funerals of John F. Kennedy Jr. and the Bessette sisters, family members found themselves on their way to another somber gathering after the death of Anthony Radziwill, who had died on August 10.

The funeral was in East Hampton, where his mother, Lee, owned Dune Cottage, an oceanfront mansion on three acres. Kennedy set out at 6:00 a.m. to drive there from Westchester County. Traffic in the posh summer enclave was heavier than usual as reporters surrounded the Most Holy Trinity Church on Buell Lane in the heart of the village, although it was nothing like the swarm that had turned out for the funeral of John F. Kennedy Jr. just a few weeks before in Manhattan, Kennedy observed. Many of Anthony's colleagues from ABC and HBO, where he had been an award-winning producer, were in attendance, noted Kennedy, who described the "sweet" eulogy that the journalist Diane Sawyer delivered, likening Anthony to a knight and echoing Sir Thomas Malory's tribute to the fictional Sir Lancelot in the fifteenth century.

James Rubin, then assistant secretary of state for public affairs and chief spokesman for Secretary of State Madeleine Albright, told

Mary that his wife, CNN international correspondent Christiane Amanpour, was not able to come because she had just landed in Kosovo and there was no way for her to get onto a commercial flight to make it on time for the funeral. "I couldn't think of a credible reason to fly her out on a government plane, and I was scared if I did, someone in the room would report it," he told Mary.

Caroline Kennedy gave the main eulogy, and, according to Kennedy, she had spent the previous day with Anthony's wife, Carole, at the Mark Hotel in Manhattan consulting with Ed Schlossberg and Charles O'Byrne, the priest and close friend of the Kennedy family, to plan the Mass. John Jr. was to have done the eulogy for his best friend and cousin and had started to put together notes before he died. Although Caroline was reluctant to take his place, she finally agreed, feeling that both John and Anthony would have wanted it, according to Kennedy. "Her eulogy was beautiful," he said. She opened by wondering how Anthony could possibly have won so many Emmys when he always seemed to be playing practical jokes on his friends. She recalled that he had called her days before her own wedding, pretending to be a gardener, florist, and caterer with "frightening news and developments." But the best joke, she said, had been his calling her in the guise of the German publisher of the world's largest bodybuilding magazine to ask if her husband would pose on the cover with her cousin by marriage Arnold Schwarzenegger, who had already agreed.

Following the service and a reception at Lee Radziwill's sprawling waterfront home, Anthony's body was flown by helicopter to Islip, where he was cremated. Kennedy and his wife headed to his aunt Patricia Kennedy Lawford's estate in Southampton, where he spent the afternoon in the pool. The ashes were returned to the family the same day, and family members reconvened at the Radziwill beach house to sprinkle the ashes into the Atlantic Ocean. "Lee and Carole were pummeled by the waves," wrote Kennedy, as they waded out into the ocean accompanied by a somber procession that included Sawyer's husband, the film director Mike Nichols, as well as Ed and Caroline, among other close family members.

Again braving summer traffic, Kennedy and Mary drove back to Westchester County and had a "great" Japanese dinner along the way. But their time together was marred by a call from Emily Black asking Kennedy about their two children. Mary fell into a rage when they got home and demanded that Kennedy leave the house with his older children. The next day, he bundled up Kick and Bobby, but she warned that he would not be allowed to take the other children—"Her kids"—and headed to Hyannis Port. "I'm really in despair," he wrote on Saturday, August 14, as he drove with his children to the cape. "She says the cruelest things. She says I only wanted kids to show off and wasn't willing to take care of them and that this is what Emily used to say."

But his escape to the cape, the scene of so many happy summers, was a bad idea. He arrived at midnight in "a dreary rain." After putting his children to bed, he walked to the end of the dock and noticed that the lights were on in John Jr.'s home. As he walked closer to the house, called Brambletyde, the summer home of President Kennedy and his family, Kennedy half expected to see John Jr.'s friends preparing for one of their famous midnight dinners. But no one was home. When he looked through the porch window, he spotted the harpoon that he and John Jr. had used when they had dressed up as ghosts to scare the Kennedy children. "I thought, 'This is all that's left here—the ghosts,'" he wrote, noting that he had attended four funerals that summer. "And I walked home in the downpour. It was one of the saddest moments of my life."

After a difficult summer, Kennedy headed into a busy and eventful fall, with his classes at Pace University's Environmental Litigation Clinic and a consulting gig with Vice President Al Gore, who was putting together his campaign for the top job. He also met with Hillary Clinton, who arrived at his home surrounded by Secret Service agents, to get a briefing—"A quick seminar"—on New York's watershed agreement, which Kennedy and Cronin had been only marginally a part of during their time together working against Hudson River polluters. In between, he recorded "walking on eggshells" as Mary began a new course of antidepressants that hadn't yet kicked in.

Things were definitely weighing on him. At the end of a day of hawking with his son Conor and a few friends, he confessed to his diary that the deaths in his family and his difficulties with Mary were bringing him down. On September 19, his friend and former Harvard classmate Peter Kaplan came by his home in Bedford and told him he was mired in a midlife crisis. Kaplan was dating one of the editors at the *New York Observer* and enmeshed in a divorce from his first wife, Audrey Walker, the mother of his three children. Both men had turned forty-five that year, and although outwardly they seemed to be at the top of their game, they both confessed to feeling trapped by their insecurities. Kaplan, who had worked as a reporter for *The New York Times* and producer on *Charlie Rose*, was now in his fifth year as the editor of the influential weekly, whose salmon-colored pages had become required reading for anyone interested in New York's power elite.

"He wonders, as do I, if he's added value, if he's used his life and his gifts to maximize his service to others," wrote Kennedy about his friend, adding that he had told him that the greatest measure of his life and service was how he treated those closest to him. But even as the words had come out of his mouth, he had wondered if he had followed his own counsel. "I've lost the sense of certitude since the early days of my sobriety when I had all the answers and saw God in everything." Back then, when he had gotten serious about dealing with his addiction in 1984, even the death of his younger brother David had made some sense because "it brought my family together." It had also led him into Alcoholics Anonymous and his work with Riverkeeper.

In the same way, his "painful divorce" from Emily had led to his love for Mary, he wrote. "But now I feel shattered, like nothing has meaning and nothing makes sense, and 'things fall apart.' The title to that book rings daily in my ears as I think of a relationship I've lost." The book in question was Chinua Achebe's *Things Fall Apart*, the Nigerian writer's 1958 novel about colonialism in his native country. Achebe had taken his title from William Butler Yeats's poem "The Second Coming," which would have particularly appealed to Kennedy as it describes a world in which "The falcon cannot hear the falconer;/ Things fall apart; the centre cannot hold."

For Kennedy, it may have indeed seemed as though his life was spiraling out of control and that much of it was his own fault. "My defects are like weeds," he wrote. "You cut them and they stay down a while. Then they come back. You pour pesticides on them and they come back. You pull them by the roots, they come back. They pop up through the cracks."

He had broken with close friends and some family members. His old partner John Cronin was now persona non grata. During a Pace University class on a boat in the Hudson, Cronin "was unrecognizable," Kennedy wrote. "He has gained 35 pounds and cut his hair short. . . . He has had some spiritual awakening." Kennedy went on to say that Cronin had confided in Mary Beth Postman, his "chief of staff," at Pace University, that he was sad that their relationship had ended. "MB tells me that he mourns the end of our relationship and laments that though we will never be the same recalls how happy we all once were when I was first dating Mary," he wrote. "He blames everything on the fact I changed. He believes me to be dishonest and manipulative."

In addition to Cronin and his old mentor Bob Boyle, Kennedy enumerated his failing relationship with Mary and the frustration that none of his political ambitions was leading anywhere. He suspected that Mary was trying to make him look like "an insensitive lout" and wrote that it was clear that "she's trying to establish a record in case we get divorced. When I call her on it, she confesses and begs forgiveness. But the moment I forgive, she starts again."

Although Mary was trying to deal with what Kennedy referred to as her "anger and control" issues, he felt that he was losing patience with her. "I'm discovering the well of resentments I am holding against her," he wrote. "All the love I felt and how she destroyed and abused it pitilessly for five years. I'm desperate to let it go and start again but I still don't trust her. I'm scared she will erupt any day and start it all again. But we are praying every morning."

Still, life went on. Two days after his musings about the value of his life with Kaplan, he was sitting in a private dining room at the Hay-Adams hotel in Washington, DC, across from President Clinton and Gore at a small dinner party to plan strategy for Gore's presidential campaign. Nearly a year after his impeachment by the House of Representatives over his affair with former White House intern Monica Lewinsky, Clinton, dressed in a blue suit, blue shirt, and bright yellow tie, looked great, Kennedy wrote. "He looked like a playboy. He was tan and fit and spoke well and laughed a lot and was very charming."

Clinton spoke about his visit to China the previous year, months before the impeachment vote in December 1998. He laughed as he recalled a cartoon in an English-language newspaper depicting him talking to the Chinese about political freedoms in the United States. The cartoon noted that under the Chinese system, Kenneth Starr, the independent counsel who had authored the report that had served as the basis of Clinton's impeachment, would have been shut down. "Ken Starr would be in jail making running shoes," said Clinton, laughing as he told the joke. "It made me rethink the Chinese system."

Kennedy was at the dinner with about fifteen other guests to introduce Gore to David Foster, a Canadian musician and millionaire record producer who had agreed to host a major fundraiser at his estate in Malibu for environmental philanthropists and Hollywood celebrities for Gore.

At the fundraiser two months later, Gore pledged that as president he would spend $2 billion over the next decade to preserve open spaces across the country: $1 billion in tax cuts to landowners who agreed to transfer private land for conservation and the rest to local governments to set up parks. He told the crowd of about two hundred guests, including celebrities and environmental activists who had paid $1,000 each to attend the Sunday-morning event, that he would finance the programs by amending a hundred-year-old mining law that allowed companies to extract minerals from federal land without paying royalties. "We will turn minerals we already own into new parklands and protection of open spaces and smart growth initiatives to make our communities more livable," he said, standing outdoors, framed by the towering Santa Monica Mountains in the background. California Governor Gray Davis, who was at the event, said that Gore "would be the most environmentally friendly president ever to sit at 1600 Pennsylvania Avenue."

At the September dinner, Clinton and Gore told Kennedy that Gore already had 20 percent of Democratic delegates behind him and that he was polling ahead in the key state of New Hampshire. At the time, Gore was considering Kennedy to be the chair of the White House Council on Environmental Quality. Kennedy's endorsement was important, especially in New York State, which was seen as a stronghold of New Jersey Senator Bill Bradley, his main challenger in the Democratic presidential primary. In an ad released during the campaign, Kennedy endorsed Gore on the banks of the Hudson River. "There is no American political leader in our history with a greater understanding or commitment to environmental protection than Al Gore," he said. ". . . If you care about your children's future, if you care about the future of America, there is no more important choice that you can make this year than to support Al Gore for president."

A few days after his trip to Washington, Kennedy organized a party for Mary's fortieth birthday. The occasion was a happy one, and he later reported having had a good day. "She doesn't seem angry or tense for the first time in years," he wrote. Mary had reminded him that she had been sober for five years and continued to studiously attend Alcoholics Anonymous meetings. "Mary reminded me of my early years in the program when I had been hyper paranoid. I wouldn't go out at night or ever go into NYC or cross the street against a light etc." She had also asked for his patience in dealing with her rehabilitation. "It helped me to hear that there is some self-awareness there and that maybe this is just part of a process that will improve some day," he wrote.

Kennedy rounded out 1999 with an Antarctic cruise, where guests joined the *Ocean Explorer* in Ushuaia on the southern tip of Argentina on December 28. In addition to whale and penguin watching, the cruise featured a performance by the jazz singer Diana Krall and myriad Hollywood film screenings. Kennedy was a guest speaker along with the author Simon Winchester. On December 30, while the cruise headed through the Drake Passage, he was scheduled to give an hour-long lecture entitled "Our Environmental Destiny." It would turn out to be a prophetic title for the new year as Kennedy set up to blow up Riverkeeper and forge his own path.

In the early part of 2000, Kennedy continued to crisscross the country, giving speeches on the environment. By February, he had fifty paying speeches lined up for the year, which he hoped would help him get out of debt. "I've got a wonderful life," he wrote on February 10. "I travel [and] meet great people, I'm highly regarded and am doing some good although I will not leave my kids much money. I'm leaving them good reputations and (I hope) values and a good education. I love them all and they give me such joy."

Indeed, sprinkled throughout his diaries are notes from a proud father, recording how great his children are. "Kyra is so sociable and fun, and everyone loves her," he gushed about his daughter in the summer of 1999, when she was four years old. "She is so delightful and loves the adventure of meeting new people and latching onto them for fun. Teddy fell in love with her and entertains her all day," he said, referring to the senator from Massachusetts.

When he had put his older children Bobby and Kick into a limo to Boston at the end of their time together in Hyannis Port, he noted, they had hugged him close, especially his eldest. "He said 'see you Friday,' and 'I love you' and he cried," wrote Kennedy about Bobby, who was then just shy of his fifteenth birthday. Kick was eleven.

Conor, his eldest with Mary, was a terrific skier, and Finn, who suffered from a host of maladies, such as asthma and food allergies, would surely come out of everything all right, he felt. "Mary is very upset, but I tend to look at the bright side," he wrote. "These children are so incredible in so many ways. They are tough, funny, resilient, athletic." And perhaps taking inspiration from his own mother, he noted, "The asthma is part of the bump in the road which will make them tougher and bring us all closer together."

He often confessed that his greatest regret was that he was so busy with so many speeches that he was not always home to eat dinner with his kids and put them to bed at night. And he seemed to be getting closer to Mary. At the beginning of 2000, at least, Mary "had acted like she loves me."

In between campaign stops on behalf of Al Gore, Kennedy was consumed with the politics of Riverkeeper. Cronin had resigned in February as the group's executive director, and momentum was building toward a showdown between Bob Boyle and his most famous protégé. Everything came to a head during what he called an "armageddon board meeting" on June 20. Kennedy was so sure he had the board votes needed to unseat Boyle as president that he prepared to go to battle.

The conflict between the two men had been building for a long time but flared up when Kennedy insisted upon hiring William Wegner, who had gone to federal prison for smuggling rare birds from

Australia into the United States, which many board members, including Boyle, considered an environmental crime. "Riverkeeper has always had clean hands when it went into court," said Boyle, under whose leadership the organization had expanded with chapters across the country under the umbrella of the Waterkeeper Alliance. "It calls into question very strongly the reputation of the organization." He demanded that Kennedy fire Wegner immediately. "You don't hire a child molester to run a nursery school," he quipped, adding that he would resign if Wegner were brought on as a staff scientist. He also wrote letters to the board of directors. "Can you imagine what Mayor Rudolph Giuliani, a former hardball United States attorney who has taken some hard knocks from Bobby over the watershed, would do if he discovered that Wegner was working for us?" he asked. "It boggles the mind."

Wegner had been released from prison in August 1999 after serving three and a half years of a five-year sentence for tax fraud, perjury, and conspiracy to violate wildlife protection laws. According to prosecutors, he was the kingpin of a group of at least ten smugglers who had taken cockatoo eggs out of Australia. The group had incubated the eggs using Styrofoam and hair dryers, although if the eggs hatched en route to the United States, the smugglers had instructions to flush the chicks down the airplane toilet, according to reports. Once in the United States, the eggs were hatched and the birds were sold for between $1,500 and $12,000 "under the guise that they had been produced by captive parent birds," according to a 1995 Department of Justice press release.

Kennedy refused to fire Wegner, arguing that he was a good scientist who had had a great deal of experience working for environmental consulting firms in the Hudson Valley before his illegal activities in Australia—a contention that was disputed by prosecutors, who said that they could find no evidence of Wegner's previous environmental work before his foray into bird smuggling. Kennedy also saw in Wegner a kindred spirit, a master falconer who brought his

Barbary falcon to work with him, according to his diary. Kennedy felt that Wegner deserved the same chance at rehabilitation that he had once enjoyed when he had entered the environmental movement following his heroin bust.

Moreover, Wegner could be hired cheaply because he was hard-pressed to find a job elsewhere after his time in prison, said Kennedy. On top of that, he said, cockatoos were not an endangered species in Australia, where they were considered pests. That wasn't entirely true, prosecutors argued. "These arguments are either untrue or irrelevant," they said. "Of the seven species at issue, several are genuinely rare and probably endangered in Australia."

Boyle and his closest allies on the board wanted nothing to do with Wegner, and the confrontation landed the entire board of directors in a lawyer's office for the "armageddon board meeting."

"The meeting was at the lawyer's office, and it was at that point that we were really trying to work with the board to come up with a resolution that wouldn't result in people leaving the board," said a former Riverkeeper board member who resigned over the Wegner situation. "Bob [Boyle] was a very strong-willed guy, and the idea of hiring this guy wasn't sensible. A lot of people agreed with him." Kennedy was also strong-willed, the former board member said. "I think basically that Bobby is a very intelligent guy, but once he got an idea in his head, there was something about being a Kennedy that he got stuck on his point of view and screw anyone who thought differently. He had this kind of sense of entitlement. It was a real problem."

In his diary, Kennedy devoted nearly four pages to the board meeting, giving a blow-by-blow description of the vote. "Finally the question was called and the first eight votes were 'no' votes (I was preparing my resignation speech)," he wrote. "Then we got ten 'yes' votes." Three more votes came over the phone, and Kennedy's side won. Boyle and his six supporters walked out, and board member Karen Klopp was elected chair—"I didn't want it," Kennedy wrote—while Kennedy was made vice chair. Then the whole crew went out to dinner to celebrate. "I felt very good, like two years of struggle was over and that the board will be purged of some very negative forces."

The next day, June 21, Kennedy reported that Boyle had gone to the press "with angry venom." A reporter from the Gannett newspaper chain called him to read him a quote from Boyle, who had said that Kennedy was "consumed" by ambition. Kennedy wrote that he had taken the "high road" but not before he had given the reporter a quote of his own. "Part of Bob's charm has always been that he's an ornery curmudgeon and he's become increasingly charming with age," he said, adding that he had never wanted to take over Riverkeeper, an accusation unfairly leveled at him by Boyle and his followers.

According to Boyle's son, Alex, Kennedy had been tolerated by the old guard at Riverkeeper largely because his last name had brought in donations and attracted celebrities and moneyed philanthropists, such as Lorraine Bracco, Alec Baldwin, and Anne Hearst, to the board of directors. But once he had begun pushing his bottled water initiative, he had begun to clash with Boyle, who was vehemently against monetizing Riverkeeper's activities on the Hudson. Ousting Kennedy could have resulted in the loss of nearly one third of the group's annual $1.5 million budget, according to a former treasurer for the group. "What we've succeeded in doing now is putting together a strong enough leadership in the organization that it will flourish with or without my presence," said Kennedy in an interview with *The New York Times*, adding that he would not rule out accepting a post in a Gore administration if Gore were elected president that year.

Riverkeeper's staff settled down to work after Kennedy's victory in the power struggle. In his diary after the vote, Kennedy reported that he had acquired a cormorant and nine starlings as well as two crows to add to Wegner's falcon at the nonprofit's office in Garrison, which one staff member likened to a scene from an Alfred Hitchcock movie.

Days after the highly publicized Riverkeeper battle, Kennedy waded into another controversy when he decided to accompany his cousin Michael Skakel on his "perp walk" to court in Connecticut to face charges in the murder of his former Greenwich, Connecticut, neighbor Martha Moxley in 1975. In the unusual case, he had been charged as a juvenile in January 2000 and surrendered to police. He had been released on $500,000 bail and arraigned in March in a juvenile court, since he had been fifteen years old at the time of Moxley's murder. He was thirty-nine years old when he was charged with the crime. "Tomorrow I'm going to do the perp walk with Michael Skakel," wrote Kennedy on June 27. "I think it will hurt me with Gore, with funders, with the public. But it's the right thing to do so I'm going to do it. The best thing about it is that it probably won't even be appreciated by M.S. who will just devise a paranoid conspiracy theory to explain it. That means it's a pure act of altruism!"

His younger brother Douglas had come to the same conclusion and was just as determined to attend even though he told his brother that other Kennedy family members would be "pissed off." He also asked his brother what he thought the trial would be like. Kennedy responded with one word written in capital letters: "PAIN!" Still, he urged his brother not to back out because he felt that Skakel was innocent of the crime.

Michael Skakel is the son of Ethel's brother Rushton Skakel and his wife, Anne Reynolds Skakel, who died of cancer in 1973, when Michael was thirteen years old. He grew up in typical boisterous and entitled Skakel fashion in Belle Haven, a wealthy Greenwich enclave, with his six siblings, who were largely left to their own devices after Anne's death. On October 30, 1975, Moxley, a pretty blond high school student who, like Skakel, was fifteen years old, failed to return home after spending the night hanging out with friends, including Skakel's older brother Tommy, who was seventeen at the time. She had last been seen "falling together" with Tommy behind the fence near the pool in the Skakels' backyard. Her body was later found bludgeoned and stabbed in the woods near their home. A broken golf club that was later linked to the Skakel family was found nearby. At the time, Tommy Skakel was considered a potential suspect, although he managed to pass a lie detector test.

The case lay dormant for decades until June 1998, when Mark Fuhrman, a former Los Angeles police detective known for his work on the O. J. Simpson case, published a book naming Michael Skakel as the likely killer. Eighteen months later, in January 2000, the state of Connecticut appointed a rare one-man grand jury. Kenneth Littleton, a former live-in tutor of the Skakel children, testified in exchange for immunity from prosecution. Other witnesses had also testified that during his time at the Élan School in Poland, Maine, for children with mental health and substance abuse problems in the late 1970s, Skakel had blurted out during a group therapy session that he had killed Moxley. The school's owner, Joseph Ricci, denied that such a confession had ever taken place.

But a boyhood friend of Skakel's later testified that on the night that Moxley had been killed, Skakel had admitted that he had been in a tree directly above where her body was found the next morning. Andrew Pugh said that his friend had had "an infatuation" with Moxley and believed that he had killed her. In 1991, when Pugh had confronted Skakel about his suspicions in a telephone conversation, Skakel admitted that he had been in the Moxleys' yard on the night of her death, masturbating in the tree. The story corresponded to one that Skakel had told private investigators hired by his father in the mid-1990s. Rushton had hired a team of investigators to look into the Moxley case in an effort to clear the family name. The results, which became known as the Sutton Report, backfired when investigators named Tommy, Littleton, and Michael as potential suspects. In Michael Skakel's case, the report found that he had initially lied to police when he had told them that he had returned home with his two brothers and a cousin at about 11:15 p.m. on the night of the murder. He had told the private investigators that he had sneaked out of his bedroom window around that same time and walked across the way to the Moxley house, where he had climbed the tree to throw pebbles at Moxley's window. When she hadn't responded, he had masturbated, he said.

The testimony of witnesses twenty-five years after the murder proved crucial to prosecutors' "reasonable cause" hearing to convince a juvenile court judge to transfer the proceedings to Connecticut Superior Court, thus enabling Skakel to be tried as an adult.

Despite the evidence against his cousin, Kennedy became obsessed with his defense and was determined to do everything he could to prove he was innocent even after Skakel was convicted of the murder in 2002 and sentenced to twenty years in prison.

In addition to fighting for his cousin's innocence, Kennedy's summer was largely taken up with attending campaign events for Gore and his older sister Kathleen Kennedy Townsend, who was running for reelection as lieutenant governor of Maryland. One of the fundraisers was held at the Kennedy compound at Hyannis Port in August with President Clinton as the keynote speaker. The event, held under a tent on Ted Kennedy's lawn, raised $700,000 from four hundred top Democratic Party donors, Kennedy wrote. Clinton was accompanied by two of his former ambassadors as well as Democratic National Committee Chair Terry McAuliffe and former New Jersey Governor Brendan Byrne. He also took along his friend and former Georgetown University roommate Tom Caplan, who had traveled with him on his first visit to the cape when they had been at university. "I nearly drowned, actually, swimming off the waters here," he joked in his speech.

It was Clinton's first visit to the fabled compound, and the family swarmed around him, taking him on a tour of the houses and showing him family photographs, with Eunice Kennedy Shriver pointing out all the photos of herself and Ted Kennedy chiding her for taking up Clinton's time. "The President has a schedule," he told her.

"Clinton was breathtaking as usual," wrote Kennedy in his diary. "He is the best speaker I've seen. He is smart and sincere and so thoughtful and brilliant. He touched everyone in the room. He had me in tears."

Clinton opened his speech with remarks about the Kennedy matriarch, Ethel, jokingly letting her know that he might want to stay with her. "Now, let me say—Ethel, you may have to put me up tonight—and if so, that would tickle me, because Ethel's been sending me these raunchy Valentine cards for years," he joked. "And I'm completely in love with her, and I keep trying to get some tabloid to write something sleazy about it, and I haven't been able to so far."

Clinton went on to say that he had been doing so much campaigning for the Kennedys, from Patrick Kennedy's congressional reelection campaign in Rhode Island to Ted's Senate campaign and Kathleen's run in Maryland, that he had neglected his own wife's campaign for the Senate. "'But it's your wife that's running for Senator from New York in 90 days, where it costs $30 million–plus to run,'" said Clinton, imitating Hillary. "'Maybe they'll just put you up tonight.'"

Clinton also thanked Ted Kennedy—"An inspiration . . . not only to me but to people in the Congress, just reminding them that nobody's got a right to be in the majority; nobody's got a right to be in office. . . . But we do if we have the office, a responsibility—we have a responsibility to get up every day and make something good happen." He then went on to say that Ted was among the ten greatest senators that the United States had ever produced before going on to praise his vice president's platform on gun safety, global warming, and the economy. He ended on a warning: "Do not blow this election." Maybe he had a premonition that all would not be well, especially since Gore refused to allow him and Hillary to campaign on his behalf. Whatever lay behind Clinton's threat, his warning proved prescient.

That was the message that Democrats seemed to take to the

Democratic National Convention in Los Angeles later that month. Kennedy traveled to the city with his eldest son, Bobby, and Conor, who had just turned six years old. They stayed as guests of Julia Louis-Dreyfus and her husband, Brad Hall, at their home in Pacific Palisades. Kennedy and Conor slept together in one bed while Bobby slept on a futon on the floor in Louis-Dreyfus's home office. The couple's young son, Henry, came in to breakfast the next morning announcing that a strange man was asleep in the office and kept saying "Go away!" Kennedy captured the funny moment in his diary on August 15.

Before the convention, Kennedy did an early-morning television special and emceed a panel of environmentalists. Later, he picked up Bobby and Conor and headed to the convention, where he reported having been "mobbed everywhere," with delegates taking photos and asking for his autograph. In addition to Kennedy, three other members of his family were scheduled to address the delegates: Kathleen Kennedy Townsend, Ted Kennedy, and Caroline Kennedy. "I got my three minutes and I made the most of it," he wrote, adding that he had been interviewed by all the big television networks. The next day, he noted that Caroline "did not speak brilliantly," although she still managed to give an inspiring speech.

After the first day of the convention, Kennedy, Louis-Dreyfus, and Peter Kaplan, who was also in Los Angeles for the event, went to a celebrity party for more than five hundred people at the home of Arnold Schwarzenegger and Maria Shriver.

At the party, where Ted Kennedy forced Secretary of Energy Bill Richardson to sing, they introduced themselves to *New York Times* political columnist Maureen Dowd. "She's written terrible stuff about us, including Julia," wrote Kennedy. "We shook hands and she said in a catty way, 'What did you say your name was?'" Later, he saw his cousin Maria Shriver telling Dowd what a brilliant writer she was "and wondered if they read the vicious stuff she's written about our family. It was fun getting a look at her."

Although he reported having had fun at the party and doing "tons of laughing," he did get stuck with the family of Gore's vice presidential candidate, Connecticut Senator Joe Lieberman. "We got trapped for a while by Joe Lieberman's family who surrounded us in a horseshoe formation uphill so we couldn't escape. They were very sweet but not too many laughs."

The next night, Kennedy went to another celebrity fundraiser featuring the actor Michael Douglas and his wife, Catherine Zeta-Jones. He ended his time in Los Angeles with a trip with Bobby and Conor to Will Rogers Beach in Pacific Palisades, where they went body surfing before catching a plane back to New York.

Gore secured the Democratic nomination and prepared to square off against Republican Texas governor George W. Bush and his running mate, former Defense Secretary Dick Cheney, in the presidential election.

Back home, Kennedy continued with his busy schedule, delivering speeches at environmental fundraisers in the Hamptons and trying to raise money for various Riverkeeper projects. During an event in Southampton that he attended with the socialite Anne Hearst, he sat next to Richard Hilton and his "wild daughters," Nicky and Paris. He also started back at school teaching, although he confessed to "struggling to keep my thoughts pure and my words and deeds . . . moral." There is no indication in the diaries that he was involved with any of his students. "Every day for me is a struggle with surrender," especially as one of his new hires at Riverkeeper became "flirtatious" with him in the office.

In the ledger at the back of his diary, he recorded "victory" on eight consecutive days at the beginning of the month—a trend that ended on August 9 when he entered a woman's name followed by the number 3, which meant that he hadn't gone all the way, according to Mary Kennedy's reckoning of what the numbers meant. On August 21, however, the ledger featured another woman with a "10" next to her name, followed by nine days of "victories." The same woman's name was repeated on September 22, with another "10" next to her name.

Following the fundraiser, he drove back to the cape with Conor in tow and the next morning attended an AA meeting, where he ran into some childhood friends, who told him that Candy Kelley had died, likely of a drug overdose. Candy had been a regular at the Centerville AA meetings. Kennedy made a point of attending her funeral. He had dated her sister Kim when he was a teenager. The other Kelley sister, Pam, had been David Kennedy's former girlfriend. She never recovered from the 1973 jeep accident with Joe Kennedy. "Every time I've walked into an AA meeting on the Cape, I've scanned the crowd for her face, hoping to see her," he wrote of Candy, the woman he had once considered to be like a sister to him. "She was so adorable with beautiful skin and frizzy blond hair as thick as a horse's tail. I also haven't seen Kim, probably since 1976 after she bumped her head and had to have brain surgery and woke up afterward not knowing who I was, even though we were sweethearts for seven years, since I was 14." Kim's husband had died in an accident, run over with his own truck, he wrote.

Kennedy said that he still prayed for the family every day and had been overwhelmed by the service, where he had sat in the back and wept. "This was a lot of sadness for me," he wrote on August 30.

That fall continued with more endorsements for Hillary Clinton and Al Gore. Kennedy flew to West Virginia in September to speak at Bethany College and meet with its president, Duane Cummins, who cried as he spoke about how much Kennedy's father had meant to him. He flew to Kansas City for a meeting with the city's top trial lawyers as he prepared to join them in a lawsuit against hog factories. There were more trips to Bakersfield and San Juan, where he argued an environmental case before flying to Omaha for a speech on biodiversity and then was off to Ottawa.

The Kennedys endured another near tragedy in October when Eunice Kennedy Shriver, Kennedy's seventy-nine-year-old aunt, was readmitted to Johns Hopkins Hospital after she developed a postoperative infection following the removal of a benign pancreatic tumor. Kennedy claimed that the doctor who had performed the operation had gone to a conference and could not be reached when Eunice's condition grew worse. The unnamed doctor had left Eunice in the care of interns, who had failed to read her test results properly, according to Kennedy. When a doctor had finally showed up, "she was dying in front of us," wrote Kennedy, adding that they had put a catheter through her neck too fast and ruptured her lung, causing it to collapse. Teddy Kennedy arrived at the hospital and said that it was the worst day of his life, with Bobby Shriver, one of Eunice's sons, "screaming" at the doctor when he finally returned from his conference. According to Kennedy, the intern thanked Bobby for screaming at the doctor, saying he needed to be "taken down a notch."

Press reports at the time noted that Eunice was in critical condition but there was never any mention of the Kennedy family's desperation and fury at Johns Hopkins for Eunice's treatment. In his diary, Kennedy described his elderly aunt crying and in agony as her left lung filled with bacteria-filled fluid. At one point, her husband, Sargent Shriver, a few days shy of his eighty-fifth birthday, was in tears and asked the family assembled in Eunice's hospital room to say the rosary at her bedside. "I noticed the patch in the back of his suit pants and it made me so sad," wrote Kennedy. "I remembered what he said about practicing charity in marriage and poverty when you're wealthy. I thought of Sarge when we were all young. How he talked about getting back from World War II. He was a waterski instructor in Hawaii and then had come to New York and couldn't hail a cab because he was so dark they mistook him for a black man." Sargent Shriver had spent five years on active duty in the navy during the Second World War, even though he had been opposed to the United States' entering the conflict. He had been awarded a Purple Heart for injuries sustained during the bombing of Guadalcanal. After meeting Eunice at a party in New York City, he had been hired by Joseph Kennedy to manage the Merchandise Mart in Chicago.

"If they treat the Shrivers like this, pity the poor wretch who wanders in off the street," wrote Kennedy in his journal. Eunice, a philanthropist, had founded the Special Olympics in 1968, whereas her husband was the founder and first director of the Peace Corps. He had also been a vice presidential candidate in 1972 and run in the Democratic presidential primary in 1976.

Eunice survived her ordeal at Johns Hopkins and would live another nine years. While Eunice was in the hospital, Ethel Kennedy's car broke down, and she was forced to hitchhike from Baltimore, where she had gone to visit her sister-in-law in the hospital, to Hickory Hill. She was picked up by a Mormon, who tried to convince her to join the Church of Jesus Christ of Latter-day Saints. Kennedy ended up driving her to Washington, DC, the next day, impressed that his mother knew "every trick and every short-cut and which lane was the fastest."

Following Eunice's ordeal, Kennedy was off to Japan for a speaking tour with his chief of staff at Pace, Mary Beth Postman, and his young daughter Kyra. He was away for the presidential election on November 7, although he was sure that Gore would win despite Clinton's ominous warning in Hyannis Port. The election turned out to be one of the closest and most controversial in US history. On election night, networks initially called the key swing state of Florida for Al Gore but then called the election for Bush. At one point Gore called Bush to concede defeat, only to call him again to retract the concession.

It would be more than a month before the vote was decided following a controversial Supreme Court ruling that ended the recount with Bush winning Florida by 537 votes. During the legal challenge, Kennedy described Gore as "star-crossed" and compared him to Odysseus. "The Gods and Fates were plotting his destiny," he wrote. "[Green Party presidential candidate] Ralph Nader, butterfly ballots, state police stopped Blacks from voting and Tom DeLay's Brownshirts bullied the election commission into halting the count in Miami-Dade," he wrote. At the time, Democrats blamed Nader, a third-party candidate, for splitting the vote for Gore. Republican Texas Congressman DeLay, the majority whip in the House of Representatives, sent out a memo to congressional Republicans telling them they had the right to challenge Electoral College votes in any state where the presidential election was in dispute.

Kennedy also directed his fury at the press, accusing them of giving Bush a free ride—"This shallow, lazy, one-dimensional man. They ignored his gaffes and lies and pounced on every tiny error by Gore as if it were murder. It was like some bizarre conspiracy." He was disappointed that his friend Peter Kaplan and journalists such as Tom Brokaw and *New York Times* editorial page editor Howell Raines, who had been sharply critical of the Clinton administration and had savaged Kennedy's first book, were focusing on Gore's "personality deficit as if it's anything that matters."

The Gore recount was still on his mind as he flew to Vail with all of his children at the invitation of the billionaire Adam Aron, the CEO of Vail Resorts. Kennedy had sat beside him at the premiere of *102 Dalmatians* a few days earlier, and the entrepreneur had offered to foot the bill for his family to spend Thanksgiving skiing in Vail—"Best snow in 15 years." Each family member received the services of a ski instructor, free of charge, noted Kennedy, as well as luxury accommodations and meals. The highlight of the trip was that Finn, all of three years old, was developing into a fine skier without the use of a beginner's harness. "Finn is a very strong boy with great balance," noted his proud father. "People marvel when they see him ride his scooter and last week I got him to stand on a skateboard for a ride down the driveway."

Soon he was back in Los Angeles for a National Resources Defense Council speech and socializing with his new set of Hollywood celebrity friends that revolved around the crew of Larry David's *Curb*

Your Enthusiasm. He had lunch with Laurie David, "who I love for her energy and commitment and humor." Aaron Sorkin, a producer and screenwriter and the creator of the popular television series *The West Wing*, was also at the lunch and gushed about the recent birth of his daughter, Roxy. Later, after his speech, Kennedy hobnobbed with Billy Crystal and his wife before heading to House of Blues with Fran Drescher and her boyfriend to meet up with Dan Aykroyd and the comedian Jon Lovitz to hear the blues great Keb' Mo'.

But it was within the *Curb Your Enthusiasm* fold that he seemed most at home, largely because both Laurie David and Julia Louis-Dreyfus were committed to helping save the planet. Another actress, the blond screen wife of Larry David in the series, began to emerge as a celebrity in her own right when *Curb Your Enthusiasm* turned into a series in the fall of 2000. While Larry David is credited with introducing Cheryl Hines to Kennedy in 2002, they had likely known of each other years before. It was the beginning of a deep attraction that would destroy both of their marriages.

CHAPTER 8

"My Voice Is Gone"

Black mold spread silently into the house, blooming from standing water after a rainstorm flooded the basement. It spread silently in fuzzy patches, staining the walls a sick dark green as it crept up inside the aluminum siding that encased the sprawling 1920 clapboard structure, infecting every room. Soon the children fell ill, and for the next two years every effort to get rid of the creeping fungus ended in failure. "When visitors with hacking coughs fled our home for fresh air, I taunted them from the front steps to come back and 'man up,'" Kennedy joked in a book that chronicled his family's struggles with fixing their old home.

The Kennedy family's very sick house in Bedford suddenly became a metaphor for a host of other problems, from Kennedy and Mary's failing marriage to Kennedy's health struggles and his growing disenchantment with the Democratic Party leaders he had once looked up to.

Kennedy's hero Bill Clinton, who had moved him to tears in the speech he gave at Hyannis Port just a few months before, quickly fell from Kennedy's favor after he pardoned a host of shady businessmen and drug dealers in the final hours of his second term in office without consulting the prosecutors who had worked on their cases. Among them was Clinton's half brother, Roger Clinton Jr., who had served time in federal prison after being convicted for drug trafficking in 1985. The fugitive financier and Democratic Party donor Marc Rich and his partner, Pincus Green, were also pardoned despite having been indicted in 1983 on fifty-one counts of tax evasion and fraud as well as running illegal oil deals with Iran during the hostage crisis in 1979–1980. They had both fled to Switzerland, although Rich's ex-wife Denise, a songwriter and herself a major Democratic donor, maintained a palatial 12,000-square-foot penthouse in New York City. Denise had made $450,000 in donations to the William J. Clinton Presidential Library and Museum and $1 million to the Democratic National Committee and had given Hillary Clinton's Senate campaign more than $100,000 in the years preceding the pardon.

The "Pardongate" controversy led to a criminal investigation by the FBI and the Manhattan District Attorney's Office. Mary Jo White, US attorney for the Southern District of New York, announced that she was looking into whether the Rich and Green pardons had been quid pro quos, made in exchange for cash donated to the Clintons. A bipartisan congressional House Reform Committee probe found that the pardons of Rich and Green "sent a message that individuals can go from the FBI's most wanted list to a presidential pardon if they spend money and have the proper connections. This message undermines U.S. efforts to apprehend fugitives abroad." Denise Rich refused to testify when she was called before the committee, citing her Fifth Amendment protection against self-incrimination. The criminal probe was quietly closed in 2005 without any charges being announced, although it left a black mark on President Clinton's legacy.

"I defended the Clintons to all comers on every issue and was never shaken," said Kennedy, referring to Rich as "that gangster" in his diary. "But now I'm disgusted. [Clinton] really is a flawed character—dramatically and for trinkets and whatever else he got for those pardons, and I think of all the good deeds he didn't do."

Ethel Skakel and Robert Kennedy dancing in Hyannis Port, circa 1948–1950. The couple, who met on a ski trip in Quebec in 1945, would go on to have eleven children.

Ethel and Robert Kennedy on their wedding day in June 1950. The couple married in a lavish ceremony in Greenwich, Connecticut, and their wedding was blessed by the pope.

Robert and Ethel Kennedy with three of their children study a map in Hyannis Port in 1955. Robert Kennedy Jr. is at left beside his older sister, Kathleen Hartington Kennedy, and Joseph Kennedy II.

Robert Kennedy Jr. and his schoolmate Peter Jenny pose with their hawks at the Millbrook School in 1968. RFK Jr. said he was attracted to the all-boys school in the Hudson Valley for its on-site zoo.

In April 1982, Kennedy married his fellow law student Emily Black, the mother of his two eldest children, Kathleen and Bobby III. He sought a quickie divorce in the Dominican Republic to marry Mary Richardson in 1994.

Kennedy and his coauthor and fellow environmentalist John Cronin worked together to clean up the Hudson River when they were both part of Riverkeeper. After several years, Cronin left the group along with Riverkeeper's founder, Robert Boyle, over disagreements with Kennedy.

Kennedy was arrested for civil disobedience while protesting the navy bombings on Vieques. During the month he spent in prison in Puerto Rico in the summer of 2001, he reevaluated many of his political views in the diary he kept on a series of yellow legal pads.

Two volumes of RFK Jr's diary from 2000 and 1999, which his second wife, Mary Richardson, gave to a source. Kennedy used the oversize date books to record his secret thoughts.

Left: A view of the 1999 diary featuring a sticker in support of Al Gore for president in 2000. Kennedy became a consultant on environmental matters to the former vice president's unsuccessful campaign in 1999.

Right: A Kennedy diary featuring a sticker of Vieques.

RFK Jr. and his second wife, Mary Kennedy. The couple married in 1994 on a research boat in the Hudson River. Mary was already pregnant with the couple's oldest child, Conor Kennedy. They would go on to have three more children before she died by suicide in 2012.

Kennedy and his younger sister Kerry shared a close relationship until Kennedy began to embrace vaccine skepticism and ran for president. When Kennedy was writing his scathing book on Anthony Fauci, the former medical advisor to the president, Kerry made sure to honor Fauci with a Ripple of Hope Award from the Robert F. Kennedy Human Rights Center in July 2020.

RFK Jr. married his third wife, Cheryl Hines, in a ceremony at the Kennedy compound in Hyannis Port two years after his second wife's suicide.

Robert F. Kennedy Jr. speaks at an anti-vaccine rally in Times Square in 2021.

Kennedy faced tough questions about his views on vaccines and legal work suing drug companies during his hearings before the Senate in January 2025.

The Rich pardon was so radioactive that many other Democrats sought to distance themselves from the Clintons. Andrew Cuomo, Kennedy's brother-in-law, had been scheduled to announce his bid for governor of New York at Denise Rich's Fifth Avenue home. His campaign scrapped the idea at the last minute and held the announcement at his brother-in-law Kenneth Cole's clothing store in Rockefeller Center, Kennedy revealed in his diary. Cole is married to Cuomo's sister Maria Cuomo, and Kennedy had been his guest at the Super Bowl along with Macy's CEO Terry Lundgren in Tampa just the day before. Not a die-hard football fan like many of his forebears, including his mother, Ethel, Kennedy had contemplated selling his ticket to the event outside the Raymond James Stadium when he was approached by ardent football fans offering him thousands of dollars, he wrote. "I thought of it, but obviously it couldn't be done." He sat beside New York City Mayor Rudy Giuliani, "who I like despite his violent and forbidding character and his narrow eyes."

Following Kennedy's trip to the Super Bowl, he "blew off" his brother-in-law's historic announcement to stay home with his youngest children and read Roald Dahl's *The Twits*, which he was enjoying with Conor. Instead, Mary went to the event with her neighbor and best friend, Kerry Kennedy, and Cuomo himself. Except for a few select journalists, the gathering—a major news event announcing a gubernatorial run—was by invitation only for the 250 guests who attended and closed to most media. Andrea Bernstein, a reporter for the *New York Observer* and WNYC radio, was initially barred from entering and was escorted by black-suited security guards to the back of the store, where she was eventually allowed to listen to Andrew Cuomo's speech.

"Upstairs, shoved between racks of micro-mini shorts and the spring camisole line, was a lovefest for Mr. Cuomo," noted her report in the *Observer*. In addition to Mary, guests included Hillary Clinton's Senate campaign manager, Bill de Blasio, who would go on to be mayor of New York City, as well as Caroline Kennedy Schlossberg; Cuomo's father, former Governor Mario Cuomo; and Martin Luther King III, who headed up the Southern Christian Leadership Conference and had come to New York City all the way from Atlanta to introduce Cuomo at his historic announcement. "My plan is, my intention is, I'm going to run for governor," he declared as waiters weaved among the racks of clothes, bearing trays of champagne and hors d'oeuvres of lobster on toast, foie gras, and shrimp. "I'm going to have a formal announcement later on. The race is in 2002—just about two years. I wanted to be clear that that's what I'm planning to do, and I don't want undue speculation."

The announcement foreshadowed what would turn into a highly competitive Democratic Party primary including New York State Comptroller H. Carl McCall, who was seeking to become the first Black governor of the state and was scheduled to formally announce his own intention to run for governor later that week. Kennedy, who had previously confessed to his diary that his brother-in-law "lacks humanity and doesn't love people," had little faith that he could win the primary. Cuomo eventually withdrew from the race less than a week before the Democratic primary, when McCall's lead was in the double digits.

While Kennedy blew off his own brother-in-law and the New York Democratic establishment, he was curious about the new Republican administration in Washington, mulling over a dinner invitation to the White House from President Bush to watch the film *Thirteen Days*, a dramatization of the Cuban Missile Crisis featuring Bruce Greenwood as President Kennedy and Steven Culp as Kennedy's father. He discussed whether he should accept the invitation, which included dinner with the Bush family with the comedian Al Franken, "a truly great and smart man," whom he saw at his local gym. Franken would later become a US senator representing Minnesota. "It's being billed as a brilliant political move by Bush to show he can get along with Democrats," Kennedy wrote, although he did not record in his diary whether or not he and Mary had accepted the White House invitation.

The year started on a somber note with yet another funeral—this one in Birmingham, Alabama, after the sudden death of Kennedy's friend David Whiteside Jr., a lawyer and nephew of Judge Frank Johnson, who had died in 1999. Kennedy had kept close to the Johnson family since his time with Peter Kaplan in Alabama in the mid-1970s. During his work on Ted Kennedy's 1980 presidential campaign in the state, he had spent six months living with Whiteside and his family. He had even been at the hospital when Whiteside's son, David Whiteside III, had been born in 1979 and had became his godfather. David III would later follow in his godfather's footsteps, breaking ground in the environmental movement, founding Black Warrior Riverkeeper in Birmingham several months after his father's death. Whiteside, fifty-one, was killed in a car crash on a rain-slicked road as he returned from a deposition. He was on his cell phone with his wife, Roseanna, during the accident. She told Kennedy that she had been horrified when the phone had gone dead. She had tried calling her husband back for twenty minutes but realized he was dead when he had failed to pick up. According to Kennedy, it took her five hours to find him. After he got the call from his godson, Kennedy rushed to Birmingham and prepared to deliver a graveside eulogy for his friend. "He had the most selfless sense of justice, but he was never self-righteous and never angry or bitter or mean," he wrote, adding that "God was with me so I spoke well. . . . I am godfather to David and I will do my best to give him the kind of . . . love that I know he needed from his father."

In addition to Whiteside's funeral, Kennedy also rushed to the side of his University of Virginia Law School colleague and Rhode Island attorney general, Sheldon Whitehouse, when his father died in June. Charles Whitehouse had been ambassador to Laos and Thailand in the 1970s as well as a CIA official and decorated marine dive-bomber pilot who had served in the Pacific theater during the Second World War and later during the Vietnam War. In 1966, the tall, elegant Whitehouse had been named one of the "Ten Most Attractive Men in Washington" by *The Washington Post*.

"Sheldon delivered a fantastic eulogy with cold steel and elegance," noted Kennedy, adding that a military guard had escorted the casket and Whitehouse's fellow members of the Orange County Hounds, a prestigious equestrian association and hunt club, had blown their horns. "The Plains church was overflowing with Old Guard Republican WASPs who are all fleeing the Republican Party. This is the noblesse oblige guard."

Members of Kennedy's more immediate family also needed his attention. His cousin Michael Skakel visited him in Bedford while he was preparing for his upcoming murder trial in Connecticut. "I told him I'd never done anything except my best to help him—which is true," wrote Kennedy, who had insisted on doing the "perp walk" with his cousin when Skakel had been arraigned on the murder charges the previous year. "I loved him and forgave him, but that I would have a hard time trusting him. He walked away from a 16-year friendship without explanation and spread lies about me and my family."

Nevertheless, Kennedy forgave Skakel during their meeting, and they hugged when he left, Kennedy wrote. After Skakel was convicted of the murder of Martha Moxley in 2002, Kennedy launched a campaign to prove his innocence, beginning with a long article that appeared in *The Atlantic* a year later, which began "The tragedy of Martha Moxley's death, twenty-seven years ago, has been compounded by the conviction of an innocent man."

Kennedy went on to relate how his cousin had helped him get sober in 1983 and, largely because of what he believed to be his good character, couldn't possibly have killed Moxley when he was a teenager. Skakel was being targeted only because he was a member of the Kennedy clan, he later said in a book he wrote about his cousin. "We attended hundreds of alcoholism-recovery meetings together," he wrote. "In that context and others we have shared our deepest feelings. For fifteen years we skied, fished, hiked, and traveled together, often with my wife and children. During that time I sometimes spent as many as two or three weekends a month in his company. Like nearly everyone else who knows him well, I love Michael. If he were guilty, I would have testified against him. He is not."

Like the creeping mold, Kennedy's health problems, some of them diagnosed when he was in college, set off alarm bells while he was traveling the country at his usual frenetic pace, giving speeches and meeting donors in 2001. Just before a speech in Seattle in May, his heart went into atrial fibrillation and began to beat furiously. He was so worried about the onset of the heartbeat abnormality, which could lead to a stroke or heart failure, that he asked a woman who had attended the lecture to take him to the nearest hospital. It turned out to be a false alarm, but he spent the night under medical observation. Two days later, he reported waking up with hallucinations from a migraine and "wondered if my life is a little too stressed!"

He had begun having difficulties with his heart in his early twenties. "It came up in college," he said in a deposition. "It feels like there's a bag of worms in my chest. I can feel immediately when it goes out." He added that he had to avoid caffeine and stress and that the condition had resulted in the loss of his short-term memory.

He had also been diagnosed with hemochromatosis, a genetic disorder that causes excessive iron absorption in the body and can lead to damage of organs such as the liver and heart. "It may account for my heart problems; my heart feels like a gerbil cage several hours a day these days, and the Captain Winky problems that began five years ago when my Hepatitis C was first discovered due to blood tests in which I took for the Captain, in which high iron levels were also noted," he wrote in his diary. "Anyway, the doctor urged immediate treatment which is blood removal—the old religious medieval practice of bleeding. Mary says I've entered the ranks of rock stars."

Then his voice started to falter. "My voice is gone," he wrote in his diary on May 20, 2001. "I can speak five minutes and it disappears completely." He was diagnosed with spasmodic dysphonia, a neurological disorder that causes involuntary spasms in the muscles of the larynx. Later, he would claim that the disorder had resulted from a flu vaccine, but his sister Kerry also suffers from the same malady, for which there is no known cure. When he was first diagnosed with the condition, a doctor treated him with botox shots in his vocal chords. But the injections made his voice sound "like I'd sucked down a helium balloon. I am breathless—I can't swallow," he wrote. "I choke and I can't talk. So far, the care is worse than the disease." The doctor had told him that the condition would last another ten days but could stretch out for four months. In the end, he would be plagued with the condition for years to come. "I'm embracing my fate," he wrote, adding that perhaps God didn't want him to speak and instead spend more time with his children and doing more productive things, such as learning management techniques.

Still, he continued to work in his legal clinic at Pace and entertain new and old celebrity friends. On the evening of May 21, he and Mary hosted the economist Jeffrey Sachs and Leonardo DiCaprio for dinner at their home. DiCaprio played with the children and Kennedy's pet raven and was a good sport when Finn, fascinated by the actor's ponytail, asked him if he was a girl. "Leo was very sweet and cautiously explained," he wrote. Later, DiCaprio asked him for advice on environmental issues while Kennedy drove him back to Manhattan. "He wants to spend his life and resources on a clean environment," Kennedy wrote. "I told him to . . . pick one area where he could develop an expertise and speak with authority." DiCaprio had already established an eponymous foundation in 1998 to give out grants to environmental causes for everything from preserving oceans and wetlands to raising awareness of climate change.

After he dropped off DiCaprio in the city, Kennedy was off to a late meeting with a law firm at the Trump Hotel to discuss upcoming litigation. "Got mugged on the way home," he wrote, using his code word for seduction. "I've got to do better," underlining the verb for emphasis.

Kennedy's disenchantment with high-ranking Democrats continued before and during his incarceration in Puerto Rico over the Vieques trespassing charges as he tried to mobilize lawmakers on both sides of the aisle to help end the bombings on the island. When he failed to secure assistance from outgoing members of the Clinton administration, Hillary Clinton helped set up a call with Donald Rumsfeld, the newly installed secretary of defense. "I got a returned phone call from Donald Rumsfeld," he wrote on January 16, 2001. "Hillary [Clinton] told me to call him. He was very jolly and told me a lot about his mother and how much he loves her, and how 'tickled' she was over his appointment. I gave my rap on Vieques."

Perhaps the call to Rumsfeld did some good. The timing may have been right, for in conjunction with the protests on the island, some Republican lawmakers were also getting in on the act and beginning to lobby the federal government to end the navy's bombing on Vieques, which, analysts said, was costing President George W. Bush critical support among Hispanic voters, many of whom were against the bombings. In the spring of 2001, New York Republican Governor George Pataki demanded an end to the bombings during a visit to Puerto Rico. He followed up with a visit to the Bush White House in June. "My goal is not to have it stopped two years from now," he told reporters at a news conference in New York. "My goal is to have it stopped now." Pataki, who planned to seek another term in 2002, knew that he needed the support of Hispanic New Yorkers, most of whom opposed the Vieques bombings.

Bush's plan, which was announced ahead of a referendum on the bombings in Puerto Rico, called for ending all military exercises on Vieques by May 2003. Like Pataki, supporters of ending the bombings wanted an immediate halt to the military exercises, while opponents in the military felt the plan was wrongheaded and would jeopardize US military preparedness. In the end, the military had a partial victory as the terrorist attacks on September 11 pushed the United States onto a war footing and postponed the end of the Vieques bombings yet again. The US Navy finally ended the bombing runs on the island in May 2003 and later turned the practice range into a nature reserve.

After his release from prison in Puerto Rico, Kennedy dived into the last month of summer on Cape Cod, packing in boat races, games of capture the flag, fishing, and waterskiing at the family compound in Hyannis Port with his children and most of the Kennedy clan. Despite the skin condition that had erupted while he was in prison, he was thrilled to be home. "My face looks like a teenager's with a very bad acne case now," he wrote. "I'm invisible to women, which is a good thing."

In August, he went on a lavish excursion with his Hollywood pals Larry and Laurie David on the billionaire philanthropist Theodore Forstmann's 140-foot yacht. Kennedy noted in his diary that the Hollywood power couple was nervous about being on "any kind of boat" and that Larry David's parents would never have boarded any kind of yacht. David's father's family were Jewish immigrants who had settled in the United States in the nineteenth century, while his mother's family were Polish Jews from what is now Ukraine.

"Our family is exactly the opposite of yours," Larry David told Kennedy on the lunchtime cruise, which also included Arianna Huffington and other celebrities. "The Davids are antithetical to the Kennedys. With the exception of politics, we have nothing in common. We are appalled by the things you do, the way you people live your lives." He wrote in Forstmann's guest book, "People and boats, what a terrible combination." Kennedy recorded David's comments on August 10, 2001.

In addition to the David couple, Kennedy hosted Susan Sarandon and Tim Robbins, who had a home on the cape nearby. Other boldface names sought his counsel. Alec Baldwin called Kennedy to talk about his impending divorce from Kim Basinger and his concerns about their daughter, Ireland, who was then five years old. "He is directing his first movie when she presented him with divorce papers . . . and moved to LA, a town he hates," Kennedy wrote of Baldwin.

At his aunt Eunice Kennedy Shriver's eightieth birthday celebration on July 10, he gave an impromptu toast, and spent most of his time speaking to his cousin Maria Shriver and her husband, Arnold Schwarzenegger, about marriage and divorce as well as health and wealth, he noted in his diary. The family had much to celebrate after Eunice's near-death experience at Johns Hopkins Hospital the previous year. Following the party, Kennedy seemed to gain a new appreciation of his mother, noting in his diary that "it occurred to me that I've never heard my mother use a curse or say a bad word. That's something!"

There were also meetings with his uncle Ted Kennedy in Hyannis Port over their fight against the Bush administration's plans to drill for oil in the Arctic. "Met with Teddy after church and meeting on ANWR," he wrote, referring to the Arctic National Wildlife Refuge, a 19.6-million-acre protected area in Alaska. "Been trying to hold together the labor/enviro coalition. John Podesta [former chief of staff to President Clinton] told me the Teamsters endorsed ANWR drilling in exchange for White House calling off the investigation. Bush fired Mary Jo White a day after the ANWR vote."

In August, Congress backed the drilling plan, which had been a central issue in Bush's 2000 election campaign. Teamsters president James P. Hoffa, the son of the legendary former labor leader who had disappeared in 1975, backed the drilling plan, saying it would create tens of thousands of jobs for union members. At the time, Hoffa was lobbying to end the union's federal monitor. The union had been under federal oversight by the Southern District of New York since 1989 in order to eliminate mob influence. At the same time, US Attorney White had been investigating a fundraising scandal related to the union's former president Ron Carey's 1996 reelection campaign. Carey was indicted in January 2001 for perjury and providing false statements to a grand jury investigating his re-election campaign. The monitor invalidated his narrow victory, ordering a new election, which Hoffa won. Following the vote, Hoffa intensified the union's campaign to end the monitoring, saying that the union had gone a long way toward cleaning up corruption and ending mob influence. After their support for drilling in Alaska, Bush suddenly came out in public support of Hoffa. "He's running a good union," he said in a Labor Day 2001 speech at a Teamsters picnic in Detroit. "And in an aboveboard manner, in an aboveboard way. And make no mistake about it, people are beginning to notice, particularly in Washington, D.C."

While Bush may not have entirely called off White's investigation of the Teamsters, as Kennedy described in his diary, he was seemingly open to supporting an end to the federal oversight of the union after it backed him on the Alaska drilling initiative. In the end, the Senate did not vote to approve the ANWR drilling.

While Kennedy spent the rest of that summer working on environmental issues at Pace University and Riverkeeper, he drove back and forth to Hyannis Port to be with his extended family and his friends, among them the actor Glenn Close. He was relieved to be home after his time in prison and gushed in the pages of his diary about how wonderful his family was. "I've got the best family ever! They love each other and love their lives and love the adventure. God bless us!" The pages of his diary are crammed with descriptions of clamming and fishing for bluefish as well as waterskiing and boating with the children, as well as fossil-hunting excursions in the Catskills and numerous games of capture the flag. "Kyra insisted that she be in Kick's film," he wrote on Saturday, August 11, describing a video that his eldest daughter, Kick, was making. "'You must put me in it,'" she said. "'I'm a drama queen. Dad said so.'"

Kyra, who was six years old at the time, was "inseparable" from her great-uncle Teddy. "He is charmed by any pretty face and she is absolutely in love with him and she's with him on his boat every day," wrote Kennedy. Earlier, while still in prison, he had written after the birth of his youngest child, Aidan, that he "couldn't be happier with the life and wife God has given me."

But as the summer wound down, so, too, did the twentieth century, at least in Kennedy's telling of the events on September 11, 2001. He was at a meeting with John Sweeney, the director of the American Federation of Labor–Congress of Industrial Organizations in Washington, DC, when terrorists flew two planes into the World Trade Center and attacked the Pentagon. "Armageddon!!" he wrote. "Today, the 20th century ended."

The meeting, which also included John Podesta and John Adams, a cofounder and the founding director of the Natural Resources Defense Council, ended abruptly when Sweeney said the World Trade Center had been attacked. Looking out of the window of the AFL-CIO headquarters, "I saw crews bringing stinger missiles to the roof of the White House and then there was an explosion as another plane hit the Pentagon," Kennedy wrote. "We watched the smoke billow out."

Kennedy and Adams walked across a "paralyzed" DC as all buildings were being evacuated. They managed to share a rental car with a Department of Justice attorney who happened to be one of their opponents in a legal case and drove to New York through the Delaware Water Gap because every other route was closed. The drive took nine hours, enough time for Kennedy to reflect on how much the world had changed since the previous day, when he had gone to Manhattan to make a speech and "do TV stuff" before attending the Marc Jacobs show at Pier 54. The Fashion Week event was also a promotion for

Riverkeeper, and Kennedy had taken his friend Peter Kaplan to the party in order to personally thank the rock star Deborah Harry for pledging $10,000 to his nonprofit. Kennedy had been shocked by the excesses of the Fashion Week party with "thousands of beautiful... bodies" crowding the venue at Pier 54. He described the party scene as "the excess of the age and the flesh and the money," like something out of Sodom and Gomorrah, the biblical cites that were centers of sin and depravity. The events also reminded him of the chaotic Russian roulette scene in *The Deer Hunter* in which American prisoners of war, surrounded by their Vietnamese captors, are forced to play the deadly game of pointing a loaded pistol at their head and pulling the trigger. As he turned to leave, "Donald Trump leapt up to hug me," he wrote, adding that Kaplan had introduced him to Tina Brown, then the editor in chief of *Talk* magazine, who had once commissioned a hit piece on him. Kennedy said that he had greeted the editor politely. "Peter was delighted," he wrote. "She is scared of him because her advertisers read his paper and he keeps saying she is failing." The magazine, which was bankrolled by producer Harvey Weinstein's Miramax as well as the Hearst Corporation, ceased publication just a few months later, in February 2002.

Kennedy continued to chronicle the effects of the 9/11 attacks in his diary. "Today the city is covered in ashes," he wrote, describing how his younger brother Max had driven all night from Boston to deliver film cameras that could spot bodies through rubble. "He spent the day at the World Trade Center with the police and fire squads." He added that another brother, Douglas, had moved into his and Mary's Bedford home after his Lower Manhattan apartment building had been evacuated.

The World Trade Center deaths hit close to home for Kennedy and his family. George Morell, a bond broker with Cantor Fitzgerald, had died in the attacks. The father of four had been on the 105th floor of the World Trade Center when one of the planes had hit. He had been on the phone with his wife at the time. He had told her he loved her and yelled at someone not to open a window. Then the phone went dead, Kennedy wrote. A few days later, he went to Morrell's memorial service. "The church was overflowing," he wrote. "Like Christmas." He took one of Morell's children to hunt for fossils near his home in Westchester County with his own kids and their Kennedy and Cuomo cousins.

If Kennedy had had any respect for President Bush, it disappeared on 9/11. He was disappointed that Bush had been evacuated to Nebraska, leaving Vice President Dick Cheney and Secretary of Defense Donald Rumsfeld in the White House. "Our president fled to Nebraska and mumbled embarrassing platitudes read from cue cards about war," he wrote. "Our president is an idiot and a puppet and it's painful watching him on TV." Later, when Bush announced plans to attack Afghanistan, Kennedy wrote that he was promising revenge and a crusade against Osama bin Laden. "He will get Bin Laden 'dead or alive.' He will drop million dollar bombs on $10 homes in Kabul and bomb back to the dirt age a nation that has already been bombed back to the stone age. He is such an utter simpleton. It's agonizing having him as our leader and I know the forces of darkness in his administration will turn this national tragedy to their advantage, using it to enrich their friends in the military production industries, jump start the Cold War, drill in the Arctic and blame the economic woes covered by their tax cuts for the rich on the Taliban."

Still, for Kennedy, some positive things came out of the attacks. "The raw number of dead here alone are [sic] not impressive," he wrote on September 23 after attending the funeral of the New York real estate developer Lewis Rudin along with Bill and Hillary Clinton, Rudy Giuliani, and others. "The effect comes from the fact that they were our friends; the towers were an important symbol. Perhaps this will give us some empathy for the suffering of others around the globe. It has brought us together as a nation and as a community in ways unimaginable a month ago, and God has blessed us with an enemy who is truly evil. Here is a gift, an opportunity to do better with someone truly bad and to solve a problem for this generation that affects the entire world. My original fears that we would bomb civilians in Kabul and make ourselves as bad as them seem to have been averted by Bush's speech last night. Our response will be more measured and probably appropriate, I pray."

The next day, after his class at Pace and a surprise birthday party for Riverkeeper board member Ann Colley, he headed to Ground Zero to pass out McDonald's hamburgers and Chicken McNuggets to the firemen who were digging through rubble, with one of his colleagues quipping, "Haven't they suffered enough?"

With many planes still grounded throughout the country, Kennedy drove with his assistant Mary Beth Postman to North Carolina for a Riverkeeper event several days after the terrorist strikes. "People talk of nothing but the bombing," he wrote on September 20. They drove back by way of Hickory Hill. The next day at the gym in nearby Tysons Corner, "my heart went into palpitations." But rather than seeking treatment in Washington, where he feared media exposure, he drove back to New York City, where he was scheduled to make a speech at an event in Central Park. It was only after the speech that he drove to Westchester and checked himself into a hospital, where his doctor was waiting for him. "Got EKG'd," he wrote, adding that he had also been given a shot of blood thinner and another drug that, he noted, had a chance of sending him into heart failure. Doctors, he noted, don't normally prescribe the treatment, but his doctor "knows I won't tell on him." He reported that he had returned home at 4:00 a.m.

Kennedy's personal life continued to be chaotic. By the end of 2001, he had recorded trysts with thirty-seven women, sixteen of whom had received a 10 next to their names in the ledger at the back of his diary, which Mary believed was his code for intercourse.

In June 2003, his younger sister Kerry and her husband, Andrew Cuomo, announced that they were separating. The breakup occurred after Kerry's alleged affair with the playboy businessman Bruce Colley, who often played polo with members of the British royal family. Cuomo, who lost his bid to win the Democratic primary in the 2002 gubernatorial election, had allegedly caught the pair together. Kennedy and Cuomo's father, Mario, tried to intervene to keep Kerry and Andrew together, to no avail. The couple, who had three young daughters, also tried counseling, but could not work out their differences, reports said. At the same time, Colley's wife, Ann, was allegedly involved with Kennedy (which Ann Colley has vehemently denied), according to Mary, who was said to be heartbroken over her husband's infidelities, especially after the birth of their fourth child, Aidan, born while Kennedy was serving time in prison in Puerto Rico and writing odes to his "beautiful wife" on the yellow legal pads that doubled as his diary. The situation was particularly fraught because the alleged affair had begun while Kennedy had been trying to play peacemaker to bring Kerry and Andrew back together.

Mary was so distraught about her husband's alleged affair with Ann Colley that she tried to get her thrown off the board of her husband's charity. But Ann, who was in charge of the philanthropic arm of the hedge fund billionaire Louis Bacon's Moore Capital Management, was not going anywhere. The hedge fund had donated more than $1 million to Riverkeeper over the past several years, and the nonprofit, which had gone through the upheaval and bad publicity of losing its founder, Bob Boyle, in the past year, needed to keep its donors happy at all costs. Both couples—the Colleys and the Cuomo-Kennedys—eventually divorced.

That summer, while he vacationed with his family in Hyannis Port, Kennedy suddenly found himself embroiled in another cause: linking common childhood vaccines to autism in young children. The new cause would cost him his relationships with fellow environmentalists as well as most of his friends and family, who would practically disown him as he dived deep into what became an all-encompassing obsession to challenge common vaccines and the entire medical establishment.

Kennedy's initial interest in mercury in childhood vaccines arose after an encounter with Sarah Bridges, a pretty blond mother with a doctorate in neuropsychology who showed up on Kennedy's doorstop in Hyannis Port with a Bankers Box of documents in high summer 2003. She was hoping that the environmental attorney would lend his famous name to her campaign against the vaccines that she believed had caused her son's brain damage. "It wasn't totally random," she said. "I went to college with one of his brother's wives, and she said that Bobby worked on environmental mercury and that planted the seed in my head. I said I was just going to show up to see him in Cape Cod." Bridges had attended Brown University with Victoria Anne Strauss, who has been married to Max Kennedy since 1991.

Bridges, who said she is not against all vaccines, nevertheless believes that mercury in a vaccine given to her son was the cause of his severe health problems. Bridges's son Porter Bridges had developed normally until he had turned four months old. Then he had been given vaccines for diphtheria, tetanus, and pertussis (whooping cough). The night of the last shot, he had woken up with a fever, which had developed into a two-hour grand mal seizure. He had never been the same afterward, his mother said. By the end of his second year, he had been hospitalized fourteen times to stop recurring seizures, some of which had gone on for hours at a time. He had later been diagnosed with brain damage and severe autism—"A bad reaction," doctors concluded, to the pertussis vaccine. He was hyperactive and unmanageable, according to Bridges, adding that her son had ended up needing specialized care. In 1994, she filed a lawsuit in the National Vaccine Injury Compensation Program, often called "vaccine court." Americans cannot sue vaccine makers directly because Congress, worried that pharmaceutical companies would stop developing vaccines if they had to defend costly lawsuits, made a law forbidding it in 1986. That same year, Congress established the National Vaccine Injury Compensation Program to handle claims against vaccine makers.

When Bridges sought out Kennedy, her son was eight years old, and she had been waiting for compensation for most of his life. With severe autism, he wore a helmet most of the time, and caring for him had proved to be untenable. Bridges's marriage had fallen apart as a result, and her other two children were having a hard time. But Kennedy had no time for Bridges. He had summer houseguests, he told her, and needed to go sailing. "So he left and I stayed on the porch," Bridges said. When he came back three hours later, she was still there. The annoyed Kennedy promised to read the documents. "He said, 'If I read it will you leave?'" said Bridges. "I left it with him. That night he read a huge portion, and he said that 'Something is wrong here. I'm going to look into it and make a few phone calls.' Three to four weeks later, he told me he was getting involved."

Although Kennedy had vaccinated all of his six children, he soon saw in Porter's case a new crusade that he could trumpet and perhaps make millions of dollars from along the way. After the "armageddon board meeting" that had resulted in the ouster of Boyle and his supporters from the board of directors of Riverkeeper two years earlier, Kennedy was still having trouble pushing his commercial plans to bottle Riverkeeper-branded water to raise money for the nonprofit. Perhaps he needed an entirely new campaign, especially now, three years after he had started an environmental legal practice with a fellow attorney, Kevin Madonna, a graduate of Pace Law School and former executive director of the Waterkeeper Alliance. Madonna had also worked with the New York State Department of Environmental Conservation and the United Nations Environment Programme. The partnership meant that Kennedy could now move beyond the nonprofit work that he had been involved with in the environmental clinic at Pace Law School and move into more profitable environmental litigation, not only against big polluters but also against pharmaceutical giants.

Among Kennedy and Madonna's first major cases was a class action lawsuit against DuPont on behalf of a group of West Virginia residents living near one of the company's zinc smelters, which had spewed dangerous chemicals into their homes and nearby sources of water. The firm joined other lawyers in the landmark lawsuit, which argued that the chemical company had been negligent when setting up its 112-acre toxic waste site. For more than ninety years, the smelter had produced more than 400 million pounds of zinc dust, exposing local residents in the town of Spelter to dangerous levels of arsenic, lead, and cadmium. A jury in the Circuit Court of Harrison County, West Virginia, awarded the plaintiffs more than $396 million in damages and ordered DuPont to conduct medical testing on eight thousand residents for forty years.

For Kennedy, the victory in West Virginia was an important one, especially as it related to his family's legacy. In his own way, he was following in both his uncle's and his father's footsteps. After all, West Virginia had been of paramount importance in his uncle's primary campaign for president in 1960, giving him a decisive victory against Hubert Humphrey and proving that a Roman Catholic could win election in a state that was overwhelmingly Protestant. It had also been important to Kennedy's father, who had spent six weeks there with his wife, Ethel, campaigning for his brother before the Democratic primary. "My family basically migrated into this state," recalled Kennedy years later. "And, you know, they claim to have shaken the hands of almost everybody in the state of West Virginia at that time."

A few years later, after President Kennedy's assassination, Robert Kennedy had returned as attorney general and "sloshed through deep mud in isolated hollows. He played with ragged children. He had visited schools to urge students not to drop out" during a visit in April 1964 to promote a federal government program to train young people for jobs and clean up impoverished neighborhoods. In doing so, he had shed light on the hardscrabble communities of Appalachia, where children often had no access to education, clean water, and food. "My father used to say West Virginia should be the richest state in the country because of the resources that are under the ground," said Kennedy. "But it's usually between the poorest and fourth poorest state in America."

As he continued his crusade for the environment, Kennedy's fans openly asked if he would one day consider running for president. "If you ever run for president, I'll set up a local committee," said one man who had attended a speech about cleaning up Long Island Sound in Glen Cove, New York, hosted by the city's then mayor, Tom Suozzi, in the summer of 2001. Another audience member at the same event hoped that he would consider running for his father's old Senate seat, challenging Republican Senator Alfonse D'Amato. But Kennedy wasn't ready to campaign for public office—not yet, anyway. As one reporter for a nature magazine noted, Kennedy was more interested in the dead seagulls that they passed on a road as they crisscrossed Long Island, where Kennedy continued to give speeches, than he was in campaigning for Democratic politicians. "I'd like to pick up some of these dead seagulls for my skull collection," he said following his event in Glen Cove. But he was on his way to yet another speaking engagement—a favor for another Democratic lawmaker—and there was no time to stop.

At home in Westchester County, Kennedy and Mary continued to fight their battle against the creeping mold. By 2005, they realized that they would have to tear down their house and rebuild from scratch if they were to get rid of the scourge for good. The mold spores had infested the heating units and were blowing mold back into the house. The children began to develop asthma and other breathing problems, many of them chronicled in Kennedy's diary. And in order to stay true to their green principles, they were going to rebuild the house to be as energy efficient as possible. The stress of rebuilding their green mansion while raising four children virtually on her own as her husband continued to crisscross the country increased Mary's depression. It would eventually destroy the couple's already faltering marriage.

Mary, who had trained as an architect and had worked for Parish-Hadley Associates, an influential design firm in New York City, "was eager to turn her talents to greening her own crib," said Kennedy. "I was stoked to use my home as a showcase of cutting-edge technologies and as a proving ground for the 'new energy' economy."

At the time Kennedy was on the board of VantagePoint Venture Partners, the country's largest green tech capital firm. At one point, the company paid him $340,000 for his board seat, plus hundreds of thousands of dollars more for speeches, according to court documents. The couple took advantage of tax breaks for making the home environmentally friendly and worked with a green demolition company to recycle the scrap materials and donate them to a nonprofit in the Catskills. They harvested the roof tiles from a demolished mental institution in Wassaic. "My children, accustomed to the bedlam in our home, often remind me how appropriate it is that we will literally live beneath the reclaimed roof of a former insane asylum," wrote Kennedy in the forward to a book written by Robin Wilson, an eco-designer from Texas who oversaw the Kennedy building project. "Our client was faced with building a new house, maintaining carrying costs for the original property and living in a rental home," wrote Wilson in the introduction to the book, *Kennedy Green House: Designing an Eco-Healthy Home from the Foundation to the Furniture*. "Yet building had to go on . . . even as the global financial services market was imploding."

To help the family with the cost of the new environmentally friendly building materials they needed to complete the project, Wilson created "sponsored product donation relationships" and helped them secure more than $1.3 million in goods, including dual-flush toilets, fireplaces, sinks, solid brass and zinc faucets, and even a hybrid hot water heater. "We all reduced our fees for this project because we believed in the premise of creating a LEED-certified home for the Kennedys," she wrote.

Contractors and vendors donated their services or slashed their rates for the promise of gaining free publicity by being associated with the home of a Kennedy. There were offers of "platinum sponsorships" and talk of tours to showcase the mansion and its products. The home improvement TV host Bob Vila started filming a show chronicling the construction, *Our Green House*, for NBC. "He didn't think he should pay for anything; even the suits he wears were donated," a source said of Kennedy. "He felt people should pay for him. He had an enormous sense of entitlement." Kennedy had grown used to the perks of being a Kennedy, or at least a prominent board member of environmental nonprofits. Riverkeeper paid his cell phone bills, and the NRDC paid for his and his children's travel around the world, he said in the deposition during his divorce from Mary.

The kitchen was designed for free, and the carpenter who built the bookcases and fireplace mantels charged half his regular rate. Contractor Jim Blansfield, who led the two-year building project, said that he had charged "very, very much less than what I would normally charge. I felt the project had great merit." He said that the job had not resulted in any increase in his business.

At one point, Mary called up Franken, now a Democratic senator from Minnesota, to try to get free energy-efficient windows from Marvin Windows and Doors, a firm in his home state, which was already giving them a discount of more than $100,000. Free Benjamin Moore paint for the twelve-room mansion did not go far enough for the Kennedys; they also wanted enough paint for their vacation house in Hyannis Port and to cover a float in the village's annual July Fourth parade, another source said.

In the end, Wilson herself was stiffed. Mary fired her just as the project was winding down and paid only part of her final bill. Perhaps as a result, Mary garnered only a fleeting mention in Wilson's 2009 coffee table book about the transformation of the Bedford house. Only Kennedy mentioned her briefly in a foreword he wrote for Wilson's book. Wilson referred to her only as "the client" in her book, although she did acknowledge her as "the thought leader" without ever naming her.

Perhaps Mary tried to wrest back control in at least one ad for some of the property's free interior finishes. In a promotional video for Gant Home's 2010 fall/winter collection, she appears serene and happy, dressed casually in red Gant boating shoes, a checkered shirt, and blue chinos, alternately strolling through her new home and sitting in the living room. At one point, she is reading a dog-eared copy of *The Ten Books on Architecture* by Vitruvius, an ancient Roman military engineer and architect. The video, entitled *The Home That Kennedy Built*, zooms in on close-ups of details throughout the new house: pillows woven with American flag patterns, fluffy quilts, a silver bowl of hydrangeas, leather chairs, framed boards of pinned butterflies, and stationery emblazoned "Robert F. Kennedy Jr."

"You learn about yourself by getting out into nature and that nature teaches us about the world that we live in and about ourselves," reads one of the captions in the nearly two-minute-long video, which is attributed to Mary.

But perhaps Mary had already learned too much about herself and her philandering husband, who had already begun his relationship with the Hollywood actor Cheryl Hines, Larry David's on-screen wife in *Curb Your Enthusiasm*. In the spring of 2010, Hines was in the process of separating from Paul Young, her husband of eight years. The divorce petition was filed in July of that year. "Cheryl was introduced to Bobby by Larry, and the kids were just swept up by her," said a source who was close to Mary.

Hines was so giddy about her relationship with the Kennedy scion that she tweeted that she had become friendly with Kennedy's sister Kerry and their family friend Glenn Close. On the day Kerry posted a photo of Hines with Kennedy, Close, and herself, Hines tweeted, "I got to tell #GlennClose what an inspiration she has always been to me." She also boasted that she was becoming close to Mary and Kennedy's youngest child, Aidan. "Rabid, unhinged New England zealotry by 10-yr-old Aidan Kennedy has nearly turned me into Pats fan," wrote Hines in the series of tweets that was hastily taken down after Mary's death.

In her memoir, *Unscripted*, Hines also revealed that Kyra, Mary's only daughter, had gone to live with her in Los Angeles several months before Mary's suicide. "I had developed a special friendship with Bobby's sixteen-year-old daughter Kyra," writes Hines. "Kyra was struggling in school, and Bobby asked if I would consider allowing her to live at my house while she attended school in Los Angeles. I loved Kyra and was happy to take her in." Kyra moved to Los Angeles in the fall of 2011—a situation that left Mary "completely shattered," a friend said.

The Gant video appeared as Mary's life was spiraling out of control and she and Kennedy were already separated. Perhaps it's telling that she is largely alone in the video, with a few frames devoted to following some of her children through the model green home. Friends say that she grew to hate the stately house after it was rebuilt. "It wasn't a private place for her and the kids," said a source close to the Richardson-Kennedy family. "It was like living in one of the windows at Macy's."

It didn't take long for Mary's private life to become very public. On Sunday, May 9, 2010—Mother's Day—Kennedy told his wife he was going to file for divorce, the source said. A day later, police were called to the newly rebuilt home and reported that Mary was "intoxicated." They remained for nearly an hour at the house, where Mary told them she had had an argument with family members. They also showed up during a second incident, responding to a call about a squabble among the Kennedy children.

On May 12, Kennedy filed for divorce in New York Supreme Court in Westchester County. Three days after that, on May 15, Mary was arrested for drunk driving. Bedford police officer Andrew Klein was directing traffic for a local carnival at about 9:00 p.m. when he stopped Mary in her Volvo outside a school near the Kennedy home after he saw the vehicle jump the curb. Kennedy told the officer that she had gone to the school to pick up people from the carnival. But Klein had noticed the smell of alcohol in the vehicle and later reported that her speech was slurred. A breathalyzer found that she had a blood alcohol level of 0.11 percent, police noted in their report. The legal limit is 0.08 percent. "Bobby used it all against her," said the source who was close to Mary. "He, of course, would complain that she was drunk and that he had to help the kids with their homework."

Mary appeared alone in Bedford Town Court, where she pled not guilty in the last week in May. The judge suspended her license, released her without bail, and ordered her to undergo an assessment by a private agency to determine if she was struggling with addiction.

The arrest was covered across the country and around the world. For a woman who had appeared in the gossip pages of glossy magazines, photographed at film premieres and fundraising dinners with her husband and their children and before that alongside the artist Andy Warhol and other glitterati, the new level of scrutiny and notoriety was unnerving, said a friend.

At the end of her first court appearance, Bedford Town Justice Kevin Quaranta said, "Ms. Kennedy, good luck to you." But all the luck in the world couldn't save Mary Richardson Kennedy.

CHAPTER 9

Vaccine Warrior

Mary did not want a divorce, and she did not want to lose custody of her children. Following her arrests, she diligently attended AA meetings and continued with her yoga classes, but most of all she pored over Kennedy's diaries. In many ways, she was trying to reassure herself that she wasn't crazy and that she had been married to a chronic philanderer for nearly twenty years.

"Mary presented as someone who was under his thumb," said a source who was close to her when she was going through her separation from Kennedy. "He definitely gaslit her. He told her she was crazy, that her accusations about other women were fantasies, but she learned with certainty in the diaries that that was a lie."

It's not clear when Mary decided to take the diaries to bolster her case against her husband or use them as leverage when Kennedy was trying to be coy about his assets during his February 2012 deposition with her attorneys. During that deposition, he admitted that he had taken out a $1 million contingent liability on the couple's home in Hyannis Port on Irving Avenue—a transaction that, he admitted, he had not disclosed to his wife, largely because he was planning to leave the house to his oldest children, Kick and Bobby. "My older kids won't be in the same house with her," he said, adding that "she follows me everywhere, and she did that until the court ordered her not to." Things got so bad, he said, that he had to leave the Irving Avenue property on the cape whenever Mary spent any time there.

The deposition revealed how much Kennedy made from his speeches each year—about $1.5 million—as well as legal fees on settlements on environmental litigation made by his law firm, Kennedy and Madonna—about $700,000 in 2011. He had also taken in $10,000 a month from the Technical Career Institutes in New York, a for-profit college that offered associate degrees in education, business, and engineering, among other disciplines. "I did a lot of lobbying for them in Washington," he said. "I essentially saved the company. I obtained the biggest loan for them—a $1.2 million loan from the Department of Education."

He also revealed that Cheryl Hines, now divorced from her husband, had bought him a boat valued at $55,000. In a few instances during the deposition, Kennedy claimed that he had little understanding of his own net worth or his expenses because everything was handled by the Kennedy family's accountants, who worked for the Park Agency corporation that his grandfather Joe Kennedy had set up in New York in 1949 to invest the family's assets. That willful ignorance was reminiscent of his mother's encounter with the police when she had been caught for speeding and demanded that the ticket be sent to "the New York office"—the amorphous institution—that handled Kennedy matters. But it was also emblematic of his negligence. He was someone who carelessly left things lying around, from the food wrappers that he casually discarded on a conference table during a legal meeting to a volume of his diary that he lost on a train in the late 1990s. One source claimed that he was also negligent about private video calls, sometimes forgetting to turn off his phone when another person came onto the scene. It's not clear how Mary obtained the diaries, but it's more than likely that they were not very hard to find lying around their home.

Meanwhile, Mary was trying to keep up her spirits, even as the negotiations dragged on. She visited Nicholas Mavroleon, the brother of her former beau, to help him on what he said was "a very important project with great environmental implications. I could sense her sadness then and, although she alluded to it, I was not aware of the immense pressure that she faced," Mavroleon later wrote.

"Mary was waiting and hoping for Bobby," said a source who had spoken to Mary daily during her struggles in the last year of her life. "She was in no shape to date. She had gained weight. She wasn't the knockout she had been. And Bobby was cruel about her weight, telling her that she had squandered her beauty, squandered her gift. He would put his arm around her and criticize her. It was ugly."

And she was terrified of his bullying, another friend said, especially during the negotiations for their divorce. "She was petrified of his wagging finger," said the friend, describing how Kennedy had violently pointed his index finger in her direction when he was making a point. But no matter what had happened between them, Mary fiercely wanted to remain married and continue to be part of the Kennedy family, her friends said. "It was the Kennedys or nobody," said the source. "That's where it all was for her. She couldn't go to Hyannis, and Ethel wasn't embracing Mary anymore. She had been so much accepted, and suddenly *boom!* she was yesterday's news."

According to the Bedford Police report on Monday, May 14, 2012—two days before Mary was found dead—someone (their name is redacted in the report) arrived unexpectedly, interrupting an evening session with her psychiatrist Carol Weiss, who sometimes made house calls to talk to her patient. The report noted that Mary was under "a tremendous amount of pressure . . . that day." This likely did not help her state of mind.

For his part, Kennedy leaked a sixty-page affidavit to a Kennedy biographer that outlined all the ways Mary had allegedly abused him. "She had [our youngest son] Aidan call me to tell me," he wrote in the 2011 document that was sworn before a notary. "He was disconsolate and crying. I asked to speak to Mom and Mary came on the phone. She said I should come over and spend the night in my old room with the kids who were distraught. She said she intended to kill herself unless I called off the divorce and unless I promised to recommit to the marriage. She promised that if I came over she would stay in her room and wouldn't see me or harass me." When he had returned home, he said, his wife had been drunk. "I opened the door and she leapt out of her bed and hit me with a roundhouse punch that, had I not blocked it, would have undoubtedly broken my face," he wrote. "Pointing to Aidan, she screamed, 'You told this child you didn't love me?' and hit me again, raining blows down on me as I backed down the hall. She struck me maybe 30 more times or more."

Mary denied Kennedy's version of events, and her family, in a rare public statement after her death, said that Kennedy's account was full of "vindictive lies."

Mary, dressed in black workout clothes and sandals, was found dead on Wednesday, May 16, 2012, about 1:30 p.m., according to a police report. A rope noose was tied around her neck, and she was hanging from a beam in the garage of the newly rebuilt Bedford property. The fifty-two-year-old mother of four and devout Catholic didn't leave a suicide note—at least not one that was ever made public. Two computers were found in her bedroom, along with her glasses, which she usually wore around her neck on a chain. A black wallet in her Longchamp bag contained $2,094 in cash, according to the Bedford police incident report. Mary, who had been cash-strapped after Kennedy had canceled her credit cards, was sometimes without cash to pay for gas. Two days before she died, she had spoken with her housekeepers who had told Kennedy about her buying a treadmill, a massage seat, and a cappuccino machine, according to the police report. "I told her that he probably found out by the credit card company," one of the housekeepers told the police, who redacted some of the names in the report. "She looked mad, and a little upset. I think she thought that we told [Kennedy] about the purchases. . . .

She asked me if I spoke to [Kennedy] about the machines and the purchases. I told her that I didn't speak to him."

By the time the police and Westchester EMS arrived on the scene at 1:51 p.m., rigor mortis had set in, which indicated that Mary might have been dead for several hours before she was found.

An individual who helped her in the months before she died said that she had not been talking about suicide; she had been sober and trying to resist Kennedy's pressure to end the divorce negotiations in his favor. "It's conceivable that she didn't want to die," the individual said. "It's conceivable that it was a rehearsal. A lot of times people put a bag over their head and see what it might feel like. She stood on a chair and put a rope around her neck."

It was Kennedy, accompanied by Mary's friend Shannon White, who found her body in the barn after the housekeeper alerted him that Mary was missing. It was Kennedy who made the 911 call, according to the police report.

White told the police that she had received a call from Kennedy, who had been looking for Mary on the morning she died. He had arrived at the South Bedford Road property after their housekeepers had called him to report her missing. "He was worried something had happened to Mary and that she may have hurt herself." White also said she had received a phone call from Mary, whom she described as "tearful," two days before she had died. She told police that she had spoken to her for a half hour on Monday, May 15, a day after Mother's Day, and said that she had had "a rough time that day."

Still, Mary was doing well, according to White. "I told [Kennedy] I was surprised because she had been blossoming in front of my eyes with the work she had been doing with AA," she said, according to the police report.

Hours after her death, when some of her siblings showed up at the house on South Bedford Road and rifled through her drawers, desperately searching for a suicide note—anything to explain her violent demise—they were met by Kennedy and his brother Chris. The

Richardsons asked the Kennedys to leave the house, and a confrontation ensued. "You have killed my sister," said the grief-stricken Nan Richardson.

In the autopsy report, the Westchester County medical examiner said that Mary had died from asphyxiation from hanging. No traces of alcohol had been found in her system, although the lab had found antidepressants: trazodone, o-desmethylvenlafaxine, and venlafaxine. Mary's remains were taken to the Medical Examiner's Office with "a beige rope around the neck" and "the knot present on this rope lying on her back with 9 loops." Perhaps significantly, the report noted, her fingers were caught between the neck and the noose when she was found dead. "Maybe she really didn't want to die," Mary's doctor said.

After her death, an ugly court battle played out in New York Supreme Court in White Plains with Mary's siblings, led by her brother Thomas Richardson, fighting against the Kennedys, represented by Conor Kennedy, who was just shy of his eighteenth birthday, to gain control of her remains. A Westchester judge met the two sides of the warring family in her chambers and signed an order directing the medical examiner to turn over the body to Clark Associates Funeral Home in Katonah, which had been hired by Kennedy to prepare for Mary's funeral. The Richardson siblings had wanted to bury her in Vermont but lost the battle. The judge sealed the case.

Three days after Mary's death, a private funeral was held at St. Patrick's Church, a small stone Roman Catholic church on the Bedford town green, attended by most of Kennedy's family and high-profile friends, including Susan Sarandon, Larry David, Glenn Close, and Edward James Olmos, among others. Maria Shriver, Ethel Kennedy, and Caroline Kennedy Schlossberg also attended the funeral, which Mary's six siblings and other close Richardson family and friends boycotted.

Kennedy and his sister Kerry gave the main eulogies, with both of them focusing on Mary's selflessness and her mental health struggles. Kerry recalled a rafting trip to Colombia with Mary and other friends in 1977 during which everyone's packed clothes had been soaked except for Mary's. She had had the foresight to pack everything in plastic, Kerry said. She had shared her dry clothes with everyone else on the trip and continued in her own wet garments. "She didn't care about herself; she cared about everybody else, and she loved, loved limitlessly."

Mary, who cared deeply about her place in the Kennedy family, might have been pleased by the outpouring of grief from the part of the family she had been desperate to be a part of since she had been a teenager. "She died his wife," said the source who was close to Mary in the final year of her life. The divorce had never been finalized.

The Richardsons held their own private memorial for Mary two days later in the trendy Boom Boom Room at the Standard hotel in New York City, owned by her friend André Balazs. The two-hour memorial featured a slide show, and guests were given memorial cards with a photo of a beaming Mary in happier times. "In celebration of her radiant life," read the cards. On the back were words inspired by the English theologian Henry Scott Holland: "Death is nothing at all—Nothing is past, nothing is lost/One brief moment and all will be as it was before./How we shall laugh at the trouble of parting when we meet again!"

Donations in her name were sought to establish a Mary Richardson Kennedy Award "to change the world for good and beauty" at the Putney School in Vermont, where she had once boarded with Kerry. As a measure of the hostility between the two families, the Richardsons did not invite Kennedy to the memorial, although Kerry and her brother Max crashed the event. "The mood there was quite hostile," said one of the guests. "The Richardsons were furious, and they were doubly furious when Bobby claimed the body. Kerry was certainly not welcome."

Mary was originally buried in a plot at Saint Francis Xavier Cemetery in Centerville next to Eunice Kennedy Shriver and Sargent Shriver, but several days later Kennedy moved her remains to the edge of the cemetery, burying her in an unmarked plot of land where, he said, he was negotiating to buy dozens of other plots for the Kennedy family. The Richardsons were not informed of the move and were furious, said a lawyer representing the family.

After the funeral, the Richardsons hired a high-powered private investigation firm and a former homicide detective to help answer some of the "unanswered questions" surrounding Mary's death. The firm wanted to know where she had obtained the rope used in her hanging and whether she knew how to tie a nautical knot. They also asked about Kennedy's movements and his relationship with his estranged wife, according to sources who were interviewed by the firm.

But the probe turned up little of any consequence, and any hope of launching a wrongful death suit against Kennedy or anyone else over their treatment of Mary was dashed, according to sources. The Richardsons were clearly angry with the Kennedys, but they vowed to put everything behind them and move on with their lives. Mary's siblings decided never to speak publicly about her death again. "Tom, who was sort of the leader of the siblings, decided they were not talking about it anymore," said the source who was close to the family.

Two months after her best friend died, Kerry Kennedy was arrested for driving her Lexus SUV under the influence of Ambien, a sleeping pill, on Interstate 684, narrowly missing other vehicles before she slammed her car into a tractor-trailer truck. Dressed in workout clothes, she was on her way to her Westchester gym and kept on driving until she was found by a highway patrolman slumped over the steering wheel, barely able to walk, much less stand up. She failed several sobriety tests at the scene of the accident, according to police, but passed others several hours later at a police station. She told the officer that she must have mistakenly taken an Ambien instead of her thyroid medication. A couple of days later, her lawyers announced that doctors believed that she had suffered a "complex partial seizure." No one had been hurt in the accident, and toxicology tests had revealed traces of Ambien.

In the days before her trial, which drew so much media attention that it had to be moved to a large courtroom in White Plains, Kennedy called *New York Post* columnist Andrea Peyser, pleading for compassion for Kerry, who if found guilty of a misdemeanor could be sentenced to a year in prison and be barred from entering foreign countries where as the president of the Robert F. Kennedy Center for Justice and Human Rights she was desperately needed. "Kerry's been instrumental in freeing political prisoners and dissidents from around the globe from imprisonment and torture," he told Peyser.

At her trial, Kerry leaned on her family's history, telling the jury that she had been eight years old when her father had been assassinated. A six-member jury acquitted her of driving under the influence of the sleeping pill.

Was Kerry's reaction with the Ambien a response to Mary's suicide, an episode of delayed grief?

As for Kennedy, friends say that the death of his estranged wife weighed heavily on him, even though he had already moved on with his relationship with Cheryl Hines. The man who was so concerned about death, never missed a funeral of his friends' parents, and was frequently called upon to give eulogies was torn apart, said a former close friend who has known him for more than twenty years. "I know Bobby well enough to know that Mary's suicide is a weight he will carry for the rest of his life," said the friend. "That's going to haunt him. He takes death very seriously."

To the rest of the world, the Kennedys seemed to move on quickly from Mary's death. During her funeral, newspapers and magazines were full of photos of the pop singer Taylor Swift hanging out with Conor Kennedy, who would celebrate his eighteenth birthday that summer. Swift had maneuvered her way into the Kennedy orbit when she had written "Starlight" in 2011 after seeing a photo of the young

Ethel Skakel dancing with Bobby Kennedy before they were married. When she told Rory Kennedy about the inspiration for the song after one of her concerts, Rory offered to introduce her to her mother. Ethel and Swift posed together at the Sundance Film Festival in January 2012, and later Swift would date Conor Kennedy. They spent the summer after Mary's death hanging out in Hyannis Port, where Swift even bought a home near the Kennedy compound, although she sold it after the romance ended.

Less than six months after Mary's death, Kennedy put the eco-friendly home in Bedford onto the market for just under $4 million. Despite the shadow that hung over the property after Mary's suicide in the barn, the house generated a great deal of buzz. After the house sold, Kennedy told reporters that he had decided to move to California to be with Hines. Perhaps he also wanted to leave behind the painful memories of Mary's suicide. The move across the country would also enable him to start anew and remake himself on the West Coast, far from the negative publicity and the anger of Mary's family and friends that surrounded her death.

Peter Kaplan's death from lymphoma a year and a half later made his decision that much easier. Kaplan, fifty-nine, died in November 2013, and his funeral in Larchmont drew New York City's literati. A year after Kaplan's death, at a memorial for him at the Cooper Union in Manhattan, Kennedy confessed how much he missed his former Harvard roommate. "The trench coat and slouched fedora was his uniform, his governing zeitgeist was angst," Kennedy said. "Most of all he was my moral compass, and every day I feel a deep sense of loss. . . . He was my best friend."

Still, Kennedy was determined to be happy and embark on his new life with Hines. He said he had first met her at a ski weekend in 2002 at the Fairmont Banff Springs hotel, where Waterkeeper Alliance held an annual weekend fundraiser, hosted by Kennedy and his friend Glenn Close. That year, the star-studded event, which auctioned off a winter hunting trip to Mongolia with Kazakh tribesmen as well as Kennedy and Close and golf outings with other Kennedys, raised more than $700,000 for the Waterkeeper Alliance. Although Mary had accompanied her husband on that trip, Kennedy later claimed to have developed a serious crush on Hines soon after he had met her. He had loaned her his ski hat, said Hines, who had not been equipped for a ski vacation when she had shown up in Banff. In her memoir, Hines puts that first meeting at 2005.

Hines, who is twelve years younger than Kennedy, grew up in what Kennedy described as "total poverty" in Tallahassee, Florida. Her father lived in a trailer park, and Hines slept in the same bed with her mother until she graduated from high school. She was active in community theater and eventually earned a degree in radio and television production from the University of Central Florida in 1990, working as a waitress to pay her tuition. She drove to Hollywood in a beat-up Toyota Tercel and worked for fifteen years as a bartender and personal assistant, scoring small parts in film and television before getting her big break in the pilot for *Curb Your Enthusiasm* in the fall of 1999.

"She has an incredible career that she put together herself," said Kennedy, adding that Larry David had told him that she is one of a handful of celebrities in Hollywood who is "universally beloved" in the industry. "She doesn't have a single enemy and she has a level of professionalism—she is never late for an appointment; she always knows her lines," said Kennedy, adding that he had sought David's approval when he wanted to start dating her. He said he had showed up at his hotel room at the Carlyle Hotel at 11:00 p.m. one night, and "I went to basically ask Larry's permission. Even though it was his TV wife, I needed to get square with him. It was like asking her parents to date."

He told *The New York Times* that he had worried about dating a Hollywood actress, but Larry David, who had introduced them, put him at ease. "She's the most solid person I've ever met," David told Kennedy. "Nothing you ever do will rattle her." In the article, the reporter quoted Kennedy as saying that he had started dating Hines while she had still been married to her first husband. Two weeks later, the newspaper appended a correction, saying in part that Kennedy had been misquoted. He had "referred imprecisely to Ms. Hines's marital status when they began dating. While she was in fact still married, as he noted, she had filed for divorce several months earlier."

Perhaps the correction was important because of Kennedy's deep-seated desire to pursue political office someday in the future. He couldn't be caught having an affair with a married woman, and precision in the date when they had first started their relationship was of great importance to him.

Still, they made plans to elope, but Hines was promptly talked out of such a course after speaking with Kennedy matriarch, Ethel. "She said we should get married on the lawn, in front of the ocean so everyone could be a part of it," wrote Hines in her memoir. "The more she talked, the better it sounded. It was impossible to argue with Ethel."

On the day of their wedding in August 2014, many of their guests arrived at the Kennedy compound in Hyannis Port in trolleys, gingerly stepping over puddles that dotted the grounds after a heavy rainfall the day before. The couple married at Ethel's house, and the reception, which featured a clambake and lobsters, took place at his uncle Teddy's old home. Hines wore a white Romona Keveza Collection dress, with delicate pearl beading and a full skirt. Guests at the wedding were presented with plush white towels embroidered with "Bobby and Cheryl Tie the Knot" and the date of the wedding in sailor blue. The towels were also emblazoned with a tasteful nautical knot, which might have reminded some guests of Mary's suicide two years before.

That same year, the newlyweds bought a Connecticut-style compound in Malibu that featured a four-bedroom main house and two guesthouses with a large pool for just under $5 million. Three years later, they put it onto the market for $6.45 million.

A year after his marriage to Hines, Kennedy's life changed drastically. Not only did he trade New York for California, he began to distance himself from the environmental movement that had defined him for decades. In 2015, he joined the board of the World Mercury Project, a nonprofit whose mission was to "educate and raise awareness of the sources and dangers of mercury" and to "hold those accountable who failed to protect our planet and people." After his fateful meeting with Sarah Bridges in Hyannis Port, Kennedy had fully embraced the growing movement to question childhood vaccines, especially the ones that Bridges believed had harmed her son Porter.

Kennedy had already been lecturing about the dangers of mercury emissions to freshwater fish across the country for Riverkeeper. By 2005, he had added the dangers of thimerosal, a mercury-based compound used as a preservative in childhood vaccines to prevent the growth of bacteria.

The World Mercury Project had been founded in 2007 by the film producer Eric Gladen, who claimed to have experienced mercury poisoning after receiving a tetanus shot. In 2014, he made *Trace Amounts*, which premiered at the Chinese Theatre in Hollywood in February 2015. Months later, the film had a special screening at the United Nations, with a panel discussion featuring Kennedy. Overnight, Kennedy seemed to become the chairman of the board of Gladen's nonprofit, and by 2017, he was being paid a salary of just over $131,000 for part-time work with the group. (That number would increase exponentially as the group drew in millions of dollars in donations, thanks in large part to Kennedy's participation.) By then the group had changed its name to Children's Health Defense, and the following year Kennedy was listed as chairman and chief legal counsel with a $50,000 bump in salary, according to public documents. Annual donations to the nonprofit jumped along with his salary. In 2015, it had taken in about $165,000 in donations. In 2019, that number was more than $1 million. And in 2022, it drew in more than $22 million.

Kennedy said that he had been inspired to join the fight against mercury in vaccines by Bridges and the other "mercury moms"—many of them professional, well-educated women—whose children had suffered as a result of vaccines and sought him out after his speeches on the environment. "They said that if I was serious about eliminating the perils of mercury, I needed to look at thimerosal," he said. "Vaccines, they claimed, were the biggest vector for mercury exposure in children. I really didn't want to get involved because vaccines were pretty remote from my wheelhouse. I'd always been pro-vaccine. I had all my kids vaccinated and got my annual flu shot every year. But, I was impressed by these women."

Kennedy might have thought back to Skip Lazell, his curmudgeonly high school biology teacher, when he took up the mantle of vaccine warrior. He had always admired independent thinkers and hadn't been entirely stoned out of his mind at Harvard when he had taken classes taught by the biologist and conservationist Edward O. Wilson and Robert Trivers, another evolutionary biologist whom *Time* called one of the greatest scientists of the twentieth century, whose theories on reciprocal altruism and parent-offspring conflict, developed while he was teaching Kennedy and others at Harvard in the 1970s, had rocked the scientific world. It was Trivers, with his unconventional views and lifestyle, who had had the most impact on Kennedy, who called him "the best teacher I ever had" in a June 13, 2001, diary entry. Trivers, who became a crusader for gay rights, joined the Black Panther Party and eventually moved to Jamaica, where he endured several near-death experiences, smoked marijuana, and studied lizards. He referred to himself as "the badass of evolutionary biology." Among his most controversial theories is that self-deception is an evolutionary strategy, that human beings fool themselves to better deceive others, which makes lying an important human trait.

Once Kennedy started digging deep into the effects of thimerosal, he quickly became the badass of the anti-vaccine community. Could thimerosal-heavy vaccines have led to the explosion in autism in children? It was a question he wasn't afraid to ask. "I was dumbstruck by the gulf between the scientific reality and the media consensus," he said. "All the network news anchors and television doctors were assuring the public that there was not a single study that suggested thimerosal was unsafe or that it could cause autism. . . . The HMO [health maintenance organization] data clearly showed that the massive mercury doses in the newly expanded vaccine schedule were causing runaway epidemics of neurological disorders—ADD, ADHD, speech delay, sleep disorders, tics and autism among America's children." He said he was stunned that children attending school in the United States were required to have as many as seventy vaccinations—a far cry from the three that had been required by schools in various states when he had been a child.

In June 2005, he published "Deadly Immunity," an article in both *Salon* and *Rolling Stone*, detailing a June 2000 secret conference of top government scientists and health officials organized by the Centers for Disease Control and Prevention at the Simpsonwood Methodist Conference Center near Norcross, Georgia. At the conference, experts in the field of epidemiology, autism, and vaccines had analyzed vaccine safety and the possible link between thimerosal and childhood autism. Kennedy claimed that the conference attendees, who had published their results three years later, in 2003, had withheld their findings from the public. He accused the government and big pharmaceutical companies of colluding to hide safety findings on vaccines and the possible link between thimerosal and autism.

Although the publications corrected several errors of science and fact made by Kennedy in the story, including that the rotavirus vaccine contained thimerosal and that one of the researchers had a patent on one of the vaccines, the article was eventually retracted and disappeared from the publications' websites. But among the vaccine skeptic activists—"The Children's Health Defense warriors," as Kennedy once called them—the article was key to their struggle and continues to be passed around like a banned samizdat. If anything, the article's disappearance only inflamed their convictions that there was a media conspiracy to keep the truth from families whose children had been injured by vaccines.

In between his work for Children's Health Defense, Kennedy continued his environmental crusades, showing up at Standing Rock near the border of North and South Dakota in November 2016 with some of his children, other celebrities, and members of Native American groups to protest the Dakota Access Pipeline. The pipeline, which would transport crude oil from North Dakota to Illinois, protestors said, would threaten sacred land of the Standing Rock Sioux Tribe, violate treaties, and contribute to climate change. Kennedy showed up when the Army Corps of Engineers threatened to evict the protestors. In photos distributed by the Waterkeeper Alliance, Kennedy, in a work shirt and faded blue jeans, pumped his fist in a show of defiance and stood with his son Conor at the Oceti Sakowin Camp amid a group of Sioux elders brandishing wooden staffs studded with feathers.

"On a recent trip to Standing Rock, I saw truck mounted facial recognition equipment tagging protestors from surrounding hilltops," he wrote. "I experienced the jarring barrage of acoustic cannons. The state and private security forces deployed water cannons against protesters in sub-freezing weather endangering their lives, tear gas bombs, pepper spray, flash bang grenades which might cost one protester her arm, and plastic bullets which felled a Sioux elder the day I left."

It would be one of his last high-profile environmental protests for the water protection nonprofits to which he had devoted so many years of his life. In March 2017, he resigned from Riverkeeper, citing his new obsession with vaccines as well as his new living arrangements nearly three thousand miles from the Hudson Valley. "I now live on the West Coast, and the weekly commute has been hard on my family, to say nothing of my carbon footprint," he wrote in his letter of resignation. "Furthermore, keeping up with the exploding growth at Waterkeeper Alliance and my work with World Mercury Project have been consuming, increasing bandwidth, leaving me little time to give Riverkeeper the attention it deserves." Two months after his resignation, Bob Boyle, his old mentor and founder of the group, died of cancer.

Riverkeeper's president, Paul Gallay, publicly thanked Kennedy, but behind the scenes the situation was very different. According to Boyle's son, Alex, Kennedy was pushed out of Riverkeeper as he became increasingly shrill about the link between vaccines and childhood autism. "He broke with Riverkeeper because they were embarrassed about his vaccine stance," Boyle said. "He was also forced to leave Riverkeeper because of his flirtations with politicians and commercializing water. He was asked to leave in January 2017. It's normal for him to go from cause to cause. He's all over the place." By November 2020, Kennedy had also stepped down from Waterkeeper Alliance.

Kennedy, whose law firm began to take on lucrative litigation against pharmaceutical manufacturers, hooked up with the film producer Del Bigtree, who had founded an advocacy group called Informed Consent Action Network in Austin, Texas. The mandate of the group is to investigate the safety of medical procedures, pharmaceutical drugs, and vaccines, according to its federal filings.

Kennedy and Bigtree, among other CHD "warriors," attended a May 2017 meeting with Dr. Anthony Fauci, the director of the National Institute of Allergy and Infectious Diseases (NIAID), at the headquarters of the National Institutes of Health in Washington, DC. The opportunity to meet with Fauci came after Donald Trump, who had been elected to his first term as president in 2016, asked Kennedy to chair the Vaccine Safety Commission, a new entity, which was compromised even before it got started after it was revealed that Trump had accepted $1 million from Pfizer for his inauguration. The meeting with Fauci didn't go well, either, according to Bigtree's account in the foreword to a book coauthored by Kennedy.

Fauci and NIH Director Dr. Francis Collins, who was also at the meeting, allegedly refused to provide them with the studies they sought about sixteen new vaccines that had been added to the CDC schedule. "Nobody knew the true risk profile of these vaccines, and nobody could say whether they were averting more problems, deaths and illnesses than they were causing," wrote Bigtree.

That first meeting with Fauci changed the course of the next several years for Kennedy and Children's Health Defense. Kennedy seemed to be on fire, writing and speaking about the dangers of vaccines. Together with board members and volunteers from the nonprofit, he doubled down on the vaccine fight. Their big break came after March 2020, when the world was plunged into a deadly pandemic and the questions surrounding vaccines—especially COVID-19 vaccines—exploded.

Suddenly, Fauci, seventy-nine at the time, became a daily fixture on news programs and presidential briefings on COVID. After all, he was "America's doctor" who had reigned over NIAID for thirty-six years, overseeing the country's response to HIV/AIDS, Zika, SARS, and other epidemics. Many people saw him as a calming influence, and he was called upon to explain on national television the science behind the spread of COVID-19. He warned the country's residents to "hunker down significantly more than we as a country are doing." Millions of people diligently followed his social distancing safety protocols and masking advice to prevent the spread of COVID-19 even as President Trump challenged much of his wisdom during the pandemic's darkest days. In one of his first tweets at the beginning of the pandemic amid widespread panic as the stock market collapsed and unemployment soared in March 2020, Trump posted on Twitter in capital letters: "WE CANNOT LET THE CURE BE MORE THAN THE PROBLEM ITSELF."

Trump wasn't the only one hostile to Fauci, who held on to the claim that COVID-19 was a product of nature and not lab generated—which would be seriously questioned in the years after the pandemic. Among his fiercest critics were the members of Children's Health Defense and Bigtree's Informed Consent Action Network. Like Children's Health Defense, Bigtree's nonprofit grew exponentially during the pandemic. Its annual donations jumped from about $3.4 million in 2019 to nearly $13 million in 2021, a year after the beginning of the pandemic, according to federal filings. Children's Health Defense grew into an even more powerful advocacy group, launching an internet TV channel and film studio, with chapters across the country and around the world. Its infrastructure was perfectly suited for a national political campaign, and before too long, Kennedy would find himself at the forefront of an exploding national movement that not only questioned the nature of vaccines and health care but was poised to expose what he saw as widespread corruption and lack of transparency in democratic institutions across the country.

Kennedy's attacks against Fauci created a deep fissure within his family. While he and the vaccine "warriors" attacked "America's doctor," his sister Kerry and his mother honored Fauci with the Ripple of Hope Award from the Robert F. Kennedy Human Rights foundation, where Kerry was president. The nonprofit had been founded by Ethel in 1968 to honor her husband after his assassination and gave out awards to those who worked to advance human rights and social justice. The award to Fauci was announced in the summer of 2020, just as Kennedy was putting the finishing touches on his bombshell book about Fauci. In December 2020, the awards ceremony went online for the first time in its more-than-fifty-year history because of the COVID-19 protocols, and a video uploaded to Facebook showed Kerry and Ethel holding up the prize—a bust of Robert Kennedy—in Ethel's living room. Fauci was honored along with the civil rights leader and longtime Georgia Democratic congressman John Lewis and labor leader Dolores Huerta, both of whom had helped with Robert Kennedy's presidential run in 1968. Awards were also handed out to Colin Kaepernick, an NFL quarterback and civil rights activist, as well as PayPal CEO Dan Schulman, among others. In his videotaped acceptance speech, Fauci spoke about having forged "a delightfully warm and productive friendship" with Ted Kennedy, "a steadfast supporter of NIH." The "liberal lion of the Senate," who had spent his life advocating for universal health care and helped pass landmark legislation to increase funding for cancer research and treatment, had died in 2009 after being diagnosed with a brain tumor. There is little doubt that Fauci's mention of Ted Kennedy was a shot directed at his nephew, who was now openly questioning everything Fauci had done during his long career in public health.

Awarding Fauci such a distinction in their father's name was likely seen as a blow aimed at Kennedy, who was upsetting his family in other ways. As the fiftieth anniversary of the assassination approached, Kennedy traveled to California to visit Sirhan Sirhan. He said he had spent months going over the investigation into his father's death and felt he needed to meet his assassin in person. He left the three-hour meeting convinced that Sirhan had been falsely accused of killing his father and publicly demanded a new investigation into the assassination. Sirhan had originally confessed to the killing after his arrest, although he had also said he had no memory of the shooting. He was serving a life sentence at a correctional facility near San Diego.

"I got to a place where I had to see Sirhan," Kennedy said. "I went there because I was curious and disturbed by what I had seen in the evidence." Witnesses to the assassination had said that Sirhan had been standing in front of the presidential candidate in the kitchen of the Ambassador Hotel, but an autopsy report had found that Robert Kennedy had been shot four times at point-blank range from behind. Kennedy pointed to new evidence showing that thirteen shots had been fired that night, but Sirhan's gun had contained only eight bullets. The theory that there had been a second gunman in the hotel kitchen was backed by Paul Schrade, a labor leader and aide in the 1968 presidential campaign, who had been shot in the head by Sirhan. Schrade had spent decades analyzing the assassination and trying to force the Los Angeles Police Department to disclose a confidential trove of documents about the shooting. Schrade pointed to evidence from an acoustics expert who had examined an audio recording made by a reporter in the hotel pantry that revealed the thirteen shots. "Yes, he did shoot me. Yes, he shot four other people and aimed at Kennedy," Schrade said in an interview on the 50th anniversary of the shooting in 2018. "The important thing is he did not shoot Robert Kennedy. Why didn't they go after the second gunman?"

Schrade and Kennedy believed that the second shooter had been a security guard who had been hired to protect Robert Kennedy on the night he was shot. Thane Eugene Cesar was standing behind Robert Kennedy when he was shot. Cesar, a plumber who worked for the Lockheed Aircraft plant in Burbank, was opposed to Kennedy's policies, once saying that if elected he would sell the country to Communists and immigrants. When he was interviewed by the LAPD after the shooting, officers did not ask to see his gun, nor did they ever consider him a suspect. Although he admitted that he had a .22-caliber pistol, which was similar to the weapon used in the assassination, he claimed that he had sold it before the shooting. Years later, in 1972, William Turner, a former FBI agent and assassination researcher, tracked down the man who had bought Cesar's gun. The receipt showed that Cesar had lied and had actually sold his weapon in September 1968—three months after the assassination. In 2018, Kennedy had arranged to meet Cesar in the Philippines, where he had retired, but had canceled the meeting after Cesar kept demanding payment to speak to him and increased the price every time Kennedy spoke to him. When he demanded $25,000 to speak, Kennedy canceled the meeting.

Both Kennedy and his brother Douglas supported parole for

Sirhan at his California parole board hearing in August 2021. "While nobody can speak definitively on behalf of my father, I firmly believe that based on his own consuming commitment to fairness and justice, that he would strongly encourage this board to release Mr. Sirhan because of [his] impressive record of rehabilitation," wrote Kennedy in a letter submitted to the board. "At 77, he is a gentle, humble, kind hearted, frail and harmless old man who poses no threat to our community. His release will be testimony to the humanity, compassion and idealism of our justice system to which my father devoted his life." The two-person board agreed to recommend Sirhan's release.

Kennedy and Douglas's six other siblings were quick to condemn the decision. "Our father's death impacted our family in ways that cannot adequately be articulated and today's decision by a two-member parole board has inflicted enormous additional pain," said a statement posted by Kerry Kennedy on social media. "But beyond just us, six of Robert Kennedy's surviving children, Sirhan Sirhan committed a crime against our nation and its people. He took our father from our family and he took him from America." A few days later, Ethel issued her own statement condemning the parole board's decision to release Sirhan, on her son Christopher Kennedy's Facebook page. "Our family and our country suffered an unspeakable loss due to the inhumanity of one man," she said. "We believe in the gentleness that spared his life, but in taming his act of violence, he should not have the opportunity to terrorize again."

A few months later, in January 2022, California's Democratic governor, Gavin Newsom, reversed the parole board's decision, citing the assassination as "among the most notorious crimes in American history" in an opinion article in *The Los Angeles Times*. He pointed to what he called Sirhan's own lack of insight and failure to address "the deficiencies that led him to assassinate Senator Kennedy."

Even before they supported Sirhan's release, Kennedy and his brother Douglas had been on the outs with their family for years for their support of their cousin Michael Skakel. They had accompanied him on his perp walk when he had first been charged with the murder of his neighbor Martha Moxley, and years later they continued by his side. In 2013, Skakel was freed on appeal after serving more than eleven years in prison on the grounds that he had not been given a fair trial due to the botched legal defense provided by his lawyer, Mickey Sherman.

In his 2016 book, *Framed: Why Michael Skakel Spent over a Decade in Prison for a Murder He Didn't Commit*, Kennedy blasted Sherman, describing him as "a slick but incompetent, dissolute and pathologically narcissistic, wannabe television lawyer" who had blown through more than $2.2 million that the Skakels had "scraped together" for Michael's defense.

It was Peter Kaplan who had encouraged Kennedy to write his book about Skakel. In 2003, he had tried to find an independent journalist willing to write the "real story of Michael Skakel's persecution," wrote Kennedy. "When those efforts failed, Peter observed, 'Every reporter is scared of appearing to have been seduced by your family. You need to write this story yourself.'" Kennedy ended up taking his advice, and shortly before Kaplan died he read one of Kennedy's chapters and encouraged him to turn it into a book. "I felt his presence every day that I worked on this project," Kennedy wrote in the acknowledgments to the book.

Kennedy also blamed the media and prosecutorial misconduct for condemning his cousin as "a spoiled brat." He wrote that when his cousin had launched his appeal, he had hired a private detective to try to get to the truth of the investigation into Moxley's murder and the handling of Skakel's case. In his conclusions, he suggested that two Black teenagers from the Bronx who had been in Greenwich at the time of the murder could have been involved in Martha's death. They denied any involvement.

In 2016, the Connecticut Supreme Court reinstated Skakel's conviction but later reviewed the decision after a request by Skakel's attorneys. Two years later, the same court overturned Skakel's conviction. In 2020, a state prosecutor announced that Skakel would not face another trial, and the charges were dropped.

In 2021, Kennedy launched his biggest attack against Fauci and, by extension, most of the Democratic establishment, with the publication of *The Real Anthony Fauci: Bill Gates, Big Pharma, and the Global War on Democracy and Public Health*. Derided by many, the book contained blurbs by the French virologist and Nobel laureate Luc Montagnier, who wrote, "Dr. Joseph Goebbels wrote that 'A lie told once remains a lie, but a lie told a thousand times becomes the truth.' Tragically for humanity, there are many, many untruths emanating from Fauci and his minions. RFK Jr. exposes the decades of lies." Lawyer Alan Dershowitz, broadcaster Tucker Carlson, and film director Oliver Stone also lauded the 449-page tome. "RFK Jr.'s story of Fauci's failure as the government's AIDS coordinator is a highly disturbing prologue to his COVID mandate as head of NIAID," said Stone. "So, who is Dr. Fauci in the end? Has American medicine truly become a 'racket,' as corrupt as a mafia organization? . . . RFK Jr. has written a strong, strong book."

The book, which is a collection of reports and chapters with titles such as "White Mischief: Dr. Fauci's African Atrocities" and "Hyping Phony Epidemics: 'Crying Wolf,'" was slammed by one critic as having "all the objectivity of *The Protocols of the Elders of Zion*," a fraudulent anti-Semitic treatise that accuses Jews of world domination. Fauci also slammed the book, invoking his friendship with Ted Kennedy and claiming that Kennedy's book would do nothing except hurt people. "And the thing that makes it even more painful about it is that ultimately that it is hurting people, that will cause disease and lose lives for the things he's saying," he said. "So, I'm so sorry that he's doing that not just because he's attacking me—that seems to be the rage among some people—but because ultimately it is going to hurt people. So it's really unfortunate that he's doing that."

Most mainstream media simply ignored the book, refusing to review it even as it climbed steadily to the top of bestseller lists across the country and stayed at number one for weeks on end. According to Skyhorse Publishing, the book's publisher, the book sold more than 1.1 million copies in its first two years.

For Kennedy and his supporters who found themselves censored on social media during the pandemic for their views, *The Real Anthony Fauci* was much more than an attack on Fauci and pharmaceutical companies; it was a rallying cry for freedom, democracy, and transparency, although Kennedy would go on to attract a great deal of negative attention when he compared US vaccine mandates to laws in Hitler's Germany at an anti-vaccine rally in Washington in 2022. "Even in Hitler's Germany, you could cross the Alps to Switzerland. You could hide in an attic like Anne Frank did," he said in reference to the surveillance state that he claimed Fauci had created during COVID.

The sentiment that Americans were being watched was a familiar theme in his book. "We can bow down and comply—take the jabs, wear the face coverings, show our digital passports on demand, submit to the tests, and salute our minders in the Bio-surveillance State," he wrote in the book's conclusion. "Or we can say No. We have a choice, and it is not too late."

Kennedy later apologized for his remarks, and Hines felt compelled to denounce her husband's comments publicly on X. "My husband's opinions are not a reflection of my own," she posted in a tweet that has since been scrubbed. "While we love each other, we differ on many current issues."

But it wasn't so much her husband's opinions that she abhorred, it was his continued philandering that was testing their relationship, said a source close to the family. A Kennedy spokesperson denied that he has had any romantic relationships outside his marriage to

Hines. "This story is untrue," the spokesperson said in an October 2024 statement to Mediaite. "Mr. Kennedy has had no romantic relationship with any woman other than his wife since their marriage."

In public, at least, she continued to support her husband, who offered to stage a separation following his Nazi remarks in order to protect her from his views. "I saw how it was affecting her life and I said to her, 'We should just announce that we are 'separated,' so that you can have some distance from me. We wouldn't really be doing anything, we would just—I felt so desperate about protecting her at a time where my statements and my decisions were impacting her," he told *The New York Times* in 2023. He even composed a press release announcing the separation, which was never sent out.

His offer to separate from his wife was little more than damage control to protect him as he prepared to launch a long-shot presidential campaign. He knew he would need all the help he could get, especially from the popular blond actress, who had as much name recognition across the country as he did. On the eve of fulfilling his lifelong dream to become president of the United States, he simply couldn't afford another negative headline about the most important woman in his life. His supporters, the "mercury moms" and other conservative cheerleaders, might not tolerate another extramarital scandal, which was likely why he did everything he could to make sure the woman he had once described as "unflappable" stayed firmly on his side.

CHAPTER 10

"They Had No Clue What They Were Doing"

Perhaps Kennedy had King Arthur and his Knights of the Round Table in mind when he addressed a raucous crowd of supporters waving red, white, and blue "Kennedy 2024" and "Kennedy Heal the Divide" signs at the Boston Park Plaza hotel on the spring day in 2023 when he announced his presidential campaign. "You give me a piece of ground, and a sword, and I'm going to take back this country," he said to thunderous applause.

It might have seemed an unusual statement for the newly minted politician, but for yet another Kennedy running for election to the country's highest office, it was oddly appropriate. For he was surely invoking King Arthur, the mythical ruler of Camelot, whose magical sword had been a symbol of both strength and virtue, signaling that he was worthy to rule over his storied kingdom, which has long epitomized chivalry, justice, honor, and democracy. Jackie Kennedy had invoked Camelot when she had quoted the popular Broadway musical in an interview with a *Life* magazine journalist shortly after her husband's assassination in 1963. "Don't let it be forgot, that for one shining moment there was Camelot," she said, pronouncing the famous lyric from the musical by Alan Jay Lerner and Frederick Loewe. Camelot was the myth that had symbolizd Kennedy's uncle and father in happier times, and it had been central to Kennedy's own lifelong desire to be a hero. This was a man who still aspired to the noble dictums set down by Holy Roman Emperor Frederick II in his treatise on falconry, as well as the teachings of St. Francis of Assisi, the Catholic saint and founder of the Franciscan Order, for whom he and his father had been named. He had named his own firstborn son with Emily Black after the saint. Robert Francis Kennedy III is known in the family as "Bobby 3."

Significantly, Kennedy's announcement took place on the 248th anniversary of the exploit of another hero: Paul Revere's "midnight ride" to Boston's Old North Church on April 18, 1775, to alert colonial militias to the movement of British troops that ultimately ushered in the Revolutionary War. The American colonists had fought against what Kennedy called the corrupt merger of the state with corporate power when they had taken on British troops—a battle he likened to his own mission to end the US government's cozy relationship with giant pharmaceutical companies, banks, and other big businesses. Everything had started in Boston, he noted, which was also the city where his Kennedy ancestors had arrived after fleeing British rule in Ireland in 1848. "My mission over the next 18 months of this campaign and throughout my presidency will be to end the corrupt merger of state and corporate power that is threatening to impose a new kind of corporate feudalism in our country, to commoditize our children, our purple mountain majesty, to poison our children and our people with chemicals and pharmaceutical drugs, to strip mine our assets, to hollow out the middle class and keep us in a constant state of war," he said.

The speech continued for more than an hour and a half in the hotel ballroom, which featured a giant US flag on the stage where Kennedy spoke, backed by a Greek chorus of supporters flashing signs and jumping to their feet and clapping at key moments during the address. Kennedy invoked God; he talked about environmental devastation and the censorship he faced when he dared to criticize fellow Democrats in the federal government, especially Fauci and his cronies for imposing lockdowns during COVID, for their evasiveness about the origins of the virus. Later, Kennedy would accuse Fauci of having "a lot of liability with coronavirus" and funding research at the Wuhan Institute of Virology in China. He railed against the war in Ukraine and chronic diseases such as obesity and neurological disorders in children that had turned contemporary America into the "sickest generation" in history. At one point, he referred to his own colorful past, alluding to his struggles with drugs and women. "I'm not an ideal presidential candidate," he said. "I'm not one of these people who said 'I've got to be really careful because one day I'm going to be in the White House.' I actually did the opposite of that. I've led a very high-risk life.... I've had a rambunctious youth and it lasted until my early sixties."

He seemed to casually laugh off his decades of addiction to drugs and casual sex that had caused him and others so much pain. Although he might not have ever worried about how his addictions might impact his ability to run for high office, others surely did. There was Lem Billings, who had worked so selflessly and diligently to inculcate the same kind of ambition and greatness that he had seen in Kennedy's uncle and father into his teenage charge. Perhaps even Ethel worried about him, although there is no evidence to suggest that of her eleven children she might have imagined that it would be her problematic third-born child who would try to follow in his father's footsteps. Of his siblings, only Douglas and Courtney Kennedy Hill (she had divorced Jeffrey Ruhe and married Paul Hill) attended the kickoff rally, as did his wife, his six children, and his three grandchildren.

Just how did Kennedy finally come to the realization that he could run for president—a dream Billings had spent so many years cultivating and a desire that had always been at the back of his mind, ever since his own father had said that of all of his children, Bobby Jr. was "most like the president."

Shortly after Instagram pulled his account in early 2021 over the Fauci attacks and his vaccine skepticism, Kennedy started to give it some serious thought. For years, his colleagues at Children's Health Defense had floated the idea. Then, months later, the pollster Jeremy Zogby conducted a national survey about American heroes. Zogby asked a sample of 26,000 Americans whom they considered a hero among a list of people that included the pope, the broadcaster Oprah Winfrey, Microsoft cofounder and philanthropist Bill Gates, Joe Biden, and Donald Trump. Kennedy was included in the mix for his opposition to vaccine mandates during COVID. Zogby said he had been shocked when Kennedy had come out on top. For Kennedy, who had grappled for so long in his diary entries with the meaning of heroism and who still aspired to Holy Roman Emperor Frederick II's dictates for heroic conduct, Zogby's findings were an important affirmation of his lifelong search for meaning. Kennedy said he had been astonished when Zogby presented his polling numbers and for the first time had felt he had a fighting chance at national office. Later, Meta shut down the accounts of Children's Health Defense for "repeatedly violating" its policies against spreading medical misinformation. "I started thinking, 'Well the one place that they couldn't censor me was if I was running for president,'" he told *The New Yorker*.

Which was how he ended up onstage in the ballroom of the Boston Park Plaza, announcing his candidacy in the Democratic primary, even as he knew he was creating an even deeper fissure within the Kennedy clan. "I bear no ill will or any kind of disappointment to any of them," he said, referring to the other members of his family who were not present. "They have different views of the politics in this country." It was a mild way to put it: Everyone else in his family was likely to support President Joe Biden if he decided to run again, and most of them backed Vice President Kamala Harris, who was eventually crowned the Democratic Party's candidate without facing a primary challenge—a decision that many people criticized as undemocratic.

Like his father in 1968, Kennedy was facing what seemed to be insurmountable odds. As he noted in his speech, his father had also been running at a time of war in a divided country and had had little support among Democratic stalwarts when he had announced his campaign for president in the Senate Caucus Room in March 1968. Although Robert Kennedy had had the support of the United Auto Workers and Cesar Chavez's United Farm Workers, the media had largely been against him, and the celebrities of the day—Paul Newman and Joanne Woodward, to name two of the most prominent—had stumped for his opponent, Minnesota Senator Eugene McCarthy, in the run-up to the Democratic primary.

Kennedy was undaunted, though, as he worked to win over even his harshest critics. And he did so by largely telling them the truth, he noted in his speech, reminding his supporters of an extraordinary address his father had given at Creighton University, a Catholic university in Omaha, a day before the Nebraska primary, which he had won in May 1968. In his controversial speech, he had chastised the four thousand students, most of them middle-class and white, for their ability to defer their military service to Vietnam because they had the good fortune to attend university. He had reminded them that as a result, 45 percent of US soldiers in Vietnam were Black, Native American, and Latino because they didn't have the means to attend college. The students, who had initially booed him, ended up applauding him. The same thing had played out at the University of Kansas when he had addressed twenty thousand largely pro-military students. "The students rushed the stage," said Kennedy. "They just wanted to hear the truth. That's it. And the day he died, he won the California primaries, the most urban state in this country. And the same day, the South Dakota primary, the most rural. He had succeeded in uniting America and building a bridge just by telling people the truth." Of course he wanted to follow in his father's footsteps and unite the country by telling people the truth—something that was becoming increasingly more difficult to do when it came to his personal life.

Wearing a tight bright blue shift dress and nude heels, her blond hair perfectly coiffed, Cheryl Hines dutifully introduced her husband at the Boston rally when he announced his run for president. It was an extraordinary performance of the supportive Kennedy spouse and was followed up less than two months later in her first interview after Kennedy hit the campaign trail.

Hines's interview with *The New York Times* seemed like preemptive damage control regarding his shaky marriage—whether at that point it was still his heterodox political views or his philandering that was threatening the union is not clear. The interview was conducted at their sprawling Spanish colonial–style six-bedroom home in Brentwood, with waxed surfboards leaning against the walls and Pop Art portraits of the couple and John F. and Jackie Kennedy painted by the Brazilian artist and family friend Romero Britto. The couple had purchased the home, which features a backyard tiki bar and a pool with a waterfall, for $6.6 million in 2021.

In the interview, Hines, a registered Democrat, declared that she would support her husband for the Democratic primary but, like First Lady Melania Trump before her, would not feel obliged to accompany him to every campaign event. "I support Bobby and I want to be there for him, and I want him to feel loved and supported by me," she said. "And at the same time, I don't feel the need to go to every political event, because I do have my own career."

In a separate interview for the same article, Kennedy emphasized the point, calling Hines "an enormous asset to me, and I don't think we've unveiled her in her true power yet."

With the rollout of the campaign, Hines indicated that her friends had been checking in on her, especially as Kennedy was increasingly appearing on Fox News shows and was scheduled to appear on Steve Bannon's *Bannon's War Room* podcast. But it was an interview with Olivia Nuzzi, the star political correspondent for *New York* magazine, that would prove to be Hines's biggest problem.

During the early part of his campaign for president, Kennedy's closest advisers "had no clue what they were doing," said political strategist Hank Sheinkopf, a veteran of political campaigns who worked with Bill Clinton, former New York City Mayor Michael Bloomberg, and Mexican President Vicente Fox, among other high-profile politicians.

Kennedy and the group that Sheinkopf described as his "rag-tag" brain trust had approached Sheinkopf months earlier to help run Kennedy's presidential campaign. Sheinkopf said that the group of strategists behind Kennedy had included his publisher at Skyhorse Publishing, Tony Lyons, who had contributed $150,000 to the campaign and would oversee one of his super PACs. Like Kennedy, Lyons was pretty fearless, undeterred by popular opinion in choosing books for his list. His company had published *The Real Anthony Fauci* as well as Woody Allen's 2020 memoir, *Apropos of Nothing*, after Hachette had refused to go forward with it after a staff walkout over the sexual abuse allegations by Allen's adopted daughter Dylan Farrow and the Me Too movement.

In addition to the Fauci book, Lyons had published several other works by Kennedy, and was also paying Kennedy as a consultant "for author introductions, book ideas and forwards to other authors' works and bonus," according to financial disclosures. Those ideas included a memoir in the works by Hines that Lyons was poised to publish, perhaps as an incentive for the actress to remain in the marriage during the campaign.

Other Kennedy supporters included Gavin de Becker, a celebrity security consultant, who was also a major donor. De Becker, a bestselling author who had cut his teeth as a teenager in Beverly Hills working for Elizabeth Taylor and Richard Burton when he was barely out of high school, had also advised President Reagan on security. He shared many of Kennedy's views on vaccines and government overreach and is himself the author of a book about the federal government's cover-up of the dangers of vaccines. *Forbidden Facts: Government Deceit & Suppression About Brain Damage from Childhood Vaccines* was published by Lyons's company in 2025. In 2024, de Becker and his family sued a Las Vegas hospital for wrongful death after it refused to use ivermectin, an antiparasitic medication that was considered by some to be a "wonder drug" in the treatment of COVID. Gavin's father, Hal de Becker, a dancer and writer who had performed with Elizabeth Taylor, Mickey Rooney, and Marlene Dietrich, among others, had died of COVID in 2021. Like Kennedy, de Becker has argued that the Emergency Use Authorization, a legal authority that allows the Food and Drug Administration to facilitate the availability of medications during a health emergency, should not have been invoked when drugs such as ivermectin had shown some success during the COVID pandemic. Instead, the government had forced on Americans what de Becker said had been a hastily produced vaccine to treat the illness. (The second Trump administration removed the authorization in August 2025, a move that was widely criticized by those who backed the availability of COVID vaccines.)

De Becker had long been obsessed with how to prevent political assassinations and was a self-described expert on both Kennedy assassinations. He backed Kennedy's campaign, making an emotional speech at Kennedy's seventieth birthday party at the London West Hollywood hotel in January 2024, an event that raised $5.8 million for his American Values 2024, the super PAC named for one of his memoirs. He billed nearly $6 million for security services to Kennedy's campaign when President Biden refused to give the candidate a Secret Service detail, which had been allocated to presidential candidates since Robert Kennedy had been assassinated in 1968. De Becker, who appealed in social media posts for donations to the Kennedy campaign to cover his security, donated a total of $14 million to Kennedy's super PAC. Kennedy was given a Secret Service escort only after the assassination attempt against Trump in Butler, Pennsylvania, in July 2024. Still, he kept de Becker close to him; he was an important adviser for his campaign who maintained close relationships with the CIA and the FBI.

Timothy Mellon, a grandson of the legendary banker Andrew Mellon, contributed more than $25 million to the campaign.

Dennis Kucinich, a progressive former Democratic congressman from Ohio who had once proposed setting up a cabinet-level Department of Peace and had twice run for president—in 2004 and 2008—was Kennedy's first campaign manager. During his first run for the presidency, Kucinich, who had been mayor of Cleveland in the late 1970s, had campaigned on a platform that included same-sex marriage rights as well as the decriminalization of marijuana and abortion rights, even though he had once opposed abortion. He had also supported single-payer health care, which Kennedy did not believe in because, he said, it relied too much on the government.

Sheinkopf said that during his first meeting with the Kennedy team, he had given them "the best advice I could" about how to run the campaign and spoken to them about needing to focus on key states such as New Hampshire, Massachusetts, Iowa, and South Carolina. But he felt that no one was really listening, and that Kucinich appeared disorganized. "In the end I wasn't interested," he said. "I didn't see how they could get organized. I didn't want to be part of a mess. It was not worth the chaos." His instincts proved to be prescient. Kucinich left his post as campaign manager on October 13, 2023, just six months after Kennedy's campaign speech in Boston in April, amid rumors of disorganization and a lack of direction in the campaign. Kucinich has never spoken publicly about his departure, although sources said that he didn't agree with Kennedy's support for Israel.

According to Kennedy, Kucinich didn't have the experience to turn his presidential run into a "billion-dollar" campaign.

Kucinich left as it was becoming increasingly impossible for Kennedy to compete as a Democrat and was poised to run as an independent candidate. For weeks he had accused the Democratic National Committee of "rigging" the primary against him. In his campaign literature, he criticized the DNC's decision not to hold debates between President Biden and other candidates. "We declare independence from the two political parties and the corrupt interests that dominate them, and the entire rigged system of rancor and rage, corruption and lies," he said at a rally in Philadelphia on October 9, 2023, when he withdrew from the Democratic primary. "I haven't made this decision lightly. It is very painful for me to let go of the party of my uncles, my father."

The majority of his family was quick to condemn him. Four of his siblings—Kathleen Kennedy Townsend, the former Maryland lieutenant governor; Kerry Kennedy; former Representative Joseph Kennedy; and filmmaker Rory Kennedy—released a statement that described Kennedy's independent run as "dangerous to our country," likely because he would split the Democratic vote in favor of former President Donald Trump. A poll had shown that in a three-way race, Biden would get 31 percent, Kennedy would get 14 percent, and Trump could win with 33 percent. "Bobby might share the same name as our father, but he does not share the same values, vision or judgment," the statement said. "Today's announcement is deeply saddening for us. We denounce his candidacy and believe it to be perilous for our country."

Weeks after his announcement an intruder was arrested twice on the same day for trespassing at the Kennedy-Hines home in Brentwood in late October 2023. A month earlier, an armed man was arrested when he showed up at a Los Angeles rally for Kennedy with loaded guns and was asking to see Kennedy. "During that time, I would stay dressed with my shoes on until I was ready to go to bed, just because I didn't know what was going to happen," said Hines in an interview with *The New York Post*.

The threats on his life and the opposition from some of his siblings didn't deter Kennedy. He moved on, hiring Bobby 3's wife, Amaryllis Fox, to head up his campaign. Fox was already a paid member of Kennedy's campaign team when he asked her to take over the campaign. She had married Bobby in 2018 and was the mother of his two children, Bobby, a girl, known in the family as Bobcat, and Cassius Watts Thoreau. She also had a child, Zoe, from a previous marriage.

Fox, a former CIA agent, had no experience running a political campaign, and many of Kennedy's inner circle found her an odd choice. "She's intelligent and she has a very high opinion of her intellectual abilities," said a source close to the campaign. Fox was born in New York City and attended private schools in Washington, DC, and London. An Oxford University graduate, she attended the Walsh School of Foreign Service at Georgetown University, where she majored in conflict and terrorism studies. She seemed to espouse many of the same values Kennedy admired: love of country and the Constitution, as well as a commitment to truth. At least that was what she wrote in a 2019 memoir, *Life Undercover: Coming of Age in the CIA*. Fox, who had lost a childhood friend in the terrorist bombing of Pan Am Flight 103 over Lockerbie, Scotland, described risking her life after 9/11 as an undercover agent posing as an art dealer to penetrate a network of Islamist extremists working to build a nuclear bomb in order to prevent a terrorist attack. She had dedicated the book, which had not been vetted by the spy agency, to "the women and men of CIA," whose work is "hard and mostly unrecognized" and for their "allegiance . . . to the truth" and the Constitution. She also dedicated the book to her mother.

Before her decade at the CIA, Fox had traveled to Thailand and Burma to work with opposition activists, who had arranged for her to do an interview with their leader, Aung San Suu Kyi. Fox, a high school student at the time, convinced a cameraman to record the interview and agreed to smuggle out the film rolled into a small plastic-wrapped cylinder that the pro-democracy leader instructed her to insert like a tampon to ensure that she would be able to smuggle it past the military police who would detain her after she left the pro-democracy activist's compound in Rangoon. The film made its way to the BBC, and Aung San Suu Kyi's message of hope to her clandestine supporters in Burma and abroad was broadcast around the world.

"Amaryllis is a woman of extraordinary intelligence and drive who I am confident will take this campaign to the next level," Kennedy wrote in a press release announcing her new role.

Fox had been introduced to Bobby 3 by mutual friends at the Burning Man festival in the Nevada desert in 2014. The marriage was considered a good match for Bobby 3, who had dabbled in acting and made a film about his family friend the gonzo journalist Hunter S. Thompson. The film, *Fear and Loathing in Aspen*, is based on Thompson's bizarre run for sheriff of Pitkin County in 1970. Shot on a shoestring budget in and around Silverton, a mountain town four hours south of Aspen, in 2018, the film featured his stepmother Cheryl Hines as Aspen Mayor Eve Homeyer and Fox as the journalist Peggy Clifford, who had encouraged Thompson to move to Aspen in 1963.

Fox and Bobby 3 married in a wedding reminiscent of his father's nuptials—at the Kennedy family compound in Hyannis Port, with a lobster and clam bake. Shortly after their wedding, they headed to Colorado to work on the film, which was released in 2021.

With Fox on board directing his campaign, Kennedy announced his independent run for president with his new running mate, Nicole Shanahan, a lawyer and Silicon Valley entrepreneur who had previously been married to Google cofounder Sergey Brin. While Shanahan, a billionaire who shared Kennedy's concerns about vaccines, was not opposed to them, she said that vaccine injuries should be openly discussed. "I think there needs to be a space to have these conversations," she said.

Shanahan's biggest contribution to Kennedy's campaign was to his super PAC American Values 2024. Shanahan gave more than

$4 million, which went toward a $7 million Super Bowl ad that created a great deal of controversy. Photos of Kennedy's face were superimposed on an ad that had been used in John F. Kennedy's run for president in 1960. The ad also used an old JFK campaign jingle. It drew immediate condemnation from Kennedy's cousin Bobby Shriver, who wrote on X, "My cousin's Super Bowl ad used our uncle's faces—and my Mother's. She would be appalled by his deadly health care views. Respect for science, vaccines, & health care equity were in her DNA."

Kennedy immediately apologized in his own post, noting that the ad had been created by the American Values PAC "without any involvement or approvals from my campaign." He noted that federal rules prevent the PAC from coordination with the campaign. The PAC had been founded by his publisher, Tony Lyons, and Mark Gorton, a hedge fund executive who supports Kennedy's views on vaccines and Children's Health Defense.

More than $11 million quickly poured into Kennedy's super PAC after he announced that he would be running as an independent. In addition to his family, environmental groups that feared that his presence in the race would only act as a spoiler for Donald Trump were quick to blast him. In an April 19, 2024, open letter to Kennedy, "Earth to RFK Jr.," published in various newspapers, Kennedy's old colleagues at the NRDC called his run for the presidency a "dangerous" and "vanity" candidacy. "For years, RFK Jr. has been spinning anti-vaccination conspiracy theories, denying science and putting lives at risk," said the letter signed by current and former colleagues and board members, including his old friend and fellow activist Laurie David, who later even attacked her old friend Cheryl Hines for "her best and most watched performance yet as the 'dutiful, adoring wife' setting women back decades."

Negative articles about Kennedy proliferated after he announced his independent run. A few weeks later, *The New York Times* reported about his "brain worm." Citing a deposition in his divorce proceedings from Mary, the newspaper reported that in 2010 he had been diagnosed with a dead parasite in his brain that was likely leading to bouts of memory loss and brain fogginess. Kennedy, who had been posting videos and photos of himself lifting weights and skiing to show that he was in good physical shape to be president, laughed off the story. Hours after the article was published, he posted on X, "I offer to eat 5 more brain worms and still beat President Trump and President Biden in a debate. I feel confident in the result even with a six-worm handicap." He later privately told *New York* magazine journalist Olivia Nuzzi that "a doctor he trusted had reviewed the scans of his brain obtained by *The New York Times*, he said, and concluded that the shadowy figure was likely not a parasite at all. He sighed. It was too late to interfere with what had already vaulted from the sphere of meme to the sphere of screwy legends . . ."

Following the brain worm incident, *The New Yorker* published a story of a road-killed bear that he had picked up in Westchester in 2014 and driven around in his van, eventually dumping it in Central Park after he had realized that he needed to catch a plane and still had the dead animal in his vehicle. He has long had a fascination with road-killed animals, which he picks up and stashes in a freezer so that he can study them later or feed them to his birds of prey. In a diary entry on November 11, 2001, he wrote about coming across one on a highway between Connecticut and New York. "I was standing in front of my parked car on I-684 cutting the penis out of a road killed raccoon, thinking how weird some of my family members have turned out to be," he wrote. For him, his cousin Bobby Shriver's and his brother Douglas's ability to hold on to "deep resentments" was its "own category of weird"—not slicing off a raccoon penis on the side of the road! "My kids waited patiently in the car."

But the Central Park bear story is perhaps more emblematic of Kennedy privilege and entitlement than any other. Kennedy reportedly told Nuzzi that leaving the bear in Central Park was a prank, a practical joke that recalled his mixing laxatives into the drinks at his brother David's birthday party following the assassination of their father. Still, he tried to get ahead of the story when he posted a video on X on August 4, 2024, telling Roseanne Barr that he had picked up the dead bear cub on the side of a highway in Goshen in upstate New York on his way to a falconry event. The idea for the media strategy came from Nuzzi, who advised him during his campaign, according to her own book *American Canto*. "How to handle such an unprecedented communication strait? My advice seemed sound to me," wrote Nuzzi. "'I guess if I were you, I would get ahead of the story.'"

Kennedy preempted *The New Yorker* magazine's big scoop. "I was going to skin the bear . . . and I was going to put the meat in my refrigerator," he told Barr. "And you can do that in New York State: Get a bear tag for a roadkill bear." New York State does allow for roadkill to be taken, provided authorities are notified. It's unlikely that Kennedy alerted authorities.

"This is a little bit of the redneck in me," he said in the video uploaded to X, going on to explain how he had developed a plan to dump the bear in Central Park along with an old bicycle he had in his van, taking advantage of numerous reports of bike accidents in the park. "The next day it was on every television station, it was on the front page of every paper, and I turned on the TV, and it was like miles of yellow tape, and there were twenty cop cars. There were helicopters flying. . . . And I was like 'Oh, my God, what did I do?'" In the video he made light of the whole affair, although he said, "I was worried because my prints were all over that bike."

It's unclear why city authorities didn't trace the fingerprints back to Kennedy.

But other than a necropsy of the six-month-old bear, the story became a kind of urban myth. Ironically, it was Tatiana Schlossberg, the daughter of Caroline Kennedy, who wrote the story of the bear for *The New York Times*. "But apart from the bear's age and weight—six months, 44 pounds—the cause of death was almost all anyone seemed to know, and almost all anyone was willing to say," she reported on October 7, 2014.

Kennedy was no stranger to "revelations" about his past spilling out, and he was certainly used to the shrill calls for him to end his campaign from groups backing the Democratic candidates, but he still faced an uphill battle to get his name onto the ballots of many battleground states. He faced numerous legal challenges, many of them bankrolled by the leaders of the Democratic Party, who wanted him off the ballots of as many states as possible to prevent him from splitting the vote in favor of Donald Trump.

Among the biggest blows to his campaign was a legal challenge in New York by Clear Choice, a Democratic super PAC. A group of New York residents backed by the group argued in New York Supreme Court that he had used a false New York address on his campaign petitions. New York was an important residency requirement for him because Shanahan had listed California as her residence. California has fifty-four electoral votes—the most in the country—and the campaign could lose them if both Kennedy and Shanahan listed California as their residence, according to the US Constitution, which sought to promote a national perspective and broad representation of candidates running for president and vice president. Despite living in California with his wife, Kennedy had claimed that he was living in New York while he was actually renting a bedroom in a home in Katonah and calling it his official residence. The case against him recalled the carpetbagging claims made against his father when he had run for senator in New York after living for years in Virginia. But the consequences for Kennedy proved more dire. New York Supreme Court Justice Christina Ryba called the bedroom a "sham address." In addition, Kennedy hadn't paid any rent to Barbara Moss, the owner of the Katonah property, nor did he have a lease for the room. He had begun paying for the room a day after the *New York Post* had raised questions about his arrangement in May 2024.

"The Court finds Kennedy's testimony that he may return to that bedroom to reside with his wife, family members, multiple pets, and all of his personal belongings to be highly improbable, if not preposterous," said Ryba in her August 13, 2024, ruling disqualifying him from the ballot. The US Supreme Court rejected his appeal a month later, by which time he had already made the decision to suspend his independent run. He hitched his wagon to that of Trump, who had been narrowly missed by a would-be assassin's bullet in Butler, Pennsylvania, in July. Although he had managed to get onto the ballot in twenty states, Kennedy promised to take himself off in swing states, where his presence could affect the election results.

Two days after the attempt on Trump's life, President Biden finally announced that Kennedy would be entitled to Secret Service protection.

In his speech backing Trump in Phoenix, he took numerous swipes against the once sacred party of his father and uncles, accusing Democratic leaders of abandoning the party's core principles. "Back then, the Democrats were the champions of the Constitution, of civil rights," he said. "The Democrats stood against authoritarianism, against censorship, against colonialism, imperialism, and unjust wars. The Democrats were the party of labor, of the working class. The Democrats were the party of government transparency and the champion of the environment. . . . I left that party in October because it had departed so dramatically from the core values that I grew up with. It had become the party of war, censorship, . . . Big Pharma, Big Tech . . . and big money. When it abandoned democracy by canceling the primary to conceal the cognitive decline of the sitting president, I left the party to run as an independent. The mainstream of American politics and journalism derided my decision."

In exchange for Kennedy's ending his presidential bid and backing Trump, the former president had promised him a seat at the most important table in the country—the president's cabinet—as secretary of health and human services. For Kennedy, the avid collector of presidential memorabilia who had been groomed by his surrogate father to lead, it was surely a dream come true.

That dream was on shaky ground, though. Less than a month

after he endorsed Trump for president, CNN reported that he had been involved in "an inappropriate relationship" with *New York* magazine reporter Olivia Nuzzi, who had spent time with him in California for a story that had appeared in the fall of 2023. Kennedy declared that he had only met Nuzzi once in person, but Nuzzi said that the inappropriate sexting relationship had gone on for a year.

Hines responded by ditching her wedding ring and heading to Europe for Milan Fashion Week with Kyra and her own daughter Catherine, where she celebrated her birthday without Kennedy on September 21. But the gesture was sheer theater. It's likely that Hines had known about Kennedy's dalliance with Nuzzi for months. She was writing a memoir, which was partly about her marriage. With her publisher, Tony Lyons, being a staunch supporter of her husband's political career, it's unlikely that she would have risked losing any part of her large advance for the book.

Hines made reference to the Nuzzi affair in her book, but never mentioned the reporter by name. She claims she decided to stay in Europe and "like many mothers do, I decided to table my breakdown until I was alone," she writes in *Unscripted*. "I didn't know what was going to happen when I returned home and saw Bobby again, but he was eager to talk to me. He picked me up from the airport and we pulled into a nearby parking lot and asked security if they could give us some privacy." The couple spoke for an hour and over the next few days "we stopped everything and drilled down on the truth," she said. "We locked ourselves in our room and laid it all on the table. . . . We went through all of the details about the last story—what was true and what wasn't. Through those soul-searching days, we tightened our ties that bind."

In her own book, Nuzzi claimed that Hines had been "hysterical" after reading the news of the sexting affair, and a public spat between the couple could upend Kennedy's chances at a cabinet seat two months away from the November election, she wrote. "It was fragile, the alliance with the president," wrote Nuzzi, referring to Kennedy's endorsement of Trump. "Nothing was certain. Any new problems could upend the whole thing."

After the wedding ring incident, Hines continued to support her husband, appearing every day at his difficult Senate hearings after the victorious Donald Trump appointed him as secretary of health and human services shortly after his electoral victory. Kennedy was ecstatic. While he wasn't going to be president of the United States as his uncle had been, he would be part of the president's cabinet, directing the country's health care policy. "Congratulations @realDonaldTrump on your historic victory," he posted on X on November 6, 2024. "Let's Make America Healthy Again."

During his Senate hearings for secretary of health and human services in early 2025, it was his old friends and colleagues who were perhaps his most vicious critics. "Frankly, you frighten people," said Sheldon Whitehouse, senator from Rhode Island, who had attended the University of Virginia Law School with him. While at law school, they had hunted, hiked, and gone on white water rafting excursions together. Kennedy had traveled to Virginia to attend Whitehouse's father's funeral in 2001.

Whitehouse was referring to a measles case in his state—the first in more than ten years. Before voting against his old friend, he noted in a press release, "Mr. Kennedy has not come remotely close to providing adequate assurances that he will follow the well-established science on vaccines, nor remedy the ways CMS [Centers for Medicare & Medicaid Services] hurts Rhode Island, so I cannot support his nomination."

Soon after Kennedy was confirmed by the Senate in a vote that was largely along party lines, he angered his critics even further by purging a vaccine advisory panel—a group of outside experts who advise the Centers for Disease Control and Prevention on vaccine schedules. Often, the group's recommendations determine which vaccines must be covered by insurance companies. For him, the group was corrupt because many of the experts had "received substantial funding from pharmaceutical companies, including those marketing vaccines." He also vowed to cut a quarter of HHS's bureaucracy of 82,000 employees.

In his determination to Make America Healthy Again, he convinced large food companies to remove dangerous dyes from a host of products and hired like-minded experts such as Casey Means to help formulate strategies to combat chronic diseases, such as the increasing rates of diabetes and obesity in children. He warned about toxic radiation levels in frozen shrimp, and he promised to study the effects of psychedelic drugs in therapeutic treatments, especially to help with depression and PTSD. In June 2025, he told Congress that psychedelics had a "tremendous advantage" in clinical settings.

Kennedy, the former heroin addict who claimed to faithfully attend AA meetings, allegedly still dabbled in psychedelic drugs for fun, according to Nuzzi's book. "He described how he waited until his wife was not home to go outside and smoke DMT [Dimethyltryptamine, a hallucinogenic drug], just as he waited until she was not home to call, or else he would call while locked in the bathroom."

In his swearing-in speech in the Oval Office, Kennedy, surrounded by his wife and some family members, thanked God for having sent him President Trump. He promised "radical transparency" and "getting rid of the people on those panels that have conflicts of interest." He also promised to get serious about child health, end the chronic disease epidemic, and help Trump return the American dream to Americans. "A healthy person has a thousand dreams," he said. "A sick person only has one. Sixty percent of our population has only one dream: that they get better."

EPILOGUE

A Work in Progress

In the years in which I have pored over Kennedy's diaries, straining to decipher his untidy collection of scribbles—the griffonage of the messy life that he sought to organize in those daily entries—I have often wondered whether he wrote with an audience in mind. This is a man who had been told his whole life that he could be president one day, that he was destined for greatness. While the diaries had been "a tool for self-examination and for dealing with my spiritual struggles," as he said when they first came to light more than a decade ago, they were surely also notes for the books he has written about himself and his family, further enshrining the vaunted Kennedy legacy while absolving himself of any real responsibility for the pain he has caused those closest to him and justifying his actions. "He thinks like a lawyer, creating evidence all the time," said a source close to the Kennedy family.

Maybe that's partly true. In more than 1,200 pages of journal entries, Kennedy meticulously chronicled all of his accomplishments—every speech, every eulogy—and made a point of listing by first and last names all the famous people he met, even those he had been seated next to at a random dinner or film premiere. And how easily those famous people invited Kennedy and his family on trips around the world and gave him lucrative speaking opportunities and seats on their boards. In many cases, he provided a short bio of those notable figures, who seemed to offer him the world. Maybe it was an effort to jog his memory should he reread his diary entries years later, but more often than not, I felt it was a reference for his reader.

For Kennedy, no achievement was too small: Every fish caught by him and his children was obsessively catalogued in his journals by type, size, and weight. He has long been obsessed with collecting things: seagull skulls, roadkill, and the presidential memorabilia showcased on a wall of his office in his old Westchester home. In his diary, he also listed payments he had received for speeches and worried about how much money he was making to support his wife and six children. But on the eve of his Senate hearings, his public disclosures indicated that he was a millionaire several times over. His disclosures showed more than $8.8 million earned from his law firm, Kennedy & Madonna, plus more than $850,000 from Wisner Baum, another law firm, for "referral fees on contingency cases" in 2024. In addition, there was a salary from yet another law firm—JW Howard Attorneys—of nearly $500,000 and another $326,000 from Children's Health Defense as well as more than $450,000 in consulting fees for finding new authors for his publisher, Skyhorse Publishing. Among those authors was his wife, Cheryl Hines, who received a $600,000 advance for *Unscripted*, a memoir about her life with Kennedy. The memoir, which detailed her acting career and her work for cerebral palsy research, was released in November 2025 but had some very stiff competition from *American Canto*, Olivia Nuzzi's tell-all about her sexually charged relationship with Kennedy, which was released a few weeks later.

But with all that cash came some serious liabilities for Kennedy and Hines, including credit card debt of more than $1 million and steep mortgages on their lavish home in California, which was likely why he insisted upon continuing to receive his contingency fees, especially from Wisner Baum, which is suing Merck over claims that the pharmaceutical giant did not properly warn consumers about its HPV vaccine. The litigation promises a huge payday for the law firm. "Upon confirmation, I will retain an interest in contingency cases that do not involve claims against the United States," he wrote in his financial disclosures released before his Senate hearings in January 2025. During the hearing, Kennedy said that he would give away his rights to any fees that might result from the cases.

Like the fish he caught and the money he made, Kennedy kept a list of the women he had bedded, mostly using only first names to describe them but including their full names if they were socially significant.

Women were easily attracted to the Kennedy scion. Shortly after endorsing President Trump in the summer of 2024, his sexting affair with *New York* magazine's Washington correspondent, Nuzzi, was publicly revealed after her fiancé, Ryan Lizza, broke off their engagement, citing what he described as her year-long affair with Kennedy in court papers. Nuzzi, who had written a profile of Kennedy for the magazine that appeared in November 2023, was placed on leave by *New York*'s editor after the affair came to light. Nuzzi, who is thirty-nine years younger than Kennedy, eventually left the magazine and spent the next year working on her memoir in Malibu. Kennedy has denied the affair and said through a representative that he had met with Nuzzi only once.

Nuzzi documents myriad FaceTime calls with Kennedy—a character she refers to as "the Politician" in her book. Among the "explicit poems" he wrote to her was one that began "I am a river. You are my canyon. I mean to flow through you. I mean to subdue and tame you. My Love."

Despite his fervent Catholicism and his three marriages, he hasn't been able to shake his addiction to women. He cheated on Emily Black with Mary Richardson before he married her and then cheated on her with Cheryl Hines. And by many accounts, his marriage to Hines is in trouble after his tryst with Nuzzi. In her memoir, Nuzzi described how he would turn down a photograph of Hines on his desk while they spoke on a video call.

During their eleven-year marriage, Kennedy seems to have drifted away from Hines. Sources say he no longer desires to spend much time with her, even as the couple made a show of moving into a lavish $4.45 million town house in Georgetown in the spring of 2025. In fact, Kennedy spends a lot of time in private conversations comparing Hines unfavorably to Mary, said a source. More than a decade after Mary's death, she is constantly in his thoughts, said the source. He speaks often about her beauty, her razor-sharp intellect, her sense of humor, her elegance, her grace. Only his political career and a possible presidential run—which he has denied that he will pursue—in 2028 is keeping him from formally separating from Hines. In death, Mary, born on the feast day of his beloved Saint Francis, has taken on a kind of saintly status for Kennedy. "There is no doubt that she was the greatest love of his life," the source said.

Despite the time that has passed since her death, Mary's friends and family continue to be furious with Kennedy, with one prominent jurist still in disbelief that he was actually granted permission by a judge to move his dead wife's body to a different part of the Centerville cemetery where many of the Kennedys are buried.

And while he may appear to have severed relations with his brothers and sisters after switching political allegiances, the strength of Kennedy family secrets has ensured an enduring bond with members of his immediate family. Kerry Kennedy, five years his junior, has publicly called on him to resign as secretary of health and human services after his firing of CDC director Susan Monarez in late August 2025. But it was Kennedy who had kept his younger sister's secret when she was having an affair with Bruce Colley—a relationship that had led to her divorce from Andrew Cuomo in the early aughts. And it was Kerry who had stood by Kennedy when he was going through his own very bitter divorce from Mary. And it was Kennedy who called up *New York Post* columnist Andrea Peyser to plead with her to go easy on his sister on the eve of her trial for driving under the influence in 2014.

Kennedy's dark side, the feral nature that some women told me they found irresistible, can also send him into a rage when he is challenged. Like a wild animal, he has been known to fight back savagely when he's cornered. "When he yelled, the soft flame of his voice roared a lithium fire, sparked anger that sparked anger and torched everything in its path," wrote Nuzzi in her memoir. "He yelled himself foreign. The man who yelled was not the man I thought I knew. The man who yelled was the man others had told me to fear."

That anger came to light at Riverkeeper and resulted in the resignation of his mentor, Robert Boyle. It arose during the divorce negotiations with Mary and their lawyers when he would menacingly wag his finger in her direction to make a point, and it surfaced more recently when he fired Monarez, whose appointment as CDC director lasted only twenty-nine days. During her second appearance before the Senate in September 2025 to answer questions about her firing, she described Kennedy as having been "very, very upset and very animated" when she had refused to do his bidding in approving directives from the White House regardless of whether the scientific evidence was flawed or not. Monarez, who has a PhD in microbiology and immunology, worried about the largest measles outbreak in thirty years, which had resulted in the death of a child, and worried that the country was unprepared for the next outbreak of diseases that are easily preventable. "If vaccine protections are weakened, preventable diseases will return," she said in her testimony. "I was fired for holding the line on scientific integrity."

Do the diaries reflect Kennedy's tortured soul, or are they covering up some deep truths? There were days when I admired his very intense soul-searching, the breadth of his knowledge of religion and philosophy, and his respect for the dead. He seemed never to miss a wake or a funeral, reaching out to a middle school friend when his father died and volunteering to act as pallbearer at others' funerals. Most recently, he flew to Boston in October 2025 to act as a pallbearer for the funeral of his aunt Joan Kennedy, who had spoken openly about her struggles with addiction and mental health after her divorce from Ted Kennedy in 1982.

Then there were other days when I felt he was just making excuses for his bad behavior and projecting a fiction of Kennedy family happiness. The diaries are full of joyful references to the Kennedy clan. "I've got the best family ever! . . . God bless us!" he wrote in 2001, going on to describes games of capture the flag, sailing, fishing, camping, and hunting for salamanders and fossils with a gaggle of children. There are few hints of the contretemps among different branches of the Kennedy family in the journals, although he does document a deep fissure between the Schlossbergs and his immediate family during the planning of the funerals of John F. Kennedy Jr.; his wife, Carolyn Bessette; and her sister Lauren. Perhaps it was one of the first signs that the Kennedys were in fact deeply divided, a division that grew into a yawning chasm and enabled Caroline Kennedy and her son, Jack Schlossberg, to make public her scathing letter to the Senate on the eve of Kennedy's hearings for secretary of health and human services at the beginning of 2025.

And if that wasn't enough to condemn him, Tatiana Schlossberg, Jack's older sister, slammed Kennedy in an article about her fight with leukemia. The article appeared in *The New Yorker* on November 22, 2025, the sixty-second anniversary of her grandfather's assassination in Dallas.

"As I spent more and more of my life under the care of doctors, nurses, and researchers striving to improve the lives of others, I watched as Bobby cut nearly half a billion dollars for research into mRNA vaccines, technology that could be used against certain cancers; slashed billions in funding from the National Institutes of Health, the world's largest sponsor of medical research; and threatened to oust the panel of medical experts charged with recommending preventive cancer screenings," wrote Tatiana Schlossberg, an environmental reporter who had previously written about the mystery of the dead bear cub in Central Park. She died in December 2025.

"There's a duality in him," said a close friend. "He can be open-minded until he chooses to close it all down. And he understands the incredible contradictions he presents."

The friend recalled Kennedy's reaction to a visitor to the Environmental Litigation Clinic at Pace University who suffered from Tourette's syndrome, a neurological disorder that causes involuntary bodily movements. As the young man jerked his head and shrugged his shoulders, displaying a host of uncontrollable tics, most of the students and lawyers in the office seemed to visibly shrink from him. All except Kennedy. "Bobby was the only one who engaged in a conversation, and he asked him about his Tourette's," the friend said. "The Tourette's kid was so delighted that someone was interested in him. One positive thing about Bobby, he was never put off by somebody's idea or belief."

As another example, the friend pointed to Kennedy's love for the southern United States where he had first traveled with his Harvard roommate Peter Kaplan to work on his undergraduate thesis in the 1970s. The friend marveled how the son of one of the biggest crusaders for civil rights could have made lifelong friends among "rednecks," former Alabama governor George Wallace, and Ku Klux Klan members, as well as the civil rights judge Frank Johnson and his extended family.

In the south, Kennedy had found people "rooted in their conviction that this country was great," he wrote in his diary. That passage, written while he was imprisoned in Puerto Rico in the summer of 2001, could have been among the first clues that he might slough off the Democrats, embrace the campaign to Make America Great

Again, and endorse a Republican for president more than twenty years later.

Robert Kennedy Jr. has spent his life trying to live up to the legacy of his father. He invokes his father in almost every speech he makes, often getting lost in a rambling family story or historic event that illustrates his dad's courage and wisdom. At seventy-two, he's likely still dealing with the trauma of his father's assassination. And he clearly views the man—much as the rest of the country and his own family do—as a saint. "My father's greatest gift to me was his character and values," he wrote in his diary on February 1, 2001. "In almost any moral dilemma I can always refer to my father. 'What would he have done here?' And I get the right answer."

After overcoming his heroin addiction, Kennedy resolved to do "something great" in the world, according to a friend. "He has always seen himself as a work in progress, working towards some big destiny," said the friend. "He's still in pursuit of it, and I'm sure there are days when he says to himself, 'What did I do to deserve this?'"

ACKNOWLEDGMENTS

On the afternoon of May 12, 2012, I was at my desk in the *New York Post* newsroom in midtown Manhattan when I answered a call from one of my sources. "Mary Kennedy is dead" came the alarmed announcement from the caller.

The name meant nothing to me, but as my source continued with their urgent, rapid-fire description of how she died, and where her body was found, I understood who Mary Kennedy was. From that moment, I began my research into the Kennedy family—a thirteen-year journey that has resulted in this book.

A year after Mary's death when the source handed me three volumes of Robert F. Kennedy Jr.'s diaries, I began writing about him for my newspaper. At first, I focused on his philandering, and on the eve of publication of that first article in September 2013, my editors and fellow reporter Melissa Klein debated why we would want to make public his sexual exploits. What public good were we serving? We came to the conclusion that the rumors of extramarital affairs had long dogged many of the Kennedy men, and here was definitive proof of their entitlement. None of us ever imagined that one day Robert Kennedy Jr. would run for president, and the diaries would suddenly provide important information about the candidate's moral code and behavior. Suddenly, after Kennedy announced his presidential run in April 2023, reporters for outlets such as *The New York Times* wanted a look at the diaries for insights into Kennedy's character.

Kennedy is anything but one-dimensional, as many of his detractors and family members insist upon describing him. He is heroic, and his life has been about overcoming great adversity and taking risks. But he is also entitled and deeply flawed. I set out to capture that duality.

Over the last year that I focused on writing this book, I was aided by numerous sources—many who have known Kennedy at different times of his life. Most of them wanted to remain anonymous.

Thank you to Melissa Klein, who helped me decipher the diaries, and the very patient librarians at *The New York Post*, for whom no research request was too obscure. A big thank-you to my fellow reporters and editors, past and present, including Shelly Ridenour, Andy Tillett, Hugh Dougherty, Margi Conklin, Paul McPolin, Steve Lynch, and Keith Poole. I am also grateful for our legal team at News Corporation, particularly the unflappable Genie Gavenchak, as well as the First Amendment attorneys at Davis Wright Tremaine, who have stood by me for years, on difficult stories too numerous to mention here. Thank you especially to Laura Handman and Adam Rich. I am also deeply grateful to Jesse Feitel at HarperCollins for all of his sound legal counsel.

A big thank-you to my agent Frank Weimann and everyone at HarperCollins, who believed in this book, particularly my editor Mauro DiPreta and Allie Johnston.

To my family and friends, scattered in Canada, the US, Brazil, and Europe, I can never say enough thank-yous. To Ray Dowd, an endless source of inspiration, wisdom, and love, my deepest gratitude.

And to my dear Hannah, whose poise, elegance, and many accomplishments continue to be my greatest rewards and sources of pride, thank you.

BIBLIOGRAPHY

Collier, Peter, and David Horowitz. *The Kennedys: An American Drama.* Simon & Schuster, 1984.
Cronin, John, and Robert F. Kennedy Jr. *The Riverkeepers: Two Activists Fight to Reclaim Our Environment as a Basic Human Right.* Charles Scribner's Sons, 1997.
Fox, Amaryllis. *Life Under Cover: Coming of Age in the CIA.* Alfred A. Knopf, 2019.
Hines, Cheryl. *Unscripted.* Skyhorse Publishing, 2025.
Kennedy, Christopher Lawford. *Symptoms of Withdrawal: A Memoir of Snapshots and Redemption.* HarperCollins, 2006.
Kennedy, Robert F., Jr. *American Values: Lessons I Learned from My Family.* HarperCollins, 2018.
Kennedy, Robert F., Jr. *Framed: Why Michael Skakel Spent over a Decade in Prison for a Murder He Didn't Commit.* Skyhorse Publishing, 2016.
Kennedy, Robert F., Jr. *Judge Frank M. Johnson, Jr.: A Biography.* G. P. Putnam's Sons, 1978.
Kennedy, Robert F., Jr. *The Real Anthony Fauci: Bill Gates, Big Pharma, and the Global War on Democracy and Public Health.* Skyhorse Publishing, 2021.
Kennedy, Robert F., Jr. *Saint Francis of Assisi: A Life of Joy.* Hyperion Books for Children, 2005.
Kennedy, Robert F., Jr., and Brian Hooker. *Vax-Unvax: Let the Science Speak.* Skyhorse Publishing, 2023.
Nuzzi, Olivia. *American Canto.* Avid Reader Press, 2025.
Oppenheimer, Jerry. *RFK Jr.: Robert F. Kennedy Jr. and the Dark Side of the Dream.* St. Martin's Press, 2015.
Oxenberg, Christina. *Trash: Encounters with Ghislaine Maxwell.* Self-published, 2021.
Pitts, David. *Jack and Lem, John F. Kennedy and Lem Billings: The Untold Story of an Extraordinary Friendship.* Grand Central Publishing, 2008.
Radziwill, Carole. *What Remains: A Memoir of Fate, Friendship & Love.* Scribner, 2005.
Rauch, Sheila Kennedy. *Shattered Faith: A Woman's Struggle to Stop the Catholic Church from Annulling Her Marriage.* Penguin Random House, 2013.
Schlesinger, Arthur M. Jr. *Robert Kennedy and His Times.* Houghton Mifflin, 1978.
Stein, Jean, and George Plimpton. *American Journey: The Times of Robert Kennedy.* Harcourt Brace Jovanovich, 1970.
Wilson, Robin. *Kennedy Green House: Designing an Eco-Healthy Home from the Foundation to the Furniture.* Greenleaf Book Group, 2010.

NOTES

PREFACE: "JUST LIKE THE PRESIDENT"

xi *"He lacks any relevant government":* Caroline Kennedy to Senators Crapo, Wyden, Cassidy, and Sanders, January 28, 2025, https://static01.nyt.com/newsgraphics/documenttools/43900493f7c3ca36/abcd0d91-full.pdf.

xii *"trading in on Camelot":* Peter Baker, "Anguish in Camelot: Kennedy Campaign Roils Storied Political Family," *New York Times*, August 6, 2023.

xii *"With global measles cases surging":* Y. Tony Yang, "The Perils of RFK Junior's Anti-vaccine Leadership for Public Health," *Lancet*, January 11, 2025.

xiii *And then, in an unforgivable betrayal:* Katherine Koretski, Ben Kamisar, Henry J. Gomez, Garrett Haake, and Dasha Burns, "RFK Jr. Suspends Campaign, Endorses Trump," NBC News, August 23, 2024.

xiii *"Bobby always aroused":* Author interview with source, June 20, 2025.

xiv *"for insurance":* Mary Richardson's statement that she wanted diaries for "insurance" and the meanings of the ledgers from source interview with the author, May 17, 2012.

xv *"The diary served as a tool":* Isabel Vincent and Melissa Klein, "Diary Bombshell: RFK's Slams Against Al Sharpton, Jesse Jackson and Gov. Cuomo," *New York Post*, September 9, 2013.

xv *reporter Olivia Nuzzi:* Mara Siegler, Anna Young, and Chris Nesi, "Olivia Nuzzi Said RFK Jr. Wanted to 'Possess and Impregnate Her' During Sexting Tryst, Her Ex Claims," *New York Post*, October 15, 2024.

xv *a former family babysitter:* Joe Hagan, "RFK Jr.'s Family Doesn't Want Him to Run. Even They May Not Know His Darkest Secrets," *Vanity Fair*, July 2, 2024.

xvi *"even coming into their bedrooms":* Cari Beauchamp, "Two Sons, One Destiny," *Vanity Fair*, January 4, 2012.

xvi *Joe Kennedy had a well-documented affair:* Cari Beauchamp, "Two Sons, One Destiny," *Vanity Fair*, December 2004.

xvi *"three girls to every man":* Ibid.

xvi *"I bought the ticket":* Robert F. Kennedy Jr., diary, July 25, 2001.

xvi *"Still trying to be a political and moral force":* Robert F. Kennedy Jr., diary, October 14, 2000.

xvii *"The thing that scares me most in life":* Robert F. Kennedy Jr., diary, May 21, 1999.

NOTES / 249

xvii *"My father, when he died":* Robert F. Kennedy, deposition in *Robert F. Kennedy v. Mary Kennedy,* February 3, 2012.

xviii *"He's just like the president":* Peter Collier and David Horowitz, *The Kennedys: An American Drama* (Simon & Schuster, 1984), 360.

xix *"It is our right":* Robert F. Kennedy speech, "Sen. Robert F. Kennedy Presidential Campaign Announcement," CBS News Special Report, March 16, 1968, rebroadcast on C-SPAN3.

xix *"I never vote for the party":* Robert F. Kennedy Jr., *American Values: Lessons I Learned from My Family* (HarperCollins, 2018), 155.

xx *"I wouldn't be a reliably liberal senator":* Mark Jacobson, "American Jeremiad," *New York,* February 2, 2007.

xx *"I live my life one day at a time":* Robert F. Kennedy Jr., interview with Roger Ailes, *Straightforward,* May 1995, https://www.youtube.com/watch?v=EU32wrSptwE

xxi *"I don't think he is inherently malicious":* Jolie Lash, "Fauci Rips 'Very Disturbed' RFK Jr.'s Attacks on His Career: 'It's a Shame Because He's a Kennedy,'" Yahoo! News, December 22, 2021, https://www.yahoo.com/entertainment/dr-fauci-says-rfk-jr-215315616.html.

xxi *"rooted in honesty, transparency":* Robert F. Kennedy Jr.'s March 15, 2021, letter to President Joe Biden was reproduced on the website of Children's Health Defense, March 17, 2021.

xxi *"It took me a long time":* "Incoming HHS Secretary Robert F. Kennedy Jr. Deep Dive, Part One—On Fauci, Vaccines and Big Pharma," *The Megyn Kelly Show,* November 27, 2024.

xxii *"He had wrappers all over":* Author interview with source, June 10, 2025.

xxii *caught for speeding by a trooper:* Robert F. Kennedy Jr., diary, July 11, 1999.

xxiii *"I felt close to these people":* Robert F. Kennedy Jr., diary, July 25, 2001.

xxiii *"For 20 years, I've gotten up":* "Remarks During a Swearing-in Ceremony for Robert F. Kennedy, Jr., as Secretary of Health and Human Services and an Exchange with Reporters," The American Presidency Project, February 13, 2025, https://www.presidency.ucsb.edu/documents/remarks-during-swearing-ceremony-for-robert-f-kennedy-jr-secretary-health-and-human.

xxiv *"The true disciples are often found":* Robert F. Kennedy Jr., diary, July 8, 2001.

xxiv *"I've been thinking about heroics lately":* Robert F. Kennedy Jr., diary, July 12, 2001.

xxiv *"There's a deeper aspect to him":* Author interview with source, June 20, 2025.

xxiv *"When people look at his position":* Author interview with source, June 20, 2025.

xxv *"It's his family-driven mission":* Ibid.

xxv *"Bobby might share the same name as our father":* Rory Kennedy, Kerry Kennedy, Hon. Joseph P. Kennedy II, Kathleen Kennedy Townsend, "Statement on Robert F. Kennedy Jr.'s Announcement Today," October 9, 2023, @KerryKennedyRFK on X.

xxv *"Other people's opinions of me":* Author interview with source, June 20, 2025.

CHAPTER 1: PRISON DIARY

3 *"You're being defiant":* Richard Lezin Jones, "Kennedy Gets Noted Defense, and 30 Days," *New York Times,* July 7, 2001.

4 *"While arch-rival Sharpton languishes":* Peter Noel, "Jesse Jackson: The Desperate Hours," *Village Voice,* July 3, 2001.

6 *"By the end of the day":* Arthur M. Schlesinger Jr., *Robert Kennedy and His Times* (Houghton Mifflin, 1978).
9 *"packed with journalists and photographers":* Robert F. Kennedy Jr., "Why Are We in Vieques?," *Outside,* January 10, 2001.
10 *"The sounds and odors of gunpowder":* "Puerto Ricans Vow to Avenge Death in US Prison," *New York Times,* November 18, 1979.
13 *"Really, I escaped my cell phone":* "RFK Speaks Out Against Bombing on Vieques," CNN, August 3, 2001, https://www.cnn.com/2001/US/08/03/robert.kennedy.jr.cnna.
14 *befriended the monk's mentor:* Thomas Spencer, "Thomas Merton and the Kennedys," Thomas Merton Center at Bellarmine University, undated.
14 *"Bobby's tragic immolation":* Thomas Merton, letter to Ethel Kennedy, June 22, 1968, Thomas Merton Center at Bellarmine University, Merton Center Digital Collections.
15 *"We ask the court to recall":* Jones, "Kennedy Gets Noted Defense, and 30 Days."
16 *In fact, he was able to spend:* Jones, "Kennedy Gets Noted Defense, and 30 Days."
17 *the guard had tears in his eyes:* Mary Mcgrory, "Credibility Behind Bars," *Washington Post,* July 28, 2001.
17 *"Vieques" as one of his middle names:* Mcgrory, "Credibility Behind Bars."

CHAPTER 2: "HISTORY WAS HAPPENING ALL AROUND US"

19 *thinking about a career in public service:* Robert F. Kennedy Jr., interview with Roger Ailes, *Straightforward,* May 1995, https://www.youtube.com/watch?v=EU32wrSptwE.
20 *"he looked me over very carefully":* James A. Oesterle, "Oral History Interview with Roy Cohn, March 24, 1971, The Robert F. Kennedy Oral History Program of the Kennedy Library.
21 *"I'm really going to get":* Ibid.
21 *In Cohn's recollection of events:* Roy Cohn, recorded interview by James A. Oesterle, March 24, 1971, Robert F. Kennedy Oral History Project of the John F. Kennedy Library Oral History Program.
21 *"In later years when he had become a 'liberal'":* Ibid.
21 *"My dad believed":* Robert F. Kennedy Jr., *American Values: Lessons I Learned from My Family* (HarperCollins, 2018), 146.
22 *"Pointing at Teamster bosses":* Kennedy, *American Values,* 147.
22 *"Teamsters backfiring in front of our house":* Robert F. Kennedy Jr., diary, July 25, 2001.
22 *do something useful instead:* Peter Collier and David Horowitz, *The Kennedys: An American Drama* (Simon & Schuster, 1984), 357.
22 *The home was decorated with shrines:* Robert F. Kennedy Jr., *Saint Francis of Assisi: A Life of Joy* (Hyperion Books for Children, 2005).
23 *"when my dad was AG":* Robert F. Kennedy Jr., diary, November 20, 2001.
24 *his Marine One helicopter:* John Cronin and Robert F. Kennedy Jr., *The Riverkeepers: Two Activists Fight to Reclaim Our Environment as a Basic Human Right* (Charles Scribner's Sons, 1997), 82.
25 *"Call Bobby, get together with him":* Anthony Lewis, "Robert Kennedy Begins One-Month Goodwill Trip Around World," *New York Times,* February 2, 1962.

25 *"Bobby is a very attractive human being":* Walter Lippman on Robert Kennedy. Lippmann made the statement on June 7, 1962, on "CBS Reports," in CIA Freedom of Information Act vault, July 21, 2000.
26 *"I have no great desire":* J.H. Meredith letter to the US Justice Department, February 7, 1961, John F. Kennedy Library.
28 *"There is nothing in the neutrality laws":* Robert F. Kennedy in a Department of Justice press release, April 20, 1961, National Archives.
29 *"We didn't see my dad":* Kennedy, *American Values*, 235.
30 *"If this country means anything":* Robert F. Kennedy speech, April 25, 1963, John F. Kennedy Library.
30 *"Governor, I'm not interested in a show":* Claudia Sitton, "Governor Leaves; But Fulfills Promises to Stand in Door and to Avoid Violence," New York Times, June 12, 1963.
30 *"When I was growing":* Mark Jacobson, "American Jeremiad," *New York*, February 2, 2007.
31 *"Justice Douglas took us kids":* Cronin and Kennedy, *The Riverkeepers*, 86.
31 *"One winter a contingent of Alaskan Inuit":* Cronin and Kennedy, *The Riverkeepers*, 86.
31 *presenting a salamander to his uncle:* Photo of meeting with John F. Kennedy, AR6420-C, President John F. Kennedy with Robert Kennedy Jr. at the John F. Kennedy Presidential Library and Museum.
32 *"the American male was still cut":* Life magazine staff, "Strike—Fury of a Wounded Whale," *Life*, December 21, 1962.
34 *"No maybe about it":* Referenced by Rebecca Aizin, "Ethel Kennedy and RFK Were Married for 18 Years. Here's the Story of Their Romance—and Why She Never Remarried After His Death," *People*, October 10, 2024.
34 *"one of the prettiest of the year":* Staff writer, "Ethel Skakel Bride of Robert Kennedy," *Boston Globe*, June 17, 1950.
35 *the "runt" of the Kennedy family:* "From 'Runt of the Litter' to 'Liberal Icon': The Story of Robert Kennedy," NPR, July 5, 2016, https://www.npr.org/2016/07/05/484780316/from-runt-of-the-litter-to-liberal-icon-the-story-of-robert-kennedy.
35 *"He was somebody who didn't seem to stand out":* Interview with Larry Tye, "From 'Runt of the Litter' To 'Liberal icon': The Story of Robert Kennedy," NPR, July 5, 2016.
35 *The affair caused a rift in his marriage:* Cari Beauchamp, "Two Sons, One Destiny," *Vanity Fair*, December 2004.
37 *"It was like being drafted":* Beauchamp, "Two Sons, One Destiny."
39 *"There's so much bitterness":* Quoted in Alan Brinkley, "Conspiracy?," *New York Times*, May 20, 2007.
39 *a controversial stop in Communist Poland:* "Kennedy's Visit Jolts Regime in Poland; His Appeal to the Crowds Breaks the Carefully Established Rules of U.S.-Polish Relations," *New York Times*, July 5, 1964.
40 *"Mr. Kennedy had lunch":* "Kennedy Meets Polish Cardinal; Talks Are Held in Spite of Warning from Warsaw," *New York Times*, July 1, 1964.
40 *Kennedy thanked the Polish government:* Robert F. Kennedy, Statement on Departure from Poland, July 1, 1964, https://www.justice.gov/sites/default/files/ag/legacy/2011/01/20/07-01-1964.pdf.

42 *"I believe it is appropriate":* Lester B. Pearson named a mountain after Kennedy in the House of Commons Debates, 26th Parliament, 2nd Session, November 20, 1965, p. 10305.

42 *It was a huge public relations coup:* "Bobby Kennedy Climbs Mount Kennedy," *Whitehorse Daily Star*, March 24, 1965.

42 *the heel of a bottle of Madeira:* Whitehorse staff, "Bobby Kennedy Climbs Mt. Kennedy," *Whitehorse Star*, March 23, 1965.

CHAPTER 3: "EVERYBODY TAKES THEIR LICKS"

44 *He faced "almost solid opposition":* Commentary by Roger Mudd, Robert F. Kennedy Presidential Campaign Announcement, CBS News, March 16, 1968, C-SPAN.

46 *"He identified with people who hurt":* Fred Dutton, quoted in Jules Witcover, "Witcover; Memories of Robert Kennedy," *Baltimore Sun*, June 7, 2019.

46 *hours holding him around the waist:* Oral interview, March 19, 1969, RFK Library, RFK Box #1, March 19, 1969.

46 *"It was as though he had prepared himself":* Jules Witcover cited in Timothy Denevi, "The Last Days of Robert F. Kennedy," Literary Hub, June 4, 2018.

47 *"I kneeled down to him":* Laurel Walmsley and Emily Sullivan, "Juan Romero, Who Cradled Dying RFK, Dies at 68," Northwest Public Broadcasting, October 4, 2018, https://www.nwpb.org/national/2018-10-04/juan-romero-who-cradled-dying-rfk-dies-at-68.

47 *"My father lay on a gurney":* Robert F. Kennedy Jr., *American Values: Lessons I Learned from My Family* (HarperCollins, 2018), 347.

48 *"hellish environment":* Peter Collier and David Horowitz, *The Kennedys: An American Drama* (Simon & Schuster, 1984), 354.

49 *"No one came after him":* Jack Newfield, quoted in Steven M. Gillon, "Inside RFK's Funeral Train: How His Final Journey Helped a Nation Grieve," History, June 7, 2021, https://www.history.com/articles/robert-f-kennedy-death-funeral-train.

50 *"He was alone":* Kathleen Kennedy, quoted in Reginald Stuart, "Robert Kennedy's Son David Found Dead in Hotel," *New York Times*, April 26, 1984.

51 *Lem was gay:* David Pitts, *Jack and Lem: John F. Kennedy and Lem Billings: The Untold Story of an Extraordinary Friendship* (Da Capo Press, 2007), 3.

52 *"That boy is just like Jack":* Lem Billings, quoted in Collier and Horowitz, *The Kennedys*, 342.

53 *"Plans for the big trip":* "Bobby Jr. in Africa," *Life*, February 14, 1969.

55 *"When I first saw him":* Peter Jenny, interview with the author, June 4, 2025.

56 *"We talked about hawks every spare moment":* John Cronin and Robert F. Kennedy Jr., *The Riverkeepers: Two Activists Fight to Reclaim Our Environment as a Basic Human Right* (Charles Scribner's Sons, 1997), 88.

57 *"the country's most admired woman":* Staff writer, "The Kennedy of Hickory Hill," *Time*, April 25, 1969.

57 *"How could I possibly do that":* Rebecca Aizin, "Ethel Kennedy and RFK Were Married for 18 Years. Here's the Story of Their Romance—and Why She Never Remarried After His Death," *People*, October 10, 2024.

58 *"Ethel's special triumph":* A profile of Ethel Kennedy as well as information about how she was managing the household at Hickory Hill appeared in "People; April 25, 1969," *Time*, April 25, 1969.

59 *"Lem used to take us to lunch":* Author interview with Peter Jenny, June 4, 2025.
60 *he took great pains to "set the record straight":* Robert F. Kennedy Jr., *American Values*, 384.
62 *"the most disorganized student":* Robert F. Kennedy Jr., *American Values*, 380.
62 *"For two dollars per week":* Cronin and Kennedy, *The Riverkeepers*, 89.
62 *"For forty-four years":* Ena Bernard's relationship with the Kennedy children is described in Kennedy, *American Values*, 163, and in Cronin and Kennedy, *The Riverkeepers*, 80.
63 *Jack Kennedy was fond of calling Ena a "saint":* Robert F. Kennedy Jr., diary, August 17, 1999.
63 *Ena was fearless:* Cronin and Kennedy, *The Riverkeepers*, 123, 166.
64 *"We taught each other how to shoot drugs":* Robert F. Kennedy Jr., diary, August 30, 2000.
64 *"We were with them all summer":* Cynthia McCormick, "Pamela Kelley Burkley Fought for Disability Rights," *Cape Cod Times*, December 3, 2020.
64 *"You had a great father":* "Joseph Kennedy Is Found Guilty of Negligence in Road Mishap," *New York Times*, August 21, 1973.
64 *Ethel visited Pam and David every day:* Collier and Horowitz, *The Kennedys*, 399.
65 *She broke her silence:* Liz McNeil, "The Tragedy and Triumph of Teen Paralyzed in Kennedy Car Crash in 1973, Who Lived Nearly 50 More Years," *People*, December 3, 2020.
65 *"Don't pretend to understand me":* Collier and Horowitz, *The Kennedys*, 374.
65 *"Buildings melted like wax candles":* Kennedy's first LSD experience is described in Kennedy, *American Values*, 383.
66 *"I know them and I think they know me":* Mark Jacobson, "American Jeremiad," *New York*, February 2, 2007.
66 *"It was Bobby who got him involved with drugs":* Jerry Oppenheimer, *RFK Jr.: Robert Kennedy Jr. and the Dark Side of the Dream* (St. Martin's Press, 2015), 265.
66 *"When Bobby came to the door":* Joanne Brode, quoted in Collier and Horowitz, *The Kennedys*, 385–86.
67 *Lazell was an expert on amphibians:* Frank Carini, "Rhode Island Zoologist Spent Lifetime Finding Rare Species While Watching Human Population Swell," ecoRI News, October 2, 2017, https://ecori.org/2017-10-2-rhode-islander-finds-rare-species-while-carefully-watching-prolific-reproducer.
68 *"Population has been a hot topic":* Ibid.
69 *"My adolescence went on until I was 29":* Jacobson, "American Jeremiad."

CHAPTER 4: "I BOUGHT THE TICKET; I TOOK THE RIDE"

70 *"I have watched him over assert himself":* Lem Billings, letter for Rhodes Scholarship, quoted in Peter Collier and David Horowitz, *The Kennedys: An American Drama* (Summit Books, 1984), 424.
70 *"I was so angry in my early life":* Robert F. Kennedy Jr., diary, May 16, 1999.
71 *"The dealer was Bobby Kennedy":* Kurt Andersen, "RFK Jr. Was My Drug Dealer," *Atlantic*, August 23, 2024.
72 *the "Bhutto leap":* Collier and Horowitz, *The Kennedys*, 388.
72 *"I write about events of our trek":* Blake Fleetwood, "Skiing the Andes—and Drawing Fire from the Border Patrol," *New York Times*, November 11, 1973.

73 *"It's great to be out"*: "Kennedy in Frankfurt After Hijacking," *New York Times*, February 24, 1972.
75 *"I can't do it the way they did"*: Collier and Horowitz, *The Kennedys*, 402.
75 *"I feel it is my destiny"*: Ibid., 409.
75 *"The trips with Uncle Bobby were exciting"*: Christopher Kennedy Lawford, *Symptoms of Withdrawal: A Memoir of Snapshots and Redemption* (HarperCollins, 2006), 212.
75 *Kennedy appointed himself the leader*: Lawford, *Symptoms of Withdrawal*, 86.
75 *"Bobby Jr. was the king"*: Ibid.
76 *In a diary that Fleetwood kept of the trip*: Collier and Horowitz, *The Kennedys*, 405.
76 *they got onto a plane to Cuzco*: Lawford, *Symptoms of Withdrawal*, 213.
76 *"Whenever he did this"*: Ibid.
77 *"We floated by Indian villages"*: Ibid., 214.
77 *"They had tied up along the bank"*: Mary Thornton, "Kennedy Chronicles: The Controversy over a New Book on the Clan," *Washington Post*, June 13, 1984.
77 *thrown into the river*: Lawford, *Symptoms of Withdrawal*, 406.
78 *"Nobody in the family had heard from us"*: Ibid., 215.
78 *"We came to the South loaded"*: Robert F. Kennedy Jr., *Judge Frank M. Johnson, Jr.: A Biography* (G. P. Putnam's Sons, 1978), 28.
79 *"still plenty of residues of racism"*: Robert F. Kennedy Jr., diary, July 25, 2001.
79 *"I found people who were sentimental"*: Ibid.
79 *"Tears filled his eyes"*: Ibid.
79 *"I spent a lot of time with Governor Wallace"*: Robert F. Kennedy Jr., *American Values: Lessons I Learned from My Family* (HarperCollins, 2018), 202.
81 *"I went down South"*: Herbert Mitgang, "Johnson Is Focus of Timely Book," *New York Times*, August 27, 1977.
82 *"who encouraged me to complete and publish my work"*: Kennedy, *Judge Frank M. Johnson, Jr.*
82 *"caste system"*: Ibid., 12.
83 *"Robert Kennedy Jr. writes about this decent"*: Kennedy, *Judge Frank M. Johnson, Jr.*, 16–17.
83 *"a plodding, disjointed analysis"*: Howell Raines, "Heroic Rulings," *New York Times*, July 30, 1978.
83 *his Harvard classmate Peter Kaplan*: Jerry Oppenheimer, "RFK Jr., His Brilliant Harvard Roommate and the Mystery of Who Really Wrote His A+ Thesis," *New York Post*, July 10, 2023.
83 *On a visit to the state legislature*: Collier and Horowitz, *The Kennedys*, 410–11.
84 *when he had helped Peter Shapiro*: David Wildstein, "How Peter Shapiro Won," *New Jersey Globe*, July 22, 2019.
84 *a move "that set off seismic shifts"*: David Waldstein, "Peter Shapiro, Former Essex County Executive and Gubernatorial Candidate, Dies at 71," *New Jersey Globe*, March 29, 2024.
84 *he started dating Rebecca Fraser*: Collier and Horowitz, *The Kennedys*, 426.
85 *Fairley's legs were blown off*: Bernard Weinraub, "Bomb Kills a Doctor near London Home of Caroline Kennedy," *New York Times*, October 24, 1975.
86 *He lived in Montgomery*: Collier and Horowitz, *The Kennedys*, 439.
86 *"I don't know about everybody else"*: David Pitts, *Jack and Lem: John F. Kennedy and*

Lem Billings: The Untold Story of an Extraordinary Friendship (Da Capo Press, 2007), 262.
87 *"Lem's house was more than a fun house":* Pitts, *Jack and Lem*, 156–57.
87 *"He felt pain for every one of us":* Collier and Horowitz, *The Kennedys*, 445.
88 *"She is lovely":* Albin Krebs and Robert Mcg. Thomas Jr., "Notes on People; Wedding Plans for Robert Kennedy Jr.," *New York Times*, October 12, 1981.
88 *"After law school":* John Cronin and Robert F. Kennedy Jr., *The Riverkeepers: Two Activists Fight to Reclaim Our Environment as a Basic Human Right* (Charles Scribner's Sons, 1997), 90.
88 *As a prosecutor:* Barbara Goldberg, "Now It's ADA John F. Kennedy Jr.," UPI, August 20, 1989.
89 *"She's interested in keeping people out of jail":* Albin Krebs and Robert Mcg. Thomas Jr., "Notes on People; Kennedy Honeymoon; Robert Kennedy Jr. and Bride Off to Caribbean," *New York Times*, April 5, 1982.
89 *"a women's lib advocate":* Cited in "Robert Kennedy Jr. Says He's a 'Women's Lib Advocate,'" UPI, April 5, 1982.
90 *"He wanted assistance":* "Robert F. Kennedy Jr. Was 'White as a Sheet,'" UPI, September 25, 1983.
90 *It was Walsh whom Kennedy called:* Tom Lawrence, "Walsh Wonders What Happened to His Friend RFK, Jr.," *Black Hills Pioneer*, November 26, 2024.
91 *"I have admitted myself to the hospital":* Cronin and Kennedy, *The Riverkeepers*, 90.
91 *Kennedy pled guilty to the felony charge:* "Robert Kennedy Jr. Pleads Guilty in Heroin Case," UPI, February 17, 1984.
91 *Kennedy's "candor and honesty":* Wayne Heck, "RFK Jr. Gets Suspended Sentence on Drug Charge," UPI, March 16, 1984.
92 *"the lowest form of journalism":* B. Drummond Ayres Jr., "A Troubled Kennedy Makes Last Trip Home," *New York Times*, April 27, 1984.
92 *the Kennedys had turned against David:* Jennifer Waters, Michael Kirkpatrick, and David Horowitz, "An Interview with David Horowitz," *Columbia: A Journal of Literature and Art*, no. 12 (1987): 95.
92 *"dragged his family's name through the mud":* Ibid.
92 *The family was so desperate to rein David in:* Collier and Horowitz, *The Kennedys*, 458.
92 *Despite his addiction:* Ibid., 452.

CHAPTER 5: THE RIVERKEEPER

93 *"My arrest generated tremendous publicity":* John Cronin and Robert F. Kennedy Jr., *The Riverkeepers: Two Activists Fight to Reclaim Our Environment as a Basic Human Right* (Charles Scribner's Sons, 1997), 90.
93 *"Sobriety is about long term commitment":* Robert F. Kennedy Jr., diary, May 21, 1999.
94 *"The purpose of life":* Ibid.
94 *"Following my arrest and my recovery":* Cronin and Kennedy, *The Riverkeepers*, 90.
94 *"I was in the first generation":* Roger Rosenblatt, "Fresh Water: Let Rivers Run Deep," *Time*, August 2, 1999.
96 *"operated like a lightweight cavalry unit":* Cronin and Kennedy, *The Riverkeepers*, 69.
98 *"From the outset Boyle's style was combative":* Ibid., 23.

98 *In a settlement negotiated by the oil giant:* Associated Press, "Exxon Is Sued by New York over Use of Hudson Water," *New York Times*, April 26, 1984.
99 *"He showed up wearing shit-kicker boots":* Author interview with source, June 20, 2025.
99 *His two-year probation was over:* David W. Dunlap and Jane Perlez, "A Quiet Victory for Robert F. Kennedy, Jr.," *New York Times*, June 4, 1985.
99 *"conveyance for industrial and municipal waste":* Cronin and Kennedy, *The Riverkeepers*, 101.
100 *One local developer:* Ibid., 97.
100 *"At that moment I knew I wanted to be an environmental lawyer":* Ibid.
101 *"Our offer put the city government":* Cronin and Kennedy, *The Riverkeepers*, 98.
101 *"We were able to stall the vote in city council":* Ibid., 112.
101 *"The results of the Quassaick Creek cases":* Ibid., 111.
103 *"I have enough friends and family":* Jacques Steinberg, "A Son Sees Reflection in the Water; Kennedy Scion Shuns Public Office for Beloved Reservoirs," *New York Times*, February 13, 1995.
103 *"Nobody else was talking to him":* Encounter with Mario Cuomo at Andrew's bachelor party Jacques Steinberg, "A Son Sees Reflection in the Water; Kennedy Scion Shuns Public Office for Beloved Reservoirs," *New York Times*, February 13, 1995.
103 *"Andrew could win because he is totally focused":* Robert F. Kennedy Jr., diary, January 1, 2001.
104 *"Bobby was never part of the negotiations":* Author interview with Dan Ruzow, June 11, 2025.
105 *speculated about how much of Amy Fisher's urine:* Steinberg, "A Son Sees Reflection in the Water."
105 *"He was very ambitious":* Author interview with Marilyn Gelber, June 11, 2025.
106 *"They all thought Bobby was a lunatic":* Author interview with Dan Ruzow, June 12, 2025.
107 *"Kennedy saw Riverkeeper as a way":* Author interview with Alex Boyle, January 27, 2025.
108 *"People used to choose the Kennedys":* Sara Rimer, "The 1994 Campaign; Kennedy's Wife Is Giving Him a Political Advantage in a Difficult Contest," *New York Times*, September 24, 1994.
108 *"In 1993 my former husband":* Sheila Rauch Kennedy, *Shattered Faith: A Woman's Struggle to Stop the Catholic Church from Annulling Her Marriage* (Pantheon Books, 1997), 1.
109 *"We had a true and valid marriage":* Scott Malone, "Ex-Kennedy Wife Says Vatican Overturns Annulment," Reuters, August 9, 2007.
110 *"Mary was as talented with the left side":* Laurence Leamer, "Exclusive: The Last Days of Mary Kennedy," *Newsweek*, June 11, 2012.
110 *remembered Mary as a detail-oriented:* Jen Just, www.maryrk.org memorial page, August 11, 2012, https://web.archive.org/web/20120827192907/http://maryrk.org/remembrances/.
110 *Another friend, Diana Kellogg:* Diana Kellogg, wwwmaryrk.org memorial page, October 5, 2012, https://web.archive.org/web/20120827192907/http://maryrk.org/remembrances/.
111 *"Fred thought Mary would be a good assistant":* Author interview with Bob Colacello, June 25, 2025.

NOTES / 257

113 *"His one true love":* Anonymous, www.maryrk.org memorial page, June 10, 2012.
113 *"in terrible trouble":* "Carlos Mavroleon, Freelancer, Killed in Peshawar, Pakistan, August 27, 1998," Committee to Protect Journalists, https://cpj.org/data/people/carlos-mavroleon.
113 *"She was always so kind":* Nicholas Mavroleon, www.maryrk.org memorial page, August 2, 2012, https://web.archive.org/web/20120827192907/http://maryrk.org/remembrances/
113 *"She was a contrarian":* Author interview with source, June 10, 2025.
114 *Kennedy "fell deeply in love" with Mary:* Robert F. Kennedy Jr., affidavit, September 16, 2011.
115 *"This is my fifth":* Nadine Brozan, "The Newest Kennedy, William Finbar, Joins the Clan," *New York Times,* November 13, 1997.
116 *"I've been given everything":* Robert F. Kennedy Jr., diary, August 5, 2001.

CHAPTER 6: "THE SIRENS WERE ON EVERY ROCK"

118 *"Someone should have edited this book":* James Gorman, "River Patrol," *New York Times,* November 16, 1997.
118 *"Michael, now is the time to fight":* Nancy Gibbs, "The Kennedy Family: Tragedy Strikes Again," *Time,* January 12, 1998.
119 *the babysitter refused to cooperate:* Sara Rimer, "A Kennedy Faces the Fallout from a Scandal," *New York Times,* July 10, 1997.
120 *the scene of so many Kennedy weddings and baptisms:* David McPherson, "Family, Friends Mourn Michael Kennedy," *Cape Cod Times,* January 3, 1998.
120 *"I ask now only that we look at Michael truly":* Excerpts from the eulogy by U.S. Rep. Joseph P. Kennedy III for his brother, Michael," *Cape Cod Times,* January 1, 1998.
121 *"I feel bad for John":* Robert F. Kennedy Jr., diary, May 15, 1999.
121 *"A partnership based on vigilance and the law":* Roger Rosenblatt, "Fresh Water: Let Rivers Run Deep," *Time,* August 2, 1999.
122 *"Cronin and the board are doing nothing":* Robert F. Kennedy, diary, March 7, 1999.
122 *"My father considered it":* Author interview with Alex Boyle, June 20, 2025.
122 *Kennedy wrote about having dinner:* Robert F. Kennedy Jr., diary, February 25, 1999.
123 *"I was struck by how small Willis was":* Robert F. Kennedy Jr., diary, February 24, 1999.
124 *"I rode 12 to 15 waves":* Robert F. Kennedy Jr., diary, February 26, 27, 28, 1999.
124 *"Roger and I gave lectures":* Robert F. Kennedy Jr., diary, March 3, 1999.
124 *"I made it through a difficult week":* Robert F. Kennedy Jr., diary, June 19, 1999.
125 *"This is how she gets in the summer":* Robert Kennedy Jr., diary, May 7, 8, 9, 1999.
126 *"She did it to embarrass and hurt me":* Robert Kennedy Jr., diary, May 30, 1999.
126 *"I couldn't be trusted with any of her children":* Robert Kennedy Jr., diary, May 30, 1999.
127 *"He definitely gaslit her":* Author interview with source, June 10, 2025.
127 *"She was just 200 percent invested":* Author interview with source, November 23, 2012.
127 *"She loved being a Kennedy":* Author interview with source, June 10, 2025.
129 *"Conor saw him the same time I did":* Robert F. Kennedy Jr., diary, June 24, 1999.
129 *"Mary is being impossible":* Robert F. Kennedy Jr., diary, June 25, 1999.
130 *"Demerol refused":* Robert F. Kennedy Jr., diary, July 9, 1999.

130 *"The passions against my father were equal"*: Randal C. Archibold, "Robert Kennedy Jr. Endorses Hillary Clinton," *New York Times*, September 7, 2000.
131 *"It's a way to access a culture"*: Anita Gates, "Television/Radio; A Filmmaker Now Known for Two Families," *New York Times*, November 28, 1999.
131 *"does a good job of showing us"*: Stephen Holden, "Film Review; A Family United by Home and Want," *New York Times*, May 26, 1999.
131 For the Kennedys, the links to the past: Robert F. Kennedy Jr., diary, May 26, 1999.
132 *"This has been a difficult year for our family"*: Robert F. Kennedy Jr., diary, July 15, 1999.
133 *"This event, and the culture"*: Alex Kuczynski, "Washington Memo; A Melding of Extremes at Correspondents Dinner," *New York Times*, May 3, 1999.
134 *"He has trouble refinancing"*: Robert F. Kennedy Jr., diary, July 15, 1999.
134 *"Mary and I resolved"*: Robert F. Kennedy Jr., diary, July 16, 1999.
135 *"Other pilots flying similar routes"*: Joseph E. (Jeb) Burnside, "Revisiting JFK, Jr.," *Aviation Safety*, December 27, 2019.
136 The NTSB later determined: Burnside, "Revisiting JFK, Jr."
136 The bickering over the bodies: Robert F. Kennedy Jr., diary, July 15–30, 1999.
140 *"Judge Johnson, really through his courage"*: Associated Press, "Judge Johnson Buried in the Alabama Hills," July 28, 1999.

CHAPTER 7: "THINGS FALL APART"

143 *"Her eulogy was beautiful"*: Robert F. Kennedy Jr., diary, August 13, 1999.
144 *"I'm really in despair"*: Robert F. Kennedy Jr., diary, August 14, 1999.
145 New York's watershed agreement: Robert F. Kennedy Jr., diary, September 15, 1999.
145 *"walking on eggshells"*: Robert F. Kennedy Jr., diary, August 30, 1999.
145 *"He wonders, as do I"*: Robert F. Kennedy Jr., diary, September 19, 1999.
146 *"My defects are like weeds"*: Robert F. Kennedy Jr., diary, August 17, 1999.
146 *"was unrecognizable"*: Robert F. Kennedy Jr., diary, August 24, 1999.
147 Although Mary was trying to deal: Robert F. Kennedy Jr., diary, May 20, 1999.
147 *"He looked like a playboy"*: Robert F. Kennedy Jr., diary, September 22, 1999.
148 At the fundraiser two months later: Matea Gold, "Gore Outlines Plan for Environmental Spending," *Los Angeles Times*, November 12, 1999.
148 *"There is no American political leader"*: CBSNews.com staff, "Gore Gets a Kennedy Nod," CBS News, February 28, 2000, https://www.cbsnews.com/news/gore-gets-a-kennedy-nod.
148 *"She doesn't seem angry"*: Robert F. Kennedy Jr., diary, October 4, 1999.
149 *"Kyra is so sociable and fun"*: Robert F. Kennedy Jr., diary, August 20, 1999.
150 When he had put his older children: Robert F. Kennedy Jr., diary, August 29, 1999.
150 *"Mary is very upset"*: Robert F. Kennedy Jr., diary, April 17, 1999.
151 *"Riverkeeper has always had clean hands"*: Robert Worth, "A Kennedy and His Mentor Part Ways over River Group," *New York Times*, November 5, 2000.
151 flush the chicks down the airplane toilet: Peter Jamison, "How RFK Jr. Hiring a Bird Smuggler Threw His Environmental Group into Turmoil," *Washington Post*, March 2, 2024.
152 *"The meeting was at the lawyer's office"*: Author interview with source, January 23, 2025.
153 *"What we've succeeded in doing now"*: Worth, "A Kennedy and His Mentor Part Ways over River Group."
156 *"I nearly drowned, actually"*: William J. Clinton, "Remarks at a Dinner for Guber-

natorial Candidate Lieutenant Governor Kathleen Kennedy Townsend of Maryland in Hyannis Port, Massachusetts," August 5, 2000, The American Presidency Project, https://www.presidency.ucsb.edu/documents/remarks-dinner-for-gubernatorial-candidate-lieutenant-governor-kathleen-kennedy-townsend.

157 *"Clinton was breathtaking as usual":* Robert F. Kennedy Jr., diary, August 5, 2000.
157 *remarks about the Kennedy matriarch, Ethel:* Clinton, "Remarks at a Dinner for Gubernatorial Candidate Lieutenant Governor Kathleen Kennedy Townsend of Maryland in Hyannis Port, Massachusetts."
158 *"I got my three minutes":* Robert F. Kennedy Jr., diary, August 15, 2000.
158 *"She's written terrible stuff about us":* Robert F. Kennedy Jr., diary, August 16, 2000.
159 *"struggling to keep my thoughts pure":* Robert F. Kennedy Jr., diary, August 28, 2000.
160 *"Every time I've walked into an AA meeting":* Robert F. Kennedy Jr., diary, August 30, 2000.
160 *The Kennedys endured another near tragedy:* Robert F. Kennedy Jr., diary, October 26, 27, 28, 2000.
162 *"The Gods and Fates were plotting his destiny":* Robert F. Kennedy Jr., diary, November 29, 2000.
163 *as he flew to Vail:* Robert F. Kennedy Jr., diary, November 26, 2000.

CHAPTER 8: "MY VOICE IS GONE"

165 *"When visitors with hacking coughs":* Robin Wilson, *Kennedy Green House: Designing an Eco-Healthy Home from the Foundation to the Furniture* (Greenleaf Book Group, 2010), xx.
166 *"I defended the Clintons":* Robert F. Kennedy Jr., diary, January 29, 2001.
167 *The Rich pardon was so radioactive:* Andrea Bernstein, "At Private Lovefest in a Shoe Store, a Cuomo Declares for Governor," *Observer*, February 5, 2001.
167 *"I thought of it":* Robert F. Kennedy Jr., diary, January 28, 2001.
167 *"Upstairs, shoved between racks of micro-mini shorts":* Bernstein, "At Private Lovefest."
168 *"It's being billed as a brilliant political move":* Robert F. Kennedy Jr., diary, January 31, 2001.
169 *The year started on a somber note:* Robert F. Kennedy Jr., diary, January 31 and February 1, 2001.
170 *"Sheldon delivered a fantastic eulogy":* Robert F. Kennedy Jr., diary, June 30, 2001.
170 *"I told him I'd never done":* Robert F. Kennedy Jr., diary, May 5, 2001.
170 *"The tragedy of Martha Moxley's death":* Robert F. Kennedy Jr., "A Miscarriage of Justice," *Atlantic*, January–February 2003.
171 *He had begun having difficulties:* Robert F. Kennedy, deposition in *Robert F. Kennedy v. Mary Kennedy*, February 3, 2012.
171 *He had also been diagnosed:* Robert F. Kennedy Jr., diary, May 20, 1999.
171 *"My voice is gone":* Robert F. Kennedy Jr., diary, May 20, 2001.
173 *When he failed to secure assistance:* Robert F. Kennedy Jr., diary, January 16, 2001.
173 *"My goal is not to have it stopped":* Raymond Hernandez, "Both Sides Attack Bush Plan to Halt Bombing on Vieques," *New York Times*, June 15, 2001.
174 *"My face looks like a teenager's":* Robert F. Kennedy Jr., diary, August 10, 2001.
174 *"Our family is exactly the opposite of yours":* Ibid.
176 *"He's running a good union":* Steven Greenhouse, "Teamsters Seek to End U.S. Oversight," *New York Times*, September 9, 2001.

176 *"I've got the best family ever!"*: Robert F. Kennedy Jr., diary, August 16, 2001.
176 *"Kyra insisted that she be in Kick's film"*: Robert F. Kennedy Jr., diary, August 11, 2001.
177 *Kyra, who was six years old*: Robert F. Kennedy Jr., diary, August 29, 2001.
177 *Earlier, while still in prison*: Robert F. Kennedy Jr., diary, July 13, 2001.
179 *"Our president fled to Nebraska"*: Robert F. Kennedy Jr., diary, September 11, 2001.
181 *polo with members of the British royal family*: Richard Johnson, "Polo 'Playboy' Was Kerry's Other Man—Bizman & Wife Vacationed with Cuomos," *New York Post*, July 4, 2003.
181 *allegedly involved with Kennedy*: Jane MacIntosh, "RFK Jr. 'Bedded' Heartbroken-wife of Sister's Loverboy: Sources," *New York Post*, May 25, 2012.
182 *"It wasn't totally random"*: Author interview with Sarah Bridges, January 25, 2025.
184 *"My family basically migrated into this state"*: Micah Leith, "In Depth: How West Virginia Plays a Role in Robert F. Kennedy, Jr.'s Presidential Plans," WOAY, January 30, 2024, https://woay.com/in-depth-how-west-virginia-plays-a-role-in-robert-f-kennedy-jr-s-presidential-plans.
184 *"sloshed through deep mud"*: "Kennedy in West Virginia," *New York Times*, April 29, 1964.
185 *As he continued his crusade*: Barry Werth, "Somewhere Down the Crazy River," *Outside*, May 2, 2004.
185 *"If you ever run for president"*: Ibid.
186 *Mary, who had trained as an architect*: Wilson, *Kennedy Green House*, xii.
186 *according to court documents*: Kennedy, deposition.
186 *"My children, accustomed to the bedlam"*: Wilson, *Kennedy Green House*, 2010, xiii.
187 *"We all reduced our fees"*: Ibid., 7.
187 *Contractors and vendors donated their services*: Isabel Vincent and Melissa Klein, "RFK Jr. and Late Wife Didn't Pay for Many of Renovations to Make Westchester Mansion Eco-friendly," *New York Post*, October 28, 2012.
187 *"He didn't think he should pay for anything"*: Author interview with source, October 25, 2012.
187 *Mary called up Franken*: Isabel Vincent and Melissa Klein, "RFK Jr. and Late Wife asked Al Franken to Help Them Receive No-Cost Home Renovations: Designer," *New York Post*, November 4, 2012.
188 *"Cheryl was introduced to Bobby by Larry"*: Author interview with source, November 23, 2012.
189 *"I had developed a special friendship with Bobby's sixteen-year-old daughter Kyra"*: Cheryl Hines, *Unscripted* (Skyhorse Publishing, 2025), 137.
189 *"completely shattered"*: Author interview with source, November 23, 2012.
189 *"It wasn't a private place for her and the kids"*: Author interview with source, October 25, 2012.
189 *It didn't take long for Mary's private life*: Katie Ryan O'Connor, "Updated: Kennedy Wife Arrested for DWI in Westchester," *Patch*, May 19, 2010, https://patch.com/new-york/harrison/reports-kennedy-wife-arrested-for-dwi-in-westchester-3.
190 *"Bobby used it all against her"*: Author interview with source, November 23, 2012.

CHAPTER 9: VACCINE WARRIOR

191 *"Mary presented as someone"*: Author interview with source, June 10, 2025.
193 *"a very important project"*: Nicholas Mavroleon, www.maryrk.org memorial page,

August 2, 2012, https://web.archive.org/web/20120827192907/http://maryrk.org/remembrances/.
193 *"Mary was waiting and hoping for Bobby":* Author interview with source, November 23, 2012.
193 *"She was petrified of his wagging finger":* Author interview with source, October 15, 2025.
193 *According to the Bedford Police report:* Town of Bedford Police Report, May 16, 2012 BP-008222-12.
193 *arrived unexpectedly:* Author interview with source, May 17, 2012.
193 *interrupting an evening session:* Author interview with source, May 23, 2012.
193 *he wrote in the 2011 document:* M. J. Lee, "Report: RFK Jr. Says Wife Abused Him," *Politico*, June 11, 2012, https://www.politico.com/story/2012/06/report-rfk-jr-says-wife-abused-him-077268.
196 *a private funeral was held:* Peter Applebome, "At a Kennedy's Funeral, Friends and Family Focus on the Lives She Touched," *New York Times*, May 19, 2012.
197 *"The mood there was quite hostile":* Author interview with source, June 19, 2025.
198 *a high-powered private investigation firm:* Isabel Vincent and Melissa Klein, "Investigators Looking into 'Unanswered Questions' About Mary Richardson Kennedy's Suicide," *New York Post*, November 25, 2012.
199 *"Kerry's been instrumental":* Andrea Peyser, "RFK Jr. Goes to Bat for Sister Ahead of Trial," *New York Post*, February 23, 2014.
199 *"I know Bobby well enough":* Author interview with source, June 20, 2025.
200 *Peter Kaplan's death from lymphoma:* Joe Pompeo, "Hundreds Gather in Tribute to the Late, Great Peter Kaplan," *Politico*, December 5, 2014, https://www.politico.com/media/story/2014/12/hundreds-gather-in-tribute-to-the-late-great-peter-kaplan-003181.
201 *"She has an incredible career":* Robert F. Kennedy on *The Megyn Kelly Show*, March 22, 2022.
202 *he had started dating Hines:* Bob Woletz, "No Curbs on Their Enthusiasm," *New York Times*, August 3, 2014.
202 *Still, they made plans to elope:* Cheryl Hines, *Unscripted* (Skyhorse Publishing, 2025), 155.
204 *"They said that if I was serious":* Rita Shreffler, "Environmental and Humanitarian Legend RFK Jr., Mainstream Media and the Very Corrupt CDC," Children's Health Defense, https://childrenshealthdefense.org/about-us/mercury-vaccines-cdcs-worst-nightmare.
205 *"I was dumbstruck":* Alexi Mostrous, "How a Kennedy Became a 'Superspreader' of Hoaxes on COVID-19, Vaccines, 5G and More," *Globe and Mail*, September 16, 2020.
206 *"On a recent trip to Standing Rock":* Robert F. Kennedy Jr., Waterkeeper Alliance, November 16, 2016.
207 *"He broke with Riverkeeper":* Author interview with Alex Boyle, January 28, 2025.
207 *Kennedy and Bigtree, among other CHD "warriors":* Del Bigtree, foreword, Robert F. Kennedy Jr. and Brian Hooker, *Vax-Unvax: Let the Science Speak* (Skyhorse Publishing, 2023), xv, xvi.
210 *"I got to a place where I had to see Sirhan":* "RFK Jr. Seeks Investigation into His Father's Assassination," CBS News, May 28, 2018, https://www.cbsnews.com/news/robert-kennedy-jr-seeks-investigation-father-assassination-sirhan-sirhan.

211 *"Yes, he did shoot me"*: Richard Sandomir, "Paul Schrade, 97, Who Was Wounded When Robert Kennedy Was Slain, Dies," *New York Times*, November 13, 2022.
213 *It was Peter Kaplan who had encouraged*: Robert F. Kennedy Jr., *Framed: Why Michael Skakel Spent over a Decade in Prison for a Murder He Did Not Commit* (Skyhorse Publishing, 2016), xii.
214 *"all the objectivity of* The Protocols of the Elders of Zion*"*: Theodore Dalrymple, "What's Up, Doc?," *Claremont Review of Books*, Summer 2022.
214 *"And the thing that makes it even more painful"*: Jolie Lash, "Fauci Rips 'Very Disturbed' RFK Jr.'s Attacks on His Career: 'It's a Shame' Because He's a Kennedy," *The Wrap*, December 22, 2021, https://www.thewrap.com/dr-fauci-rfk-jr-shame-kennedys-disturbed-individual.
215 *"Even in Hitler's Germany"*: "Robert F. Kennedy Jr. Invokes Nazi Germany in Offensive Anti-Vaccine Speech," CNN, January 24, 2022.
215 *"We can bow down and comply"*: Robert F. Kennedy Jr., *The Real Anthony Fauci: Bill Gates, Big Pharma, and the Global War on Democracy and Public Health* (Skyhorse Publishing, 2021), 446.
216 *"I saw how it was affecting her life"*: Caitlin Moscatello, "Robert F. Kennedy Jr. Wants to Be President. Cheryl Hines Is Along for the Ride," *New York Times*, June 10, 2023.

CHAPTER 10: "THEY HAD NO CLUE WHAT THEY WERE DOING"

219 *"I'm not an ideal presidential candidate"*: Robert Kennedy Jr. Announces 2024 Presidential Campaign, C-SPAN, April 19, 2023.
220 *"the one place that they couldn't censor me"*: Clare Malone, "What Does Robert F. Kennedy, Jr., Actually Want?," *New Yorker*, August 5, 2024.
222 *"I support Bobby"*: Caitlin Moscatello, "Robert F. Kennedy Jr. Wants to Be President. Cheryl Hines Is Along for the Ride," *New York Times*, June 10, 2023.
223 *"had no clue what they were doing"*: Author interview with Hank Sheinkopf, June 24, 2025.
227 *"During that time I would stay dressed"*: Sara Nathan, "Cheryl Hines Opens Up About Her Marriage—and Affair Allegations," *New York Post*, November 23, 2025.
227 *"She's intelligent and she has a very high opinion"*: Author interview with source, October 9, 2025.
228 *based on Thompson's bizarre run for sheriff*: John Wenzel, "Bobby Kennedy III Lands $300K to Shoot Hunter S. Thompson Movie in Colorado," *Denver Post*, December 15, 2016.
229 *"setting women back decades"*: Jacob Bryant, "Larry David's Ex-Wife Trolls Cheryl Hines for 'Setting Women Back Decades' with Her 'Dutiful, Adoring' Support of RFK Jr.," Yahoo News, January 31, 2025.
230 *"a doctor he trusted"*: Olivia Nuzzi, *American Canto* (Avid Reader Press, 2025), 145.
230 *Following the brain worm incident*: Robert F. Kennedy Jr., diary, November 11, 2001.
231 *"How to handle such an unprecedented"*: Nuzzi, *American Canto*, 166.
231 *"But apart from the bear's age"*: Tatiana Schlossberg, "Bear Found in Central Park Was Killed by a Car, Officials Say," *New York Times*, October 7, 2014.
234 *Hines made reference to the Nuzzi affair in her book*: Cheryl Hines, *Unscripted* (Skyhorse Publishing, 2025), 288.

NOTES / 263

235 *"It was fragile":* Nuzzi, *American Canto,* 157.
236 *"He described how he waited":* Olivia Nuzzi, *American Canto,* p. 149.

EPILOGUE: A WORK IN PROGRESS

237 *"He thinks like a lawyer":* Source interview with author, November 11, 2025.
239 *Nuzzi documents:* Nuzzi, *American Canto* (Avid Reader Press, 2025), 166.
241 *"When he yelled":* Nuzzi, *American Canto,* 250.
243 *"As I spent more and more of my life":* Tatiana Schlossberg, "A Battle with My Blood," *The New Yorker,* November 22, 2025.
243 *"There's a duality in him":* Source interview with the author, June 20, 2025.
243 *"rooted in their conviction that this country was great":* Robert F. Kennedy Jr., diary, July 25, 2001.

INDEX

Achebe, Chinua, 146
adolescence, of RFK Jr. *See also* education
  David and cousin drug use, 63–64
  falconry interest, 55–56, 65
  Hyannis Port Terrors formation, 63
  jeep accident with brother, Joe, 64–65
  Lem as surrogate father during, xviii, 51, 52, 62, 87, 219
  practical jokes after RFK Sr., death, 50–51, 65, 230–31
  troubled relationship with his mother, Ethel, 58–59
Africa trip, of Lem and RFK Jr., 51, 52
  RFK Jr., sale of pictures and text to *Life*, 53–54
Aidan. *See* Kennedy, Aidan Caomhán
Ailes, Roger, xx, 19
Alabama
  Johnson, F., segregation abolishment in, 80–81
  RFK Jr., stay in Hayneville, 79–80
  RFK Jr. as college student in, xxiii, 18, 78–79
  segregation attempt in University of Alabama, 29–30, 78–79
Albright, Madeleine, 142–43
Alcoholics Anonymous meetings, of RFK Jr., 93, 145, 160
American Canto (Nuzzi), 231, 238
American Hollow (documentary), of Rory, 130–31
American Values (RFK Jr.), 26, 221
  on arrest for spitting ice cream in police officer's face, 60
  on troubled relationship with his mother, Ethel, 58–59

Anastos, George, 64
Andersen, Kurt, 71
ANWR. *See* Arctic National Wildlife Refuge
Apurimac River rafting trip, Peru
  The Kennedys portrayal of, 77
  Lawford, David, Spooner, Stroud, Fleetwood on, 75–77
  of Lem and RFK Jr., 74–77
Arctic National Wildlife Refuge (ANWR), 175
Arlington National Cemetery, JFK and RFK Sr., burial at, 49
Armstrong, Karen, 13
Army-McCarthy hearings, RFK Sr., plan to attack Cohn at, 20–21
arrests, of RFK Jr.
  for heroin possession in 1982, 89–91
  for selling marijuana to undercover cop, 60
  on spitting ice cream in police officer's face, 60
  threatening police officer, 65
assassination, of JFK, xix, 23
  Morgenthau with RFK Sr., when Hoover called about, 38, 88
  National Archives release of original casket, 131–32
  RFK Sr., response to, 38–39
assassination, of RFK Sr., xvii, xviii–xix
  Cesar as possible second gunman, 211
  children brought to hospital, 47
  close friends and family at hospital, 47–48
  emergency neurosurgery, 47
  Ethel refusal to remarry after, 57

INDEX / 265

RFK Jr., on second gunman for, 210–11
RFK Jr., remembrance of death and
    funeral, 47–49
  Rory birth after, 56–57
  by Sirhan, xxii, 46–47, 210–12
  train and Arlington National Cemetery
    burial, 48–49
assassination attempt and paralysis, of
    Wallace, 80
Australia, Caroline as former ambassador
    to, xi
autism, vaccine-related, xiii, 181–83, 204–5

Bacall, Lauren, 31
Bad Boy lion cub, of RFK Jr., 54–55
Bailey, Mark, 121, 132–35
Barnett, Ross, 27
Barry, Bill, 46
Bay of Pigs operation (April 1961), 27–28
Beck, Dave, 22
de Becker, Gavin, 223–25
Belafonte, Harry, 31
Bennett, Joan, 107
Bernard, Ena, 62–63
Berrios, Ruben, 8, 9
Bessette, Carolyn. *See* Kennedy, Carolyn
    Bessette
Bessette, Lauren, 138
Bhutto, Murtaza, 72
Biden, Joe, 226
Bigtree, Del, 207
Billings, Kirk LeMoyne "Lem"
  absent in Ted presidential campaign, 86
  Africa trip with RFK Jr., 51–54
  Apurimac River in Peru rafting trip with
    RFK Jr., 74–75
  death of, 87
  drug use with RFK Jr., 74, 86
  Egypt trip with RFK Jr., 54–55
  as JFK friend in school, 51
  Joe reference to as son, 51–52
  Palfrey Street School enrollment for
    RFK Jr., 66
  RFK Jr., recommendation for Rhodes
    Scholarship at Oxford University, 70
  as surrogate father to RFK Jr., xviii, 51,
    52, 62, 87, 219
  visit with RFK Jr., at Millbrook, 59
Black, Emily. *See* Kennedy, Emily Black
Bobby III or Bobby 3. *See* Kennedy, Robert
    Francis, III
Bobby Sr. *See* Kennedy, Robert F., Sr.

Bonaparte, Napoleon, Schom biography
    of, 13
Bouvier, Jacqueline. *See* Kennedy,
    Jacqueline Bouvier
Boyle, Robert Hamilton, Jr., 107, 122, 146,
    241
  of HRFA and Hudson Preservation
    Conference, 96
  Riverkeepers and Wegner, 151–53
Brawley, Tawana, 7
Bridges, Sarah, xxi, 182–83, 203–4
Brode, Joanne, 66–67
Brown v. Board of Education (1954), on
    illegal segregation, 26
Buddha (Armstrong), 13
Burgos, Norma, 2–4, 16
Bush, George W., 159, 168
  RFK Jr., lack of respect for September
    11, 179
  on stop to Vieques bombings, 173–74
Buttafuoco, Joey, 104
Buttafuoco, Mary Jo, 104

Caroline. *See* Kennedy, Caroline
Carolyn. *See* Kennedy, Carolyn Bessette
Carter, Jimmy, 5–6
Castro, Fidel, xix
  Bay of Pigs operation to topple, 28
  Operation Mongoose to undermine, 28
Catskill Watershed Corporation, Ruzow
    of, 104
Cavendish, William "Billy," Kick marriage
    to, 102
  death of, 102
CDC. *See* Centers for Disease Control and
    Prevention
Centers for Disease Control and
    Prevention (CDC)
  conference on vaccinations safety, 205
  RFK Jr., purge of vaccine advisory panel
    of, 235–36
Centers for Medicare and Medicaid
    Services (CMS), Whitehouse, S.,
    concern for RFK Jr., lack of support
    for, 235
Cesar, Thane Eugene, 211
Chappaquiddick, Kopechne drowning at,
    xxv, 60–61, 86
Chavez, Cesar
  Kennedy family relationship with, 6
  RFK Sr., presidential campaign support,
    45

Cheryl. *See* Kennedy, Cheryl Hines
Chicago Merchandise Mart, Joe ownership of, 35–36, 139, 162
childhood, of RFK Jr.
  Bad Boy lion cub for, 54–55
  on Bernard as nanny, 62–63
  birth of, 19
  Caroline on, xxi
  in Colombia on ranch, 62
  description of idyllic, 22
  falconry interest, xviii, 31–32
  Hickory Hill mansion, 22–23, 26, 30–31, 58
  Hyannis Port memories, 23–24
  interest in animals and nature, 31–33
  JFK death remembrance, 38–39
  JFK presidential campaign memories, 25–26
  Jimmy sea lion gift, 31–32
  listening to Hyannis Port meetings, 26
  powerful adults relationships, 30–31
  public service ambition, 19
  requirement to read current affairs, 22
  RFK Sr., assassination and funeral remembrances, 47–49
  at RFK Sr., Senate hearings, 21–22
  Udall meeting, 31
Children's Health Defense, anti-vaccine group, xxi, 203
  Meta shut down for medical misinformation, 220
  RFK Jr., work for, 206, 208
Chile, RFK Jr., and Fleetwood shot at during ski trip in, 72–74
Civil Rights Act (1964), 41
Clean Water Act (1972), Tuck Tape company violations of, 95
Clear Choice legal challenge, to RFK Jr., independent presidential candidacy, 232–33
Clearwater Initiative, of Seeger, 95
Clearwater sloop, of Seeger, 95
Clinton, Bill, xx, 156–57
  impeachment of, 147
  at John Jr., funeral, 139
  Lewinsky affair, 147
  Pardongate controversy, 165–67
  RFK Jr., criticism of, 165–66
  Vieques bombings temporary halt by, 10
Clinton, Hillary, xx
  ask for RFK Jr., political support, 129–30
  as critic of Sharpton and Jackson, Jesse, 7

  at John Jr., funeral, 139
  visit to RFK Jr., in prison, 3, 17
Clinton, Roger, Jr., 166
Close, Glenn, 176, 188–89
CMS. *See* Centers for Medicare and Medicaid Services
coal and coke business, of Skakel, G., Sr., 33–34
Cochran, Johnnie, 4
Cohn, Roy
  pursuit of Communists in US Army, 21
  RFK Sr., friction with, 20
  as Trump mentor, 20
Colacello, Bob, 111
Coles, Robert, 82
Colley, Ann, 181
Colley, Bruce, 181, 240
Collier, Peter, 77
  David interview with, 91–92
Collins, Francis, 208
Communism
  Cohn pursuit of Communists in US Army, 21
  MLK connection to, xxv, 25
  RFK Sr., focus on, xix, 20–21
  Rosenberg, E., and Rosenberg, J., prosecution and execution, 20
Communist Poland, RFK Sr., controversial trip to, 39–41
Congress in Massachusetts, JFK run for, 38
Conor. *See* Kennedy, Conor
Consolidated Edison power plant, on Hudson River, 96–97
Corretjer, Juan Antonio, 10
Courtney. *See* Kennedy, Courtney
COVID-19 vaccinations
  Children's Health Defense and Informed Consent Action Network against, 208–9
  Emergency Use Authorization, of FDA, 224
  Fauci and, 208–9
  ivermectin and, 224
Cristobal, Angel Rodriguez, 9–10
Cronin, John, 107, 117–18
  as HRFA riverkeeper, 96
  Hudson River environmental activism, 94–102
  RFK Jr. relationship end, 121–22, 146, 150–51
Cuban Missile Crisis, xix, xxv
  RFK Sr. role in, 27–29

INDEX / 267

Cuomo, Andrew, xx, 12
  bid for governor of New York, 167–68
  as governor of New York, 103
  Kerry separation and divorce from, 181, 240
Cuomo, Mario, 181
  RFK Jr., and Rivera Vieques trial defense, 12, 15–16, 103
Curb Your Enthusiasm (television show)
  David, Larry, and, 164, 174, 200
  Hines in, 163–64, 188, 201

Dakota Access Pipeline, Standing Rock Sioux Tribe and, 206
David. *See* Kennedy, David
David, Larry, 122, 164, 174, 200
David, Laurie, 122, 164, 174
"Deadly Immunity" (RFK Jr.), 205
Democrats
  Joe connections and importance to, 36
  RFK Jr., disillusionment and break from, xiii, xx, 167–68, 173, 215–20, 232
diaries, of RFK Jr.
  on duality, 243
  financial disclosures in, 238–39
  on funeral attendance, 242
  on notable figures, 238
  Post publication of, xiv–xv
  during Puerto Rico imprisonment, xxiii–xxiv, 1–18
  study of, 236–43
  taken by Mary, xiv–xvi, 191, 193
  womanizing references, xiv–xvi, 13, 93, 239–40
DiCaprio, Leonardo, 172
Dinkins, David, 103, 104
Doar, John, xix, 82
Douglas, William O., 31
Draco Rosa, Robi, 9
Driscoll, Mary, 20
drugs, RFK Jr., and
  Alcoholics Anonymous meetings of, 93, 145, 160
  Andersen purchase at Harvard University, 71
  Caroline on encouragement of, xi
  continued use during presidential campaign of Ted, 86
  expulsion from Millbrook boarding school, 55, 58
  in Harlem with David, Michael and John Jr., 89
  heroin and cocaine use, at Harvard University, 71
  heroin possession arrest in 1982, xxii, 90–91
  heroin use with David and Kelleys, 66
  Horowitz on, 66
  Hyannis Port Terrors and experimentation with, 63
  introduction of heroin to David, 66
  Lem use with, 74, 86
  LSD use, 65
  marijuana and cocaine in Hayneville, Alabama, 79
  memoir on addiction to, 87
  presidential campaign reference to, 219
  in Summit Oaks Hospital, New Jersey drug rehabilitation, 90–91
  use and dealing at Harvard University, 70–71
  use of psychedelic drugs, 236
DuPont, RFK Jr., class action suit against, 184
Dutton, Fred, 46

education, of RFK Jr.
  admitted to New York State Bar in 1985, 89
  bar exam failing in 1982, 89
  few weeks at London School of Economics, 84
  Georgetown Prep high school, 59, 62
  at Harvard University, 69, 70–71
  Johnson, F., thesis focus, 80–81
  Lazell at Palfrey School influence on, 67–68
  Lem enrollment at Palfrey Street School, 66
  living with Brode while at Palfrey Street School, 66–67
  Millbrook boarding school expulsion for doing drugs, 55, 58, 62
  Pomfret School expulsion, 60
  Rhodes Scholarship at Oxford University rejection, 70
  thesis publication by Grann and Schlesinger, 81–82
  at University of Virginia School of Law, 86
Egypt trip, of Lem and RFK Jr., 54–55
Emergency Use Authorization, of FDA, 224
Emily. *See* Kennedy, Emily Black

environmental activism, of RFK Jr., xvi, xxii
  ANWR, 175
  class action suit against DuPont, 184
  at Dakota Access Pipeline and Standing Rock Sioux Tribe, 206
  distancing from, 203
  Exxon environmental litigation, 99
  green house renovation, after mold finding, 185–88
  Hudson River litigation, 99–102
  New York City watershed, 102, 103, 104, 106, 145
  with NRDC, 94, 106, 121–24, 162–63
  Quassaick Creek litigation, 99–101
  with Riverkeeper nonprofit, xxii, 98–99, 101, 106, 107, 118, 122, 125, 145–46, 159
  The Riverkeepers book, 100, 107, 117–18, 121
  Ruzow on, 104
  speaking demands of, 107, 117, 121, 124–25, 149
  teaching environmental law at Pace University law school, 101, 144, 180
  teamed up with Cronin, 94–102
  threaten to fire Gelber, 105–6
  VantagePoint Venture Partner board member, 186
  at Vieques, 3–4, 7–8, 11
  Waterkeeper Alliance, 151
  whale-watching expedition, 123
Environmental Protection Agency, on New York City Watershed, 104–5
Epstein, Jeffrey
  RFK Jr., relationship with, 114–15
ESK or Ethel. *See* Kennedy, Ethel Skakel
Euler, Sandy, 24
Eunice. *See* Kennedy, Eunice Shriver
Evers, Medgar, 27
Exxon environmental lawsuit, for $16 million, 98
  RFK Jr. involvement with, 99

Fairley, Gordon Hamilton, 85
de La Falaise, Henry, 35
falconry, RFK Jr., interest in, xviii, 31–32, 55–56, 65
Fauci, Anthony
  HIV epidemic and COVID-19 pandemic mismanagement, xx
  as NIAID director, 207

  RFK Jr., attack on, xx, 208–9, 219–20
  RFK Jr., meeting with, 207–8
FDA. *See* Food and Drug Administration
Fear and Loathing in Aspen (film), 228
Federal Refuse Act (1899)
  Tuck Tape violations of, 95
  violations on Hudson River, 97–98
Ferllnghetti, Lawrence, 14
Finn. *See* Kennedy, William Finbar
Fisher, Amy "Long Island Lolita," 104
The Fitzgeralds and the Kennedys (Kearns Goodwin), 108
Fleetwood, Blake, 72
  on Apurimac River rafting trip, 75–77
fluoride, health problems from, xxiii
Food Allergy Initiative, Mary volunteer for, 128
Food and Drug Administration (FDA), Emergency Use Authorization of, 224
Forbidden Facts (de Becker), 224
Fox, Amaryllis. *See* Kennedy, Amaryllis Fox
Framed (RFK Jr.), 213
Fraser, Hugh, 84–85
Fraser, Rebecca (girlfriend of RFK Jr.), 85–86
  Caroline introduction of RFK Jr. to, 84
Frederick II (emperor), 65

Gates, Bill, xx–xxi
Gelber, Marilyn
  Giuliani firing of, 106–7
  RFK Jr., threaten to fire, 105
George magazine, of John Jr., 133–34
Georgetown Prep high school, of RFK Jr., 59
Gifford, Frank, 119
Gifford, Vicki. *See* Kennedy, Vicki Gifford
Giuliani, Rudolph, 151, 167, 179
  Gelber fired by, 106–7
Gladen, Eric, 203
Glenn, John, 47, 50
Gore, Al, 107, 118, 144–45
  environmental activism of, 122, 148
  fundraiser of, 147–48
  presidential campaign in 2000 of, 148, 157, 162–63
Gorman, James, 118
Grann, Phyllis, 81–82
Green, Mark, 3
Green, Pincus, 166
Grier, Roosevelt, 31

Hack, Jinx, 47
Harris, Kamala, xiii, 220–21
Harvard University, RFK Jr., at, 69
  Bhutto leap between Halls, 71–72
  drug use and dealing at, 70–71
  shot at during ski trip in Chile, 72–74
Hayneville, Alabama, RFK Jr., stay with Russell, 79
health and human services (HHS) secretary, RFK Jr., as, xxiii, 233
  on food dyes, 236
  Kerry ask for resignation of, 240–41
  Monarez firing, 240, 241
  on psychedelic drugs effects in therapeutic treatments, 236
  RFK Jr., vow to cut employees, 236
  Schlossberg, E., condemnation of research slashed, 242
  Whitehouse, S., critic of appointment to, 235
health conditions, of RFK Jr.
  atrial fibrillation, 171, 180
  hemochromatosis, 171
  Hepatitis C, 171
  spasmodic dysphonia, 171–72
health maintenance organization (HMO) data, on neurological disorders from vaccinations, 205
heroin arrest, 89–90
  suspended sentence with drug treatment program, 91
HHS. *See* health and human services
Hickory Hill mansion, of RFK Jr., childhood, 22–23
  chaos after RFK Sr., death, 58
  powerful adults as guests, 30–31
  as White House extension, 26
Hines, Cheryl. *See* Kennedy, Cheryl Hines
HMO. *See* health maintenance organization
Hoffa, James P., 175–76
Hoffa, Jimmy, 21, 22
The Home That Kennedy Built (video), on RFK Jr., and Mary green home, 188
Hood, James, 30
Hoover, J. Edgar, 38, 88
Horowitz, David, 66, 77
  David interview with, 91–92
HRFA. *See* Hudson River Fishermen's Association
Hudson River, environmental activism at companies polluting, 95
  Consolidated Edison power plant, 96–97
  Cronin involvement in, 94–102
  Riverkeeper nonprofit, 98
  Seeger clean up efforts, 95
  Storm King litigation, 97–98
  Tuck Tape company environmental waste, 95
Hudson River Fishermen's Association (HRFA), Cronin as riverkeeper for, 96
Hughes, Fred, 111–12
Humphrey, Hubert, 38, 44, 47
Hyannis Port, Cape Cod
  children athletic training, riding lessons, sailing at, 24
  Joe Sr., home and development of, 23–24
Hyannis Port Terrors, RFK Jr. founding of, 63

"I Have a Dream" speech, of MLK, 25
An Inconvenient Truth (film), 122
Informed Consent Action Network
  Bigtree founding of, 207
  RFK Jr., connection with, 207
Israeli Olympic team, Popular Front for the Liberation of Palestine attack, 73

Jack. *See* Kennedy, John F.
Jackie. *See* Kennedy, Jacqueline Bouvier
Jackson, Jacqueline, 4, 5
Jackson, Jesse, xx, 3
  affair and out-of-wedlock child, 4
  Carter relationship with, 5–6
  Noel *The Village Voice* article on, 4–5
  presidential campaign in 1984, 5, 6
  RFK Jr., dislike for, 4–7
Japan, Caroline as former ambassador to, xi
Jean. *See* Kennedy, Jean
Jenny, Peter, 55, 140–41
  nonprofit for peregrine falcon established by, 59
Jesus Mercado, Alberto de "Tito Kayak," 8, 11
JFK. *See* Kennedy, John F.
Jim Crow laws, Johnson, F., impact on dismantling, 81
Jimmy. *See* Skakel, Jimmy
Joe. *See* Kennedy, Joseph, Sr.
Joe Jr. *See* Kennedy, Joseph, Jr.
John Birch Society, Lazell as supporter of, 67

John F. Kennedy Library & Museum, JFK and RFK Jr. picture at, 31
John Jr. *See* Kennedy, John F., Jr.
Johnson, Frank Minis, Jr., 169
   Alabama segregation abolishment and, 80–81
   death of, 140
   Doar on, 82–83
   Jim Crow laws dismantling impact, 81
   RFK Jr., thesis focus on, 80–81
   ruling on Parks and 1955 bus boycott, 81
Johnson, Lyndon B., 24, 38
   RFK Sr., strong dislike for, 39
Johnson, Rafer, 47
Just, Jen, 110

Kaplan, Peter, 13, 18, 78–79, 145, 158, 178, 213, 243
   death of, 200
   on Emily, 88
   thesis of RFK Jr., and, 83, 169
Katzenbach, Nicholas, 23, 26
   role in University of Alabama segregation attempt, 30
Kearns Goodwin, Doris, 108
Kelley, Kim (girlfriend of RFK Jr.), 60, 63–64, 160
   heroin use with RFK Jr., 66
Kelley, Pam (girlfriend of David), 63
   death in 2020, 65
   paralysis from jeep accident with RFK Jr., brother Joe, 64, 160
Kellogg, Diana, 110–11
Kelly, Beth, 108
Kennedy, Aidan Caomhán (son of RFK Jr., and Mary), 116, 177, 193–94
   birth during Vieques prison experience, 16
   Cheryl closeness to, 189
Kennedy, Amaryllis Fox (wife of Bobby III), 227–28
Kennedy, Caroline (daughter of JFK), 137
   as Australia and Japan former ambassador, xi
   eulogy of Radziwill, A., 143
   fight with John Jr., about estate of Jackie, 133
   on Kennedy, D., death, xi
   letter to senators investigating RFK Jr.., xi
   on RFK Jr. childhood and adolescence, xi
   on RFK Jr. on family tragedies publicity exploitation, xii
   at Sotheby's Institute of Art in London, 84–85
   on substance abuse encouragement of cousins by RFK Jr., xi
Kennedy, Carolyn Bessette (wife of John Jr.), 133, 134, 139
   cremation and burial at sea, 137–38
Kennedy, Cheryl Hines (wife of RFK Jr.), xv, 200, 203, 238
   affair with RFK Jr., 188–89, 192, 199
   in *Curb Your Enthusiasm*, 163–64, 188, 201
   presidential campaign support, 215–16, 222–23
   separation of, 234, 240
   wedding of, 201
   womanizing accusation, 215–16
Kennedy, Conor (son of RFK Jr. and Mary), 15, 17, 115, 125–26, 129, 150, 196
   Swift relationship with, 199–200
Kennedy, Courtney (sister to RFK Jr.), 22
   marriage to Ruhe, 85, 112
Kennedy, David (brother to RFK Jr.), 21–22, 48, 49, 160
   on Apurimac River rafting trip, 75–77
   death from drug overdose of, xi, 91–92, 145
   feelings of family exclusion, 92
   fractured vertebra from jeep accident, 65
   heroin use with RFK Jr., 63–64, 66, 89
   interview with Collier and Horowitz, 91–92
   near drowning on day of RFK Sr., death, 50
   RFK Jr., introduction of heroin to, 66
   RFK Sr., death response by, 50, 92
   sent to Austria tennis camp after RFK Sr., death, 51
Kennedy, Edward Moore "Ted" "Teddy" (uncle to RFK Jr.), xxi, 64
   Clinton, B., praise of, 157
   death in 2009 from brain tumor, 210
   divorce from Bennett, 107
   John Jr., criticism by, 133
   Kopechne drowning in 1969 at Chappaquiddick, xxv, 60–61, 86
   presidential campaigns, xxiii, 5, 85–86, 169
   Reggie as second wife of, 107–8, 137

INDEX / 271

in Senate, 103
trip to Bangladesh, 72
visit to RFK Jr., in prison, 3
Kennedy, Emily Black (wife to RFK Jr.), 12, 87, 144
  Bobby III birth, 93, 218
  divorce, 109, 114, 115
  Kaplan on, 88
  mugging of, 89
  New York Legal Aid Society attorney, 89
Kennedy, Ethel Skakel "ESK" (mother of RFK Jr.), xvii–xviii, 157, 167
  anger and depression after RFK Sr., death, 51
  dating RFK Sr., 34–35
  family of, 33–34
  impatience with RFK Jr., 56
  Merton relationship with, 14
  pride in Puerto Rico prison sentence, 3, 17–18
  refusal to remarry after death of RFK Sr., 57
  on RFK Jr., and Cheryl wedding, 201
  Swift introduction to, 200
  Time coverage of admired Kennedy woman, 57
  visit to RFK Jr., in prison, 17
  wedding ceremony to RFK Sr., 34–35
Kennedy, Eunice Shriver (aunt of RFK Jr.), 156, 197
  illness and hospital experience of, 160–62, 175
Kennedy, Jacqueline Bouvier "Jackie" (wife of JFK)
  Bobby Sr., affair with, xvi
  death in 1994, 133
  remarriage to Onassis, 58
Kennedy, Jean (aunt to RFK Jr.), 52
Kennedy, John F., Jr. "John Jr." (son of JFK)
  as assistant district attorney in Manhattan District Attorney's Office, 88
  Bessette as wife of, 133, 134
  cremation and burial at sea, 137–38
  death in plane accident, 135–36
  drug use with RFK Jr., 89
  failure to pass law exam twice, 88
  fight with Caroline about estate of Jackie, 133
  financial troubles, 133–34
  funeral for, 139
  RFK Jr., at funeral of, 138–40
  Ted criticism of, 133
Kennedy, John F. "Jack" "JFK" (uncle to RFK Jr.)
  assassination of, xix, 23
  defeat of Lodge in Senate run, 38
  Joe demand to be in politics, 37
  Johnson, L., as running mate, 24
  Lem as friend in school of, 51
  military enlistment and war hero, 37
  presidential campaigns 1960, 24, 25, 38, 52
  RFK Sr., attorney general appointment by, 24, 25
  run for Congress in Massachusetts, 38
  womanizing conquests, xvi
Kennedy, Joseph, Jr. "Joe Jr." (uncle to RFK Jr.), Operation Aphrodite and death of, 36–37, 64, 102
Kennedy, Joseph, Sr. "Joe" (grandfather to RFK Jr.)
  banking and Hollywood interests, 35–36
  Chicago Merchandise Mart ownership, 35–36
  demand for oldest son in politics, 37
  Democrats connections and importance to, 36
  heart attacks and death of, 61
  Hyannis Port home and development by, 23–24
  presidential ambitions of, 36
  reference to Lem as son, 51–52
  Roosevelt appointment of ambassador to London, 36
  Roosevelt appointment to SEC in 1934, 36
  Scotch whisky distribution rights, 35–36
  stroke in 1962, 38
  Swanson affair, xvi, 35
  womanizing encouragement, xv–xvi
  youngest bank president in US, 35
Kennedy, Joseph II "Joe" (brother to RFK Jr.), 6, 21, 47, 48, 71
  annulment request to end Rauch marriage, 108–9
  election to Congress for Massachusetts, 103
  on hijacked Boeing 747, 72–73
  jeep accident and Kelley, P., paralysis, 64
  Kelly affair with, 108
  as man of house after death of RFK Sr., 49

Kennedy, Joseph II "Joe" (*cont.*)
  political career end, 119–20
  RFK Jr., independent presidential campaign condemnation, 226
  sent to Spain after RFK Sr., death, 51
Kennedy, Kathleen "Kick" (daughter of RFK Jr., and Emily), 102, 115, 144, 191
Kennedy, Kathleen "Kick" (sister to RFK Jr.), 21, 47, 50, 102
  as lieutenant governor of Maryland, 103, 156
  RFK Jr., independent presidential campaign condemnation, 226
Kennedy, Kathleen "Kick" (sister to RFK Sr.)
  marriage to Cavendish, 102
  Wentworth-Fitzwilliam romantic relationship, 102
Kennedy, Kerry (sister to RFK Jr.), 17, 22, 128–29
  arrest for driving car under influence of Ambien, 198–99, 241
  Colley, B., affair with, 181, 240
  Fauci Ripple of Hope Award by, 209
  marriage to Cuomo, A., xx, 12
  Mary eulogy by, 196–97
  RFK Jr., independent presidential campaign condemnation, 226
  RFK Jr., introduction to Mary, 109–10, 112
  RFK Jr., relationship with, 240–41
  separation and divorce from Cuomo, A., 181, 240
  spasmodic dysphonia of, 172
  trial of, 199
Kennedy, Kyra (daughter of RFK Jr. and Mary), 15, 115, 125–26, 149–50, 176–77
  move to live with Cheryl, 189
Kennedy, Mary Richardson (wife of RFK Jr.), 2, 12, 240
  alcohol addiction, 17, 126–27, 149, 189–90, 194
  anorexia of, 111
  arrest for driving under the influence, 190
  as assistant to *Interview* magazine editor Colacello, 111
  dating Mavroleon before marriage, 112–13
  diaries of RFK Jr., taken by, xiv–xvi, 191, 193
  divorce from RFK Jr., 191–93
  as fashion model, 112
  funeral of, 196–98
  Just on, 110
  Kellogg on, 110–11
  Kerry introduction to RFK Jr., 109–10, 112
  marriage difficulties, 125–27, 143, 164
  marriage to, 17
  Maxwell friendship with, 114
  rebuilding of house with mold, 185–88
  rehabilitation treatment, 126–27, 149
  RFK Jr. affair before marriage to, 109–10
  suicide of, xiv, 194–96, 199, 200
Kennedy, Michael (brother to RFK Jr.), 22
  affair with babysitter of his children, 119
  celebrities and politicians as funeral of, 120
  drug use with RFK Jr., 89
  estranged wife, Vicki, 119
  skiing accident death, 118–20
Kennedy, Robert F., Jr. "Bobby Jr." "RFK Jr.." *See also specific topics*
  disillusionment and break from Democratic Party, xiii, xx, 167–68, 173
  identification with Saint Francis of Assisi, xviii, 22
  Kennedy, C., criticism of, xi
  siblings endorsement of Harris and Walz, xii, 220–21
  Trump endorsement in 2024, xii, xv, xxiii
Kennedy, Robert F., Sr. "Bobby Sr." "RFK Sr." (father of RFK Jr.), 184–85
  anti-Communist position, 40–41
  assassination of, xvii, xviii–xix, xxii, 46
  as attorney general, 23, 25, 40
  Chavez relationship with, 6
  climbing of Mount Kennedy in Canada to honor JFK, 41–42
  Cohn friction with, 20–21
  Communism focus, xix, 20–21
  controversial visit to Communist Poland, 39–41
  Cuban Missile Crisis role, 27–29
  deep mourning for JFK death, 39
  family lack of money at death of, xvii
  JFK campaign management, 20
  JFK death response, 38–39
  Johnson, L., strong dislike by, 39
  Lippman on ruthless action of, 25

INDEX / 273

McCarthy, J., relationship with, 19–21, 64
Mob and labor union investigations and hearings, 21–22
Monroe and Jackie affairs, xvi
Operation Mongoose to undermine Castro government, 28
presidential campaign, xix, 6, 42–46, 220–22
RFK Jr., strive to impress, xvi, 21, 244
role in University of Alabama segregation attempt, 29–30
Ruddy friend of, 23
Senate hearings of, 20–22
speech on MLK death, 45–46
Tye biography on, 35
United Farm Workers votes for, 6
US Senate of New York win, 41
wedding ceremony with Ethel, 34–35
Kennedy, Robert Francis, III "Bobby III" "Bobby 3" (son of RFK Jr., and Emily), 12, 115, 144, 191
Emily birth of, 93, 218
Fox marriage to, 227–28
Kennedy, Rory (sister of RFK Jr.), 23, 56–57
American Hollow documentary of, 130–31
introduction of Swift to Ethel, 200
marriage to Bailey, 121, 132–35
at Michael skiing accident death, 118–20
RFK Jr., independent presidential campaign condemnation, 226
wedding postponement due to John Jr. missing plane, 136
Kennedy, Rose Fitzgerald (grandmother to RFK Jr.), 33, 35, 48, 91, 102
Kennedy, Vicki Gifford (wife of Michael), 119
Kennedy, Victoria Reggie (wife of Teddy), 107–8, 137
Kennedy, William Finbar "Finn" (son of RFK Jr., and Mary), 15, 115, 128, 129, 172
Kennedy family
Chavez relationship with, 6
as devout Roman Catholics, xiii, xvi
flaws in, xxv
heroic legacy, xxiv–xxv
love of nature, 31–33
marital infidelities, xxv

proximity to power, 30–31
RFK Jr., presidential campaign rift with, 220, 226
sense of entitlement, xxii
Kennedy Green House (Wilson), 186–88
The Kennedys (Collier and Horowitz), 77, 91
Kerouac, Jack, 14
Kerry. *See* Kennedy, Kerry
Khrushchev, Nikita, 28–29
Kick. *See* Kennedy, Kathleen "Kick"
King, Coretta Scott, 47
King, Martin Luther, Jr. "MLK," xix
Communist Party connection, xxv, 25
extramarital affairs, xxv, 25
"I Have a Dream" speech, 25
RFK Sr., speech on death of, 45–46
RFK Sr., wiretapping of, xxv, 25–26, 45
Kirby, Phil, 51
Kopechne, Mary Jo, xxv, 60–61, 86
Kucinich, Dennis, 225–26
Kyoto Protocol, 118
Kyra. *See* Kennedy, Kyra

Laffitte, Hector Manuel, 1–2, 15–16
The Lancet, RFK Jr. anti-vaccine policy concerns, xii–xiii
Lawford, Christopher Kennedy (cousin to RFK Jr.), 63–64, 122
on Apurimac River rafting trip, 75–77
Lazell, James D. "Skip," xxiii, 204
biology teacher at Palfrey School influence, 67
John Birch Society supporter, 67
as YAF member, 67–68
Lem. *See* Billings, Kirk LeMoyne "Lem"
Lewinsky, Monica, 147
Lewis, John, 45
Life magazine, RFK Jr., sale of Africa pictures and text to, 53–54
Life Undercover (Fox), 227
Lippman, Walter, 25
Lives of Moral Leadership (Coles), 82
Lodge, Henry Cabot, Jr., 38
London School of Economics, RFK Jr., few weeks at, 84
Louis-Dreyfus, Julia, 122, 158, 164
Luce, Henry, 37
Lyons, Tony, 223

Madison Avenue Initiative, of Sharpton, 6
Madonna, Kevin, 183–84

Make America Healthy Again, xii, 235, 236
The Making of the President 1968 (White, T.), 75
Malone, Vivian, 30
Manhattan District Attorney's Office
  RFK Jr., as assistant district attorney in, 88
  RFK Jr., resignation after heroin possession arrest, 89–90
  run by Morgenthau, 88
Mankeiwicz, Frank, 44
Marshall, Burke, 23
Martin, Ricky, 10
Mary. *See* Kennedy, Mary Richardson
Mary Richardson Kennedy Award, 198
Mavroleon, Carlos, 112
  heroin overdose death, 113
Maxwell, Ghislaine, 114
McCall, H. Carl, 168
McCarthy, Eugene, 44, 221
McCarthy, Joseph, xix
  RFK Sr., relationship with, 19–21, 64
  Senate censure of, 21
McClellan, John, 21, 22
McNamara, Robert S., xix–xx
measles, mumps, and rubella (MMR) vaccines, xxi–xxii
measles epidemic, from RFK Jr. antivaccine policy, xii, 235, 241
Mellong, Timothy, 225
Meredith, James, 26, 82
  Barnett prevention from attending Ole Miss, 27
  lawsuit against Ole Miss, 27
Merton, Thomas, 13
  Skakel and Ethel relationship with, 14
Michael. *See* Kennedy, Michael
Millbrook boarding school, of RFK Jr.
  Bad Boy lion cub in zoo at, 55
  falconry program at, 55–56
  Lem visiting at, 59
  RFK Jr., expulsion for doing drugs, 55, 58
MLK. *See* King, Martin Luther, Jr. "MLK"
MMR. *See* measles, mumps, and rubella
Mollo, Silvio, 38
Monarez, Susan, 240, 241
Monroe, Marilyn, xvi
Morell, George, 178–79
Morgenthau, Robert, 38
  Manhattan District Attorney's Office run by, 88

Mount Kennedy, Canada, RFK Sr., climb to honor JFK, 41–42
Moxley, Martha, 154–56, 170–71, 212–14
Mudd, Roger, 85

National Association for the Advancement of Colored People (NAACP), 27
National Institute of Allergy and Infectious Diseases (NIAID), Fauci as director of, 207
National Institutes of Health (NIH), 207
  Collins as director of, 208
National Vaccine Injury Compensation Program, 182–83
Natural Resources Defense Council (NRDC), RFK Jr., environmental activism and, 94, 106, 121–24, 163–64
  on RFK Jr., dangerous and vanity candidacy, 229
Neri, Rocco, 84
Newfield, Jack, 49
New York City watershed environmental work, 102, 145
  Dinkins and, 103, 104
  Ruzow criticism of RFK Jr., on, 106
New York Legal Aid Society, Emily as attorney for, 89
New York State Bar Association, RFK Jr., sworn into, 99
NIAID. *See* National Institute of Allergy and Infectious Diseases
NIH. *See* National Institutes of Health
Nixon, Richard, 25
Noel, Peter, 4–5
NRDC. *See* Natural Resources Defense Council
Nuzzi, Olivia, 238, 241
  RFK Jr., presidential campaign and, 230–31
  RFK Jr., sexting scandal with, xv, 234–35, 239

Ole Miss. *See* University of Mississippi
Olmos, Edward James, 3–4, 9
Onassis, Aristotle, 58
The Once and Future King (White, T.), 31
On the Art of Hunting with Birds (Frederick II), 65
Operation Aphrodite, Joe Jr., death in, 36–37, 64, 102
Operation Breadbasket, Sharpton as Youth Director for, 6

INDEX / 275

Operation Mongoose, to undermine Castro, 28
Outside magazine, RFK Jr., Vieques story, 9, 11

Pace University law school, RFK Jr., teaching environmental law at, 101, 144, 180
Pacifico, Duff (girlfriend to RFK Jr.), 85
Pardongate controversy, of Clinton, B., 167
Parks, Rosa, 81
Pfeiffer, Michelle, 123
pharmaceutical manufacturers, RFK Jr., litigation against, 207
Pomfret School, RFK Jr. expulsion from, 60
Popular Front for the Liberation of Palestine
　hijacking of Boeing 747, 72–73
　Israeli Olympic team attack, 73
presidency, RFK Jr. reverence for, xxiv–xxv
　Lyons contributions to, 223
presidential campaign, of RFK Jr., 2024, xiii, xv, xxi, 218, 220–21
　American Values PAC Super Bowl ad, 229
　de Becker contributions to, 223–25
　brain worm diagnosis report, 229–30
　change to independent candidate status, 226–30
　Cheryl support of, 215–16, 222–23
　Clear Choice legal challenge to, 232–33
　drugs and sex addiction reference, 219
　Fox as new campaign manager, 227–28
　Kucinich as campaign manager for, 225–26
　Mellon contribution of $25 million to, 225
　NRDC on dangerous and vanity candidacy, 229
　Shanahan contribution to, 228–29
　Sheinkopf political strategist and, 223, 225
　suspension of, 233
　threats to life during, 226–27
presidential campaign, of RFK Sr. (1968), xix, 6, 42, 220–22
　Barry as bodyguard during, 46
　Chavez and Lewis support for, 45
　Ethel and children at announcement of, 43
　Mankiewicz as press secretary, 44
　Mudd as correspondent for, 43–44
　speech at, 44
　Vietnam War focus, 45
　Witcover coverage of, 46
presidential campaigns
　Carter 1980, 5, 85–86
　Gore 2000, 148, 157, 162–63
　Humphrey 1968, 45
　Jackson 2004, 5–6
　JFK 1960, 24, 25, 38, 52
　Johnson, L., withdrawal from 1968, 45
　Teddy 1980, xxiii, 5, 85–86, 169
　Trump 2024, xxiii
　Wallace 1976, 80
prison diary, 1–18
　on becoming better father and husband, 18
　on Jackson, Jesse, 4, 5
　on Jackson, Jesse, and Sharpton relationship, 6
　on jailed Vieques protestors, 7–8
　on prison readings, 13–14
　on Rivera and Clinton, H., as critics of Sharpton and Jackson, Jesse, 7
　on Sharpton, 5
　while political prisoner in Puerto Rico, 1
Profiles in Courage (Kennedy, John F.), xxiv
Puerto Rico Bar Association, bomb exploding at, 10
Puerto Rico political prisoner trial
　Burgos sixty day sentence, 2–3
　Cuomo, M., representation of RFK Jr., and Rivera, 12, 15–16
　Laffitte as judge at, 1–2, 15–16
　Laffitte sentencing for Vieques protests, 2
　RFK Jr., thirty day sentence, 1, 2–3
　for Vieques trespassing charge, 2

Quassaick Creek litigation, on environmental violations, 99–101

Radziwill, Anthony, 133, 136, 138
　death and funeral of, 142–43
Radziwill, Carole (wife of Anthony), 135
Radziwill née Bouvier, Lee (sister to Jackie), 133, 135, 142, 143
Rainbow/PUSH Coalition, of Jackson, Jesse, 4, 5
Raines, Howell, 83
Rauch, Sheila Brewster, 108–9, 119–20
Reagan, Ronald, 6

The Real Anthony Fauci (RFK Jr.), 223
  Cheryl criticism of Nazi remarks, 215
  criticism of, 214
  Fauci response to, xxi, 214–15
  Gates blame for African children vaccinations, xx–xxi
  on HIV epidemic and COVID-19 pandemic mismanagement, xx
Reggie, Victoria. *See* Kennedy, Victoria Reggie
Reiner, Rob, 123
RFK Jr. *See* Kennedy, Robert F., Jr.
RFK Sr. *See* Kennedy, Robert F., Sr.
Rhodes Scholarship at Oxford University rejection, 70
Rich, Marc, 166
Richardson, Mary. *See* Kennedy, Mary Richardson
Ripple of Hope Award, of Fauci by Kerry, 209
Rivera, Dennis, 2, 3, 9, 11
  as critic of Sharpton and Jackson, Jesse, 7
  Jackson, Jesse, and, 4–5
Riverkeeper nonprofit, on Hudson River, 101, 106, 107, 118, 122, 125, 145–46
  Cronin environmental work with, 98–99
  Exxon lawsuit for $16 million, 98–99
  RFK Jr., community service with, xxii
  RFK Jr., fundraiser for, 159
  RFK Jr., resignation from, 206–7, 241
  Wegner and, 150–52
The Riverkeepers (RFK Jr., and Cronin), 100, 107, 117, 121
  Gorman on, 118
Robert F. Kennedy Human Rights foundation
  awards by, 210
  Fauci Ripple of Hope Award from, 209
  Ted support of, 210
Robert F. Kennedy Memorial Tennis Tournament Dinner, 77–78
Roman Catholics
  Kennedy family as devout, xiii, xvi
  McCarthy, J., faith, 19
  RFK Jr., return to religion of, 93
Romero, Juan, 46–47
Roosevelt, Franklin D., 36
Rory. *See* Kennedy, Rory
Rose. *See* Kennedy, Rose Fitzgerald
Rosenberg, Ethel, 20
Rosenberg, Julius, 20

Rubin, James, 142–43
Ruddy, Francis, Jr., RFK Sr., friend of, 23
Ruhe, Jeffrey, 85, 112
Rumsfeld, Donald, 173
Russell, John, Jr. "Sweet Pea," RFK Jr., stay in Hayneville, Alabama with, 79
Ruzow, Daniel, 104, 106

Sachs, Jeffrey, 172
Saint Francis of Assisi, xviii, 22
Save Our Everglades campaign, 6–7
Scenic Hudson Preservation Conference, Boyle as member of, 96
Schlesinger, Arthur M., Jr., 81–82, 86
  as RFK Sr., biographer, 6
Schlossberg, Edwin (husband of Caroline), 133, 137
  John Jr., death, cremation, eulogy, 138–39
Schlossberg, Jack (son of Caroline), xi
  campaign for Congress in New York City, xii
  social media attacks against RFK Jr., xii
Schlossberg, Tatiana, 242
Schom, Alan, 13
Schrade, Paul, 211
Schwarzenegger, Arnold, 158
SEC. *See* Securities and Exchange Commission
Securities and Exchange Commission (SEC), Joe appointment by Roosevelt to, 36
Seeger, Pete
  Clearwater Initiative founded by, 95
  Hudson River clean up efforts, 95
segregation
  Johnson, F., abolishment in Alabama, 80–81
  Meredith registration at Ole Miss, 26–27
  University of Alabama and, 29–30, 78–79
September 11, 2001 attack
  Bush, G. W., and, 179
  Morell death in, 178–79
  RFK Jr. recollection of events with, 177–80
The Seven Storey Mountain (Merton), 13–14
sex addiction to women, of RFK Jr., xiv–xv, xvi, 13, 93, 125, 172–73, 180
  Cheryl accusations of, 215–16

Colley, A., alleged affair, 181
  Mary knowledge of, 127, 159–60
  Nuzzi sexting scandal, xv, 234–35
  presidential campaign reference to, 219
Shanahan, Nicole, 228–29
Shapiro, Peter, RFK Jr., campaigning for New Jersey assemblyman, 84
Sharpton, Al, 3–4, 5
  Brawley scandal and, 7
  as youth director for Operation Breadbasket, 6
Shattered Faith (Rauch), 108
Sheinkopf, Hank, 223, 225
Shriver, Bobby (cousin to RFK Jr.), 33
  RFK Jr. Super Bowl ad condemnation, 229
Shriver, Maria (cousin to RFK Jr.), 158, 175
Shriver, Sargent (uncle to RFK Jr.), 33, 161
Simpson, O. J., 4
Sinatra, Frank, 25
Sirhan, Sirhan Bishara
  Newsom response to parole of, 212
  RFK Jr., parole support, 211–12
  RFK Jr., visit with, 210–11
  RFK Jr. on assassination of RFK Sr., by, xxii, 210–11
  RFK Sr., assassination by, 46–47
Skakel, Ann Brannack (grandmother to RFK Jr.), 14, 33
Skakel, George, Jr. (uncle to RFK Jr.), 32
Skakel, George, Sr. (grandfather to RFK Jr.), successful coal and coke business, 33–34
Skakel, Jimmy (uncle to RFK Jr.), 32
Skakel, Michael (cousin to RFK Jr.), Moxley murder charge of, 154–56, 170–71, 212–14
Skakel, Patricia "Pat" (aunt to RFK Jr.), 34
Smith, Steve, 47, 52
Sotheby's Institute of Art in London, Caroline intern at, 84–85
Spooner, Doug, 75–77
Stanford, Karin, 4
Stevens, George, Jr., 25
Storm King litigation, on Hudson River, 97–98
The Story of Us (film), 123
Stroud, Morris, 75–77
Student Nonviolent Coordinating Committee, RFK Sr., presidential campaign support by, 45

Summit Oaks Hospital drug rehabilitation facility, RFK Jr., at, 90–91
Swanson, Gloria, xvi, 35
Swift, Taylor
  Conor relationship with, 199–200
  introduction to Ethel, 200

Ted or Teddy. *See* Kennedy, Edward Moore "Ted" "Teddy"
thesis publication, of RFK Jr.
  acknowledgments in, 82
  Doar writing of forward for, 82
  by Grann and Schlesinger, 81–82
  on Johnson, F., segregation efforts, 81–82
  Kaplan and, 83
  Raines criticism of, 83
Things Fall Apart (Achebe), 146
This Broken Archipelago (Lazell), 67
Thompson, Hunter S., xvi
Thoreau, Henry David, 16
Three Mile Island nuclear accident, 97
Time magazine
  coverage of Ethel as admired Kennedy woman, 57
  on Jackie marriage to Onassis, 58
Tito Kayak. *See* Jesus Mercado, Alberto de
del Toro, Benicio, 17
Trace Amounts (film), 203
Trinidad, Felix "Tito," 10
Trivers, Robert, 204
Trump, Donald, 178
  Cohn as mentor to, 20
  RFK Jr., endorsement of, xii, xv, xxiii, 233
Tuck Tape company, environmental waste on Hudson River, 95
Tye, Larry, 35

Udall, Stewart, 31
United Farm Workers, RFK Sr., votes from, 6, 45, 221
University of Alabama segregation attempt
  Kaplan and RFK Jr., trip to research, 78–79
  Katzenbach role in, 30
  RFK Sr., and Wallace role in, 29–30
University of Mississippi "Ole Miss"
  JFK dispatch of federal troops to, 27
  Meredith attempted registration at, 26–27
  riot and Meredith admission to, 27

University of Virginia School of Law, RFK Jr., at, 86
Unscripted (Hines), 189, 234, 238
vaccinations
 CDC conference on safety of, 205
 Children's Health Defense anti-vaccine group, xxi
 MMR, xxi–xxii
 National Vaccine Injury Compensation Program, 182–83
 school requirements for, 205
vaccinations, RFK Jr., and
 attack on Fauci, xx, 208–9, 219–20
 autism as vaccine-related, xiii, 181–83, 204–5
 dangerous misconceptions about, xii–xiii
 fight against COVID-19, 208–9
 on government and pharmaceutical company collusion, 205–6
 on HMO data of neurological disorders from, 205
 obsession with, xxi–xxii, 181–82, 208
 unwillingness to back, xii
Vaccine Safety Commission, RFK Jr., as chair of, 207
VantagePoint Venture Partners, RFK Jr., as board member of, 186
Vicki. *See* Kennedy, Vicki Gifford
Victoria. *See* Kennedy, Victoria Reggie
Vieques. *See also* Puerto Rico political prisoner trial
 Bush, G. W., on stop to bombings at, 173–74
 Clinton, B., temporary stop to bombings, 10
 health risks at, 11
 protesters at, 3–4, 7–8
 RFK Jr., first involvement in 2000, 11
 RFK Jr., invasion to remove US Navy from, 8–10
 US Navy bombs exploding at, 9
Vieques incarceration, of RFK Jr., 173
 Aidan birth during, 16
 civil disobedience and, xxiii–xxiv, 1–11
 readings during, 14, 16
 skin and face pustules during, 12, 13, 17, 174
Vietnam War, 15, 44
 JFK and RFK Sr., escalation of, xxv
 RFK Sr., presidential campaign focus, 45

Waeckerle, Bill, 90
Wallace, George, 7, 29–30
 assassination attempt and paralysis of, 80
 presidential campaign 1976, 80
 RFK Jr., encounters with, 79–81
Wall Street Project, of Jackson, Jesse, 6
Walsh, Bill, 90
Walz, Tim, xiii
Warhol, Andy, 111–12
Waterkeeper Alliance, 151, 200–201
 RFK Jr., resignation from, 207
Waugh, Evelyn, 16
Wegner, William, 150–52
Wentworth-Fitzwilliam, Peter, 102
White, Byron, 26
White, Theodore H., 31, 50, 75
Whitehouse, Charles, 169
Whitehouse, Sheldon, 169–70
 as critic of RFK Jr., appointment to HHS, 235
Whiteside, David, Jr., 169
Whittaker, Jim, 42
Why England Slept (JFK), 37
Williams, Andy, 47, 48, 120
Willis, Bruce, 123
Willy, Wilford John, 37
Wilson, Robin, 186–88
Witcover, Jules, 46
womanizing
 Cheryl accusation of RFK Jr., 215–16
 JFK conquests, xvi
 Joe encouragement of, xv–xvi
 RFK Jr., diaries on, xiv–xv, xvi, 13, 93, 239–40
 of Ted, 86, 107
World Mercury Project, xxi, 202, 207
 founded by Gladen, 203
 name change to Children's Health Defense, 203
 RFK Jr., as chairman of board of, 203

YAF. *See* Young America's Foundation
Young, Paul, 188
Young America's Foundation (YAF)
 Lazell as member of, 67–68

de la Zerda Alex Joseph, 10
Zogby, Jeremy, 220